RELUCTANT
REVOLUTIONARIES

RELUCTANT REVOLUTIONARIES

Englishmen and the Revolution
of 1688

❧

W. A. SPECK

Oxford   New York
OXFORD UNIVERSITY PRESS
1989

Oxford University Press, Walton Street, Oxford OX2 6DP

Oxford New York Toronto
Delhi Bombay Calcutta Madras Karachi
Petaling Jaya Singapore Hong Kong Tokyo
Nairobi Dar es Salaam Cape Town
Melbourne Auckland

and associated companies in
Berlin Ibadan

Oxford is a trade mark of Oxford University Press

First published 1988 by Oxford University Press
First issued as an Oxford University Press paperback 1989

British Library Cataloguing in Publication Data

Speck, W. A. (William Arthur) 1938–
Reluctant revolutionaries: Englishmen and the
revolution of 1688.—Oxford paperbacks
1. Great Britain. Political events, 1688–1689
I. Title
941.06'7
ISBN 0–19–285120–9

Library of Congress Cataloging-in-Publication Data

Speck, W. A. (William Arthur), 1938–
Reluctant revolutionaries: Englishmen and the revolution of 1688
/ W.A. Speck.
p. cm.
Bibliography: p. Includes index.
1. Great Britain—History—Revolution of 1688. 2. Great Britain—
History—James II, 1685–1688. I. Title.
941.06'7—dc19 DA452.S69 1989 88–34887
ISBN 0–19–285120–9 (pbk.)

Printed in Great Britain by
The Guernsey Press Co. Ltd.
Guernsey, Channel Islands

Printed in Great Britain by
Biddles Ltd.
Guildford and King's Lynn

To
the Memory of
my Mother

Preface

⌘

In this, my first serious venture into late seventeenth-century English history, I have received tremendous help to find my feet in unfamiliar territory. Above all I am indebted to John Kenyon, who generously lent me transcripts and photocopies of materials which he has accumulated over many years of studying late Stuart politics. These were a boon which saved me incalculable time and trouble, for which my gratitude cannot be adequately expressed. John Childs too helped considerably with the loan of documentary evidence which he has gathered during the research for his trilogy on the military history of the period. I also wish to thank Pat Murrell for her generosity in making available transcripts of documents relating to East Anglian elections.

Professor Kenyon suggested that an examination of the dispatches of the comte d'Avaux at the Quai d'Orsay might reap dividends. In following up this lead I was awarded a grant from the British Academy to finance two trips to Paris, where I benefited from the hospitality of the Institut Britannique and the Institut Francophone while engaged on research there. Professor Peter King and Mr Roel Vismans assisted my efforts to acquire enough Dutch to consult correspondence at the Hague, and the Twenty Seven Foundation provided financial assistance for a visit to the Rijksarchief.

As usual when commencing an investigation into an episode in English history I wrote to county archivists and other curators of manuscripts, and as usual was impressed by the care which they took to respond to my requests. Our network of local archives offers a superb professional service to historians and other enquirers. The scattered nature of the evidence involved travels throughout England and a foray into Scotland, incurring expenses which could not have been met without assistance from the research funds of Hull and Leeds Universities.

Wherever I went I was given every help. My old acquaintances Bruce Jones at Carlisle and Sheila Macpherson at Kendal made me especially welcome. I also enjoyed working again in the Bodleian and British Libraries, and for the first time in Dr Williams Library, whose Trustees I thank for allowing access to the manuscripts of Roger Morrice. One memorable visit was made to Sothebys, where, thanks to Sir Charles Graham, I was able to consult the papers of Viscount Preston before they came under the hammer.

I have benefited from opportunities to rehearse some of the conclusions of my research in lectures. The University of Newcastle upon Tyne kindly invited me to give three on the Revolution in March 1985, which greatly helped to clarify my thinking at a crucial time. In May 1987 I presented a version of the Introduction to the International Symposium on British History held in Nanjing, China.

I have profited greatly from the views of others on aspects of late-Stuart history. Discussions with Mark Goldie, who informed me of John Gother, and John Styles, who introduced me to the work of Theda Skocpol, were particularly stimulating on the subjects of religion and the state. The graduate students who attended the seminars on English history 1660–1760 at Brighton in 1984, Hull in 1985, and Exeter in 1987, and the undergraduates in my Special Subject class at Leeds 1986–7, taught me a lot.

Above all, one who has shared with me the excitement of exploring the reigns of Charles II and James II is Mary Geiter, who is working on the political career of Sir John Reresby, a man whose traces are frequently to be encountered in this study. Mary has involved herself so much in the writing of this book, reading every version of each chapter and suggesting improvements, that it would have been appropriate to have called it '1688 and All That', and to have signed it 'Williamanmary', save that any faults in it are all mine.

Knaresborough   W.A.S.
September 1987

Contents

Abbreviations   xi
Note on Dates   xii

1. Introduction   1

PART ONE

2. The Origins of the Revolution   25
3. The Reign of James II   42
4. The Dutch Invasion   71
5. The Convention   92

PART TWO

6. James II and the Revolution   117
7. The Constitutional Issues   139
8. The Religious Issues   166
9. The Social Implications   188
10. Reluctant Revolutionaries   213

11. Conclusion   241

Select Bibliography   252
Index   263

Abbreviations

∽❧✠❧∾

Ailesbury	Thomas Bruce, earl of Ailesbury, *Memoirs*, ed. W. E. Buckley (2 vols.; Roxburgh Club, Edinburgh, 1890), volume I.
Bramston	*The Autobiography of Sir John Bramston* ed. Lord Braybrooke (Camden Society, 1845)
BL	British Library
Burnet	Gilbert Burnet, *History of his Own Time* (6 vols.; Oxford, 1833)
CSPD	*Calendar of State Papers Domestic*
Clarendon	*The Correspondence of Henry Hyde, Earl of Clarendon . . . with the Diary*, ed. S. W. Singer (2 vols., 1828)
Cobbett	W. Cobbett, *Parliamentary History of England* (36 vols.; 1806–1820)
CP(A)	Correspondance Politique Angleterre, Archives du Ministère des Relations Extérieures, Paris
CP(H)	Correspondance Politique Hollande, Archives du Ministère des Relations Extérieures, Paris
Dalrymple	Sir John Dalrymple, *Memoirs of Great Britain and Ireland* (vol. i in one part, vol. ii in two parts; 1771–3)
Ellis	*The Ellis Correspondence*, ed. G. A. Ellis (2 vols.; 1829)
Grey	Anchitell Grey, *Debates of the House of Commons from the Year 1667 to the year 1694* (10 vols., 1763)
Henning	B. D. Henning (ed.), *The History of Parliament: The Commons 1660–1689* (3 vols.; 1983)
HMC	Historical Manuscripts Commission
Japikse	*Correspondentie van Willem III en van Hans Willem Bentinck*, ed. N. Japikse (vol. i in 2 parts, vol. ii in 3 parts; The Hague, 1927–37)
Lowther	Sir John Lowther, *Memoirs of the Reign of James II*, ed. T. Zouch (York, 1808)
Macaulay	T. B. Macaulay, *The History of England from the Accession of James II*, ed. C. H. Firth (6 vols.; 1914)
Morrice	Dr Williams Library, Roger Morrice, Entering Book
NLS	National Library of Scotland
NLW	National Library of Wales
PRO	Public Record Office
RO	Record Office
Reresby	*Memoirs of Sir John Reresby*, ed. A. Browning, (Glasgow, 1936)

Note on Dates

During the seventeenth century England's Old Style calendar was ten days behind the continental New Style. Old Style dates have been used throughout the text, though the year has been taken to have started on 1 January and not, as contemporaries began it, on 25 March. In the notes documents dated New Style in the original have been cited under both Old and New Style dates: e.g. 5/15 Nov. 1688.

1

Introduction

❦

I come now to the year 1688, which proved memorable,
and produced an extraordinary and unheard of revolution.

(Gilbert Burnet, *History of his Own Time*)

'THE ultimate view that we take of the Revolution of 1688',
wrote G. M. Trevelyan, 'must be determined by our preference
either for royal absolutism or for parliamentary government.
James II forced England to choose once for all between these
two.'[1] In those two sentences he summarized the Whig view of
the Glorious Revolution. Its glory consisted in the final triumph
of parliament over the Crown.

In the seventeenth century the word 'revolution' did not have
the significance which it has acquired since 1789. When
Englishmen used it to describe the events of 1688 and 1689 they
did not mean by it the violent overthrow of authority, nor the
transfer of power from one class to another. Rather it was
employed in the sense of the revolution of a wheel turning
round to a former state. Whigs insisted that there was an ancient
constitution of mixed or limited monarchy, in which the Lords
and Commons curbed the Crown's attempts to extend its
powers. James II acted unconstitutionally, in the Whig view,
when he dispensed with parliament and ruled arbitrarily. When
William of Orange became king, he agreed to maintain the rule
of law in conjunction with parliament. It was as much a
restoration as a revolution, since it restored the ancient
constitution. This is what the leading Whig historian of these
events, Lord Macaulay, meant when he claimed that, in the
Revolution Settlement, 'not a single flower of the Crown was
touched; not a single new right was given to the people'.[2] His

---

[1] G. M. Trevelyan, *The English Revolution* (1938), 245.
[2] Macaulay, vi.; 1308. Christopher Hill has recently challenged the claim
that contemporaries defined the term revolution only in cyclical terms, and

great nephew Trevelyan echoed this claim when he observed that England chose 'once for all' between royal absolutism and parliamentary government.

According to Whig historians, throughout the seventeenth century the Crown had been involved in a struggle for sovereignty with parliament. During the civil wars and the subsequent Interregnum, parliament had triumphed to the point of actually abolishing the monarchy. Under the later Stuarts, however, the royal prerogative was reasserted against the claims of parliament. The Glorious Revolution was thus the last act in a drama which began with the accession of James I, if not earlier.

Moreover it was a cosmic drama between the forces of good and evil. Of the principal characters in Macaulay's massive *History of England*, the hero William of Orange and the villain James II, it has been said that they were 'God and Satan: the great history is a kind of *Paradise Lost* and *Paradise Regained*'.[3]

Macaulay's angels were the Whigs and his devils were the Tories. His partisanship is apparent on almost every page of the *History*. He made it even more explicit in his address to the electors of Edinburgh in 1839, when he proclaimed that it was the Whig party which 'under Charles II carried the Habeas Corpus Act, which effected the Revolution, which passed the Toleration Act'. The great Whig historian saw English history as the story of progress. To him the Whigs were the agents of improvement and the Tories were the instruments of reaction. He was out of sympathy with Tory theories of divine,

cites several examples of them using it to indicate linear change too. C. Hill, 'The Word "Revolution" in Seventeenth–Century England', *For Veronica Wedgwood, These* ed. R. Ollard and P. Tudor-Craig, (London, 1986), pp. 134–151. He might have added another major instance. Charles II, in the Declaration of Breda, referred to 'the continued distractions of so many years and so many and great revolutions'. Yet, even when being used in the sense of linear rather than of cyclical change, this did not imply the kind of political transformation which is associated with the term in modern times. Thus Roger Morrice described both the execution of Charles I and the death of Charles II as great revolutions (Morrice MS P, p. 537). The first might merit the modern usage of the word, but scarcely the second. Soon after 1688 the events of that year became known as *the* Revolution. It was generally seen as the restoration of the ancient constitution, however, rather than as the establishment of a new one.

[3] G. R. Potter, *Macaulay* (1959), 31.

indefeasible, hereditary right, which in his view upheld absolut-ism. At the same time he distinguished between moderate and extreme Whiggism. He was highly critical of the first earl of Shaftesbury, leader of the Whigs under Charles II, accusing him of extremism, especially in his exploitation of mob violence. He also ridiculed the republicanism of Algernon Sidney. What he admired most was the moderation of a man like the marquis of Halifax. *The Character of a Trimmer*, with its emphasis on the rule of law, the balanced constitution, the vital role of parliament, and the desirability of religious toleration, epitomized the moderate achievements of the Revolution Settlement, which resolved the struggle for sovereignty under the Stuarts.[4]

Marxist historians also depict the events of 1688–9 as a coda to an epic work which reached its climax in the central decades of the century. To them the English Revolution, the preferred term for the period 1640 to 1689, or even 1640 to 1660, was marked by the violent seizure of power by the bourgeoisie.

Christopher Hill, the leading English Marxist historian of the seventeenth century, has provided a convenient summary of the case for seeing it as a bourgeois revolution.[5] It was not bourgeois in the sense of an urban bourgeoisie ousting a feudal aristocracy. Capitalism in England was highly developed in the countryside as well as in the towns, and capitalist methods of estate management were a marked feature of the landed economy. Nor was it a bourgeois revolution in the sense that the bourgeoisie willed its outcome. The intentions of the revolutionaries were many and varied. Few if any fought the civil wars for their results. Yet the consequences of the Revolution were to remove obstacles to the development of capitalism which the Stuarts had sustained. Thus feudal tenure, the Court of Wards, and the prerogative courts were swept away, and with them impediments to the capitalist exploitation of land. At the same time, the state actively promoted overseas commercial expansion. The Restoration temporarily held up these developments. 'After 1660 no doubt Charles II (from time

---

[4] W. A. Speck, 'Thomas Babington Macaulay', in J. Cannon (ed.), *The Historian at Work* (1980), 55–69.

[5] C. Hill, 'A Bourgeois Revolution?', in J. G. A. Pocock (ed.), *Three British Revolutions: 1641; 1688; 1776* (1980), 109–39.

to time) and James II (more seriously) dreamed of building up the absolute monarchy that their father had failed to achieve. But thanks to the Revolution, there was never any chance that they would succeed.'

'If the Revolution of 1640 was unwilled', concluded Hill, 'the coup d'état of 1688–9 and the peaceful Hanoverian succession were very much willed. The self-confident landed class had now consciously taken its destiny into its own hands.' It is significant that he describes the 'Glorious Revolution' as a mere *coup d'état*, thus emphasizing its relative unimportance by contrast with the great upheavals of the 1640s. To many historians, and not just Marxists, the fall of James II and his replacement by William and Mary represented little more than a palace revolution, having no deep social significance. The 'landed classes' simply reasserted their hegemony by getting rid of a monarch who had tried to undermine it. One indication of this generally held belief is that, where accounts of the origins of the civil war sometimes commence as far back as 1529, most studies of the Revolution of 1688 seem content to begin with the Popish Plot of 1678, or even with the accession of James II in 1685, after only a brief glance at the previous forty years or so.

Such a short-term view of the causes of the Revolution is now fashionably in line with recent revisionist interpretations of the earlier conflict, which challenge the notion that it had origins which can be traced back into the sixteenth century, or even as recently as the reign of James I. Those who adopt this approach have strongly criticized the conclusions of Whig and Marxist historians alike. At the moment both seem to be in full retreat before the attacks of their critics. There are, however, signs of a rally rather than of a rout.

The main lines of a critique of the Whig interpretation were laid down long ago by Sir Herbert Butterfield.[6] He castigated Whig historians for looking at the past from the vantage-point of the present, and for retrospectively praising those they saw as responsible for encouraging those trends which were to produce modern society and condemning those held to have impeded them. Revisionists of Stuart history sustain the same charges against those who detect long-term causes of the English

[6] H. Butterfield, *The Whig Interpretation of History* (1931).

Revolution.[7] The disadvantage of hindsight distorts the past, seeking for signs of incipient conflict long before the battle lines were drawn. Thus, to look for evidence of polarization in early Stuart or even Tudor England which foreshadowed the civil war is to assume that such an upheaval must have cast a long shadow behind it. When one examines earlier periods in their own right, and not for evidence of strains which were to culminate in catastrophe, they do not necessarily exhibit tensions which were pre-conditions of breakdown. Similarly it could be a mistake to examine the politics of Charles II's reign before the Popish Plot and Exclusion crisis in an attempt to discern the 'origins' of the Revolution of 1688. It would certainly be mistaken to identify the Whigs as being responsible for the downfall of James II and the transference of the Crown to William and Mary. Not only is it unhistorical retrospectively to take sides at any time in the past; it is particularly so in this instance, since no single party could claim responsibility for the Revolution and the subsequent Settlement.

The Whig concept of a fundamental conflict in Stuart England between Crown and parliament, resulting in the triumph of parliamentary government over royal absolutism, has been the main target of the revisionists. Parliament in this view was not seeking to share sovereignty with the Crown. In so far as there was discord between them, this was not due to a fundamental disagreement about the location of sovereign power in the constitution. Though their criticisms have concentrated on the early Stuart period, their objections have implications for the later seventeenth century too. They object primarily to the idea that parliament adopted an adversary stance towards the Crown whenever it assembled. On the contrary, they argue, parliaments met in a spirit of consensus rather than of conflict. Harmony, not discord, was the norm, and to concentrate upon disagreement distorts the reality. There were, of course, dissentient debates. But these usually reflected disagreements within the Court itself, rather than an organized opposition to the Crown. Thus the impeachments of Bacon, Buckingham, and Cranfield in the 1620s were inspired by rival courtiers rather

[7] See, for example, C. Russell (ed.), *The Origins of the English Civil War* (1973).

than by 'Country' politicians. Parliament was an arena in which Court factions carried on their jockeying for position.

Another objection to the classic Whig interpretation is that it tends to concentrate upon the House of Commons to the virtual omission of the Lords. The Upper House has been surprisingly neglected by historians, even though all the great ministers of the Stuarts, from Bacon, Buckingham, and Cranfield under James I and Charles I to Lords Danby, Godolphin, Nottingham, Rochester, and Sunderland in the reigns of Charles II and James II, sat in it. Certainly debates in the House of Lords affected the outcome of the Exclusion crisis and the Revolution Settlement. In both the Upper Chamber acted as a brake on the more extreme deliberations of the Commons.

The peers of the realm also played a major part in the events of 1688. In so far as there was any overt and active support for William of Orange in the provinces, it was led by such noblemen as Danby in Yorkshire and Devonshire in the Midlands.

It has even been suggested that the Marxist case could be stood on its head, and that what occurred under James II was a feudal reaction to a monarch intent on expediting a bourgeois revolution.[8] When he realized that he could not count on the co-operation of the Anglican aristocracy and gentry in the localities, he turned for support to Catholics and Dissenters. Those who replaced the Anglicans on the commissions of the peace and as officers in the county militias were notoriously from less affluent gentry families than their predecessors. Perhaps more significantly, James rigged the corporations in many boroughs by issuing new charters which gave the Crown the power to nominate the governing bodies. In town after town entrenched Anglican oligarchies were ousted and replaced by business and professional men who had been kept out of local government. It has been suggested that these changes replaced clients of the local landed élite with burgesses who resented their hegemony, especially if the newcomers were Dissenters who had suffered from the Anglican ascendancy in their boroughs. By placing the power of the Crown at the disposal of interests other than those of the traditional landed

---

[8] J. R. Jones, *The Revolution of 1688 in England* (1972), 15.

ruling class, especially in towns, James precipitated a reaction. Local magnates closed ranks at this threat to their privileges just as they had done in the 1650s. In 1660 this had facilitated the Restoration. In 1688 it prepared the way for the Revolution.

The lead taken by the aristocracy in 1688 is stressed by David Hosford.[9] He demonstrates the crucial roles of such noblemen as Lords Delamere, Devonshire, and Stamford in the taking of Derby and Nottingham in November 1688. This is a salutary corrective to those who have played down the significance of violent aspects of the events of that month, reducing them in some accounts to a mere palace coup.

At the same time, as Professor Kenyon observed in his inaugural lecture at Hull University,[10] nine out of ten aristocrats did not stir during it, either to join William of Orange, or, more significantly, to lift a finger for James II. This created a vital vacuum of power which William could exploit. Three years previously, when the duke of Monmouth had invaded, the landed élite sprang to James's defence. Its support proved critical, for as recent studies of the Monmouth episode have shown, the rebellion was by no means a shambles.[11] The duke himself showed remarkable talents of military leadership during his campaign, even earning the reluctant admiration of the king. Had he received any backing from the gentry, or even if they had not supported the regime, the outcome could have been very different. Certainly the change in the attitude of the aristocracy and gentry towards James II was a crucial ingredient in the success of the Dutch invasion of 1688.

The reluctance of most Englishmen to become involved in actual combat was a marked feature of the crisis of 1642 as well. Every local study has shown that, so far from there being antagonistic social groups anxious to settle scores with each other and only awaiting the signal to fight from their national leaders, the civil war was initially fought most reluctantly by men who, rather than spoiling for a fight, were desperately anxious to avoid the breakdown at the centre disturbing the

---

[9] D. Hosford, *Nottingham, Nobles and the North* (Hamden, Connecticut, 1976).

[10] J. P. Kenyon, *The Nobility in the Revolution of 1688* (Hull, 1963).

[11] P. Earle, *Monmouth's Rebels* (1977); R. Clifton, *The Last Popular Rebellion: The Western Rising of 1685* (1984).

peace of their localities. Another conclusion from local studies
has been that it is impossible to detect a cleavage in society
between opponents and supporters of capitalism, either rural or
urban. Compared with the period prior to 1642, there have been
hardly any local investigations of the Revolution of 1688. Most
of those that have been undertaken, however, scarcely support
the view of a society divided along Marxist lines.[12]

Perhaps the most telling critique of the Whig and Marxist
cases is the proposition that the later Stuarts nearly succeeded in
establishing absolutism by the legitimate exploitation of the
residual powers of the Crown. To Whig historians such a policy
was unconstitutional, while to Marxists it was futile since the
lasting achievements of the civil wars made the establishment of
absolute monarchy impossible.

The view that the later Stuarts were consciously seeking to
strengthen the power of the Crown during the 1680s was most
persuasively propounded by J. R. Western.[13] The basic thesis
which he put forward was that, 'after 1680 England seemed to
be moving inexorably towards absolutism and only the events
of 1688 led to a change of direction, perhaps at the last possible
moment'. Charles and James were able to enhance the power of
the Crown by reinvigorating traditional institutions and by
building up new financial and military resources. The traditional
machinery of the law and of local government was reinvigorated
by the extensive use of the royal prerogative. Thus both
Charles II and James II appointed judges at pleasure and purged
the county militias, the commissions of the peace, and above all
the parliamentary boroughs. It is in this respect that the 1680s
were uniform. Both kings used their powers to appoint judges
to create a compliant judicial bench which would uphold the
prerogative against parliamentary limitations on it. Both weeded
the county militias and the commissions of the peace. Above all
both used their power of *quo warranto* to recall borough charters
and to remodel the corporations, appointing mayors, aldermen,

---

[12] See C. Holmes, *Seventeenth Century Lincolnshire* (Lincoln, 1980), 235–53;
A. Fletcher, *Reform in the Provinces: The Government of Stuart England* (1986),
351–73.
[13] J. R. Western, *Monarchy and Revolution: The English State in the 1680s*
(1972).

and common councilmen who would support the Crown, especially in parliamentary elections.

Both monarchs also developed the financial machinery and the standing army. The Treasury was overhauled and made more efficient, while the farming of indirect taxes was abandoned and direct administration of the revenues was implemented. These initiatives, coupled with a trade boom which boosted the yield of the customs, enabled them to survive without extraordinary parliamentary supply. It also allowed James II to build up a standing army. Since he had no intention of fighting a foreign war, then the increase of the armed forces following the suppression of the Monmouth rebellion was aimed at further strengthening the monarchy along absolutist lines.[14]

One of the most ambitious uses of the residual prerogatives to achieve absolutism was the campaign to procure a parliament which would repeal the Test Acts and penal laws against Roman Catholics and Protestant Dissenters. This was touched on by Western but most thoroughly investigated by J. R. Jones, who concluded from his investigation that James II's aim to pack parliament could well have succeeded.[15]

Indeed both historians stress that the later Stuarts nearly got away with their schemes to strengthen the royal prerogative at the expense of representative institutions. There was not much in the way of positive resistance to their plans. On the contrary, as long as they were being implemented to consolidate the position of the established church and the Tory gentry, at the expense of Protestant Dissenters and exclusionist Whigs, they received substantial and solid support. Few complained when Charles II failed to summon parliament between 1681 and 1685 in defiance of the Triennial Act of 1664. It was only when James II reversed this trend, and employed the powers of the Crown on behalf of Catholics and nonconformists, that Anglican Tories began to protest. Even then they scarcely threatened revolution. It would have flown in the face of their doctrines of passive obedience and non-resistance to oppose the

---

[14] In addition to Western, see H. Roseveare, *The Treasury, 1660–1870* (1973); D. C. Chandaman, *The English Public Revenue, 1660–88* (1975); and J. Childs, *The Army, James II and the Glorious Revolution* (1980).

[15] Jones, *Revolution*, pp. 128–75.

monarch forcibly. Although James alienated their allegiance, it took a foreign invasion to remove him from the throne.

Moreover, according to the military historian of the later Stuarts, John Childs, even this could have been defeated.[16] James had build up an impressive standing army, numbering perhaps 40,000 all told by November 1688. William landed with about 14,000 men, not noticeably superior to the English professionals. Although some of the latter deserted to the Dutch, they probably numbered no more than 1,000. The vast majority of James's troops remained loyal to him, and these were more than enough to have beaten William in battle had the two armies engaged. That they did not do so was mainly owing to the king's panic when he learned of the desertions. Thus in the event the Revolution hinged on the personality and mental state of James II.

These have been investigated in a number of biographies, of which that by John Miller is the most important to appear recently.[17] Dr Miller argues that James was a basically simple man with a single-minded aim, to obtain toleration for Catholics. He was not aiming at the forcible reconversion of England, nor did he seek to be absolute. He only resorted to increasing the power of the Crown in order to obtain his goal when parliament refused to co-operate with him. In so far as there was any tendency towards absolutism under him, it was as a means to the end of religious toleration, not as an end in itself. Moreover, even if he had sought to make himself absolute on the French model, he simply lacked the resources which Louis XIV enjoyed to emulate him.[18] The king of France had a much larger army, vast revenues, and a paid bureaucracy at his disposal. In comparison the sinews of state in England were puny.

In this view James II's Catholicism and his religious intentions were the most important causes of the Revolution, and not his use or alleged abuse of the royal prerogative. It was simply unfortunate for the king that Protestant Englishmen had created a bogyman out of fear of a papist king. Fears of popery

[16] Childs, *The Army, James II and the Glorious Revolution*, pp. 177–81.
[17] J. Miller, *James II: A Study in Kingship* (1978).
[18] J. Miller, 'The Potential for "Absolutism" in Later Stuart England', *History*, 119 (1984), 187–207.

generated irrational delusions about the intentions of the Stuarts from the 1630s to the 1680s. They were fed on a mythology sustained by Foxe's *Book of Martyrs* that Catholic monarchs would follow Mary Tudor's example and extirpate heresy by wholesale executions. In addition to this Protestant martyrology there was also the myth which equated Catholicism with arbitrary power, a belief which received strong support from contemporary events in France, where Huguenots were suffering renewed persecution after the revocation of the Edict of Nantes. That the French king was a militant Roman Catholic and an absolute monarch reinforced the association between the two in the minds of most Englishmen. Yet, according to historians favourably disposed towards James, they were erroneous in drawing parallels between him and Louis XIV. James was a genuine convert to Catholicism but also, since he was aware that Catholics were a tiny minority in England, to religious toleration. He was not the cynical hypocrite of Whig legend, intent on wooing the Dissenters from siding with the Anglicans simply to drive a wedge between his Protestant subjects, the better to achieve the goal of recatholicizing the country. On the contrary, he was an enlightened ruler ahead of his time in his commitment to a wide measure of toleration.[19]

The debate about James's intentions in England can to some extent be resolved by placing it in the context of his aims elsewhere in his dominions. Recent studies of colonial North America, Ireland, and Scotland seem to reinforce the views of those who detect absolutist pretensions in him.

James had long been interested in America, having been granted the proprietorship of New York and New Jersey when they were acquired from the Dutch in the 1660s.[20] As Governor of New York he had stubbornly resisted demands by his colonial subjects for an assembly. It is true that he gave in to these demands in 1683, but this was only a temporary concession. After he became king, and New York was

[19] In addition to Miller, this view is also taken by Maurice Ashley. See M. Ashley, *James II* (1977).

[20] For colonial North America, see D. Lovejoy, *The Glorious Revolution in America* (1972), and J. Sosin, *English America and the Restoration Monarchy of Charles II* (1980), and *English America and the Revolution of 1688* (1982).

transformed from a proprietorial to a Crown colony, he suppressed the new assembly.

His attitudes towards representation in the colonies were more fully displayed in the arrangements which he made for the government of Massachusetts, Rhode Island, Connecticut, and New Hampshire. Of these only New Hampshire was a Crown colony. The other three all enjoyed a remarkable degree of autonomy, to the point where they were even accused of being quasi-independent republics. The government in England had determined to get a grip on this situation under Charles II, and, after investigations of flagrant violations of the navigation Acts by Massachusetts, its charter was revoked in 1684. The new charter which Charles II drew up made no mention of a representative assembly in the Bay colony.

James, who had been closely involved in the decisions affecting Massachusetts, applied them to all four New England colonies after he became king. A so-called Dominion of New England was established under a Governor-General. All colonial assemblies were suppressed, while even town meetings were severely circumscribed. James was creating a viceroyalty in North America, which he extended to include New York and New Jersey before the end of the reign. Sir Edmund Andros, whom James appointed as Governor of the Dominion, had power to make laws and raise taxes virtually at will. Those who refused to pay them could be imprisoned and fined.

This exercise in absolutism across the Atlantic was not merely the means to an end of religious toleration; it was an end in itself. To be sure, both Charles and his brother sought to make the zealous Puritans of New England more tolerant. They objected strongly when the Congregationalists of Massachusetts persecuted Quakers. But in the whole length and breadth of the Dominion of New England, from Maine to the Delaware, there cannot have been many Catholics in the 1680s. Yet James strengthened autocracy in these regions at the expense of colonial assemblies.

One of the main motives behind the creation of the Dominion of New England was defence. Stephen Webb has stressed this element in imperial policy.[21] While he might have overstressed

[21] S. Saunders Webb, *The Governors General: The English Army and the Definition of Empire, 1569–1681* (Chapel Hill, 1979).

it for other periods, there can be little doubt that his concept of 'garrison government' fits the colonial aims of James II. As Philip Haffenden has observed of them, 'the objective was the reduction of the remaining independent governments overseas, and their regrouping, with the royal provinces, to form viceroyalties comparable in size to the Spanish territories to the South and greater in military strength than the French power in the North'.[22]

Defence was a major priority in Ireland too.[23] James II's right-hand man in Ireland, Richard Talbot, who became earl of Tyrconnel, went even further than the king in promoting the Catholic cause. Tyrconnel himself, like the majority of Irishmen, was a Catholic. Moreover, he considered all Protestants to be disaffected. The accession of a Catholic monarch gave the Irish Catholics a unique opportunity to assert the ascendancy which their numbers warranted. Speed was of the essence, however, since James was not expected to live long, and would be succeeded by his Protestant daughter Mary and her Calvinist husband William. Ultimately what Tyrconnel sought to do was to build up Catholic strength to the point where an independent Ireland could resist the claims of William and Mary, even if this meant putting the country under French protection. As he was alleged to have sworn in 1686, 'the Irish would be fools or madmen if after his [James's] death they should submit to be governed by the Prince of Orange . . . or be longer slaves to England, but rather set up a king of their own and put themselves under the protection of France'.

James's attitude towards Tyrconnel's proposals was ambivalent. It appealed to his heart but not to his head. The opportunity to make at least one of his three kingdoms a safe haven for his fellow Catholics was emotionally appealing. At the same time, political calculations urged caution. The Protestants, although a minority, were an important force in Irish politics and in the economy. Those of the Church of Ireland, the Irish equivalent of the Anglican Church, formed the Protestant

[22] P. Haffenden, 'The Crown and the Colonial Charters, 1675–1688', *William and Mary Quarterly*, 25 (1958), 297–311, 452–66.

[23] For Ireland, See J. G. Sims, *Jacobite Ireland* (1969); J. Miller, 'The Earl of Tyrconnel and James II's Irish Policy, 1685–1688', *Historical Journal*, 20 (1977), 803–23.

ascendancy based in Dublin. Theoretically they enjoyed a monopoly of public office. The earl of Clarendon, whom James sent to Ireland as Lord-Lieutenant, relied on these to sustain his authority and they in turn expected him to maintain their ascendancy. The Ulster Presbyterians already played a significant role in Irish commerce. To support Tyrconnel's policies, therefore, meant alienating the important Protestant communities in Ulster and the Pale, and arousing the fears of Anglicans and Dissenters in England. Moreover, James was a stickler for the hereditary succession, and hesitated to break it in the case of Ireland, even if its independence might seem the best solution for his Catholic subjects there.

As usual ambivalence produced the worst of all possible worlds. James's indecision, his desire to have it both ways, manifested itself in the first two years of his reign by retaining Clarendon as Lord-Lieutenant but giving Tyrconnel complete control of military affairs in Ireland. Naturally this produced friction between the two men. Clarendon, the cultivated English nobleman, was aghast at the splenetic intemperate Irishman, whom he dismissed as 'a man of monstrous vanity as well as pride and furious passion'. He came to the conclusion that Tyrconnel was mentally unbalanced. Nevertheless the Irish politican undermined the authority of the English Lord-Lieutenant, rendering him virtually impotent politically even before he was recalled in 1687, to be replaced by Tyrconnel himself.

Tyrconnel disarmed the Protestant militia in Ireland, and purged the army of Protestants. As early as September 1686 40 per cent of the officers and 67 per cent of the rank and file were Catholics. By 1688 the Irish army was virtually all Catholic. In that year too almost the entire administration from top to bottom throughout Ireland was in the hands of Catholics. As David Hayton has observed, 'in the Irish context the issue was not toleration but supremacy'.[24]

The ambivalent attitudes which characterized James's approach to Ireland have also been discerned in his dealings with Scotland.[25] Paul Hopkins has recently shown that he had no

[24] D. Hayton, 'John Bull's other Kingdoms: Ireland', *Britain in the First Age of Party 1680–1750*, ed. C. Jones (1987), 263.

[25] English historians hesitate to comment upon Scottish history, all too

consistent policy towards his northern kingdom either. While projecting an image of resolute determination, he in fact vacillated between two fundamentally incompatible aspirations: to sustain social stability, and to promote Catholicism.

When he was sent into exile in Edinburgh by his brother in November 1679, he became virtual viceroy there until May 1682. Like New York, therefore, Scotland had experience of his rule while he was still duke of York. During his Scottish sojourn he stressed the necessity for a stable society. This made him popular with the landed élite and the Episcopal Church, which had felt threatened by the revival of militant presbyterianism under his predecessor the duke of Lauderdale. Whiggish accounts of the duke of York's regime dwelt on his repression of Covenanters, accusing him of presiding over a reign of terror and characterizing the 1680s as the killing time. Burnet told a story of James witnessing the torture of prisoners, which lost nothing in the telling by Macaulay, who accused the duke of downright sadism. Catholic apologists denied the truth of Burnet's allegations, and cited evidence which painted a very different picture of his regime. Thus Andrew Hay wrote from Edinburgh on 15 October 1681: 'His Highness doth carry himself with so great temper and diligence, is so just in his payments, so merciful in all penal matters, so impartial in giving his judgment in Court, so humble, so civil and obliging to all sorts of people, that he hath gained the affection of all

---

aware of the criticisms they will receive from scholars there for doing so. At one time I had intended to extend my own researches on the 1688 Revolution into its progress in Scotland, but backed off when I became aware of the mass of materials in Scottish repositories and the little use which had been made of them. In fact a scholarly study of the Revolution in Scotland has still to be written. As recently as 1983 Rosalind Mitchison had to admit that 'there is little in the general histories of Britain since T. B. Macaulay's *History of England* . . . which pays serious attention to James VII's rule in Scotland or to the impact of the Revolution there' (*Lordship to Patronage: Scotland, 1603–1745*, p. 184). Yet there is a wealth of virtually unexploited evidence for the subject. As the Keeper of Manuscripts at the NLS bluntly put it in reply to my request for information, 'the amount of material relating to the political history of the 1680s is so enormous that unless you can be a great deal more specific about what you want to see there is really very little that I can do to help you'. Paul Hopkins has shown how rich it is, and what can be done with it, in *Glencoe and the Highland War* (1986).

understanding and obligable persons.'[26] Covenanters were indeed tortured and put to death, but torture was still legal in Scotland, and their offence was more political than religious. They had virtually declared war on the government.

More recent accounts have stressed the positive rather than the negative aspects of James's stay in Scotland. He used his patronage to encourage the development of institutions there, such as the Royal College of Physicians, the Advocates' Library, and the Order of the Thistle. This patronage was the practical expression of a political ideology which stressed paternalism and order; absolute monarchy allied to a stable hierarchical society.[27]

After he became king, however, James broke the alliance by promoting the interests of his fellow Catholics. He ruled Scotland from London, relying on the earls of Melfort and Perth, converts to Catholicism, to realize his objectives there. They undermined the royalist support he had so assiduously cultivated during the last years of his brother's reign. As Bruce Lenman has observed, 'by his tactlessness, ineptitude, wooden arrogance and unpopular (if defensible) policies James threw away a position of immense strength'.[28]

Just how strong he was in Scotland was illustrated shortly after his accession as James VII by the suppression of the earl of Argyll's rebellion. This was accomplished even more easily than the defeat of the duke of Monmouth's rising in England. Although the government forces were scarcely models of competence and efficiency, Argyll showed far less military skill than did Monmouth. More important, as in England, the rebels found no significant support among the magnates. On the contrary, these rallied to the Crown in impressive numbers. As Hopkins observes of Argyll's invasion, 'it was far too soon, allowing no time for James's folly to start alienating his supporters'.[29] The political nation demonstrated its loyalty in

---

[26] M. V. Hay, *The Enigma of James II* (1938), 24.

[27] H. Ouston, 'York in Edinburgh: James VII and the Patronage of Learning in Scotland, 1679–1688', in J. Dwyer, R. A. Mason, and A. Murdoch (eds.), *New Perspectives on the Politics and Culture of Early Modern Scotland* (1982), 133–55.

[28] B. Lenman, *The Jacobite Clans of the Great Glen* (1984), 44.

[29] Hopkins, *Glencoe and the Highland War*, p. 95.

the Edinburgh parliament of 1685, which resolved that Scotland owed its blessings to 'the solid absolute authority' with which its kings were invested 'by the first and fundamental law of our monarchy'. James strained their loyalty to the limit, forcing absolutism down their throats in the preamble to his Scottish Declaration of Indulgence, which he justified by his 'Absolute power, which all our subjects are to obey without reserve'.

In the Whig view, the Glorious Revolution brought a sudden end to these absolutist tendencies in all James's dominions, replacing them in England with limited or mixed monarchy. William of Orange was cast in the role of Deliverer. The Revolution Settlement enshrined the transition from divine-right kingship to the acceptance of John Locke's concept of contractual government. Two features of the settlement allegedly upheld this shift to a Whiggish interpretation of the constitution. One was the resolution of the Convention parliament 'that king James the second, having endeavoured to subvert the Constitution of the kingdom, by breaking the original contract between king and people, and . . . having violated the fundamental laws, and having withdrawn himself out of the kingdom, has abdicated the Government and that the throne is thereby become vacant'. The other was the Declaration of Rights, which apparently renewed the contract with William and Mary, setting aside the hereditary succession and establishing parliamentary monarchy.

The Whig view of William as the Great Deliverer has been radically revised by recent historians. So far from intervening in English politics to protect liberty and property, he is now seen as aiming at the Crown before the pretext to seize it arose. Lucille Pinkham's view that he was intriguing to that end from 1686 at the latest has been discounted, since until James had a son and heir there was no need for the Prince of Orange to plot to obtain a throne which would be his wife's by right when her father died.[30] The announcement of the queen's pregnancy in November 1687, however, drastically revised his plans.

The possibility that Mary of Modena might give birth to a son in the summer of 1688 concentrated William's mind on intervening, to save not abstract English liberties but his wife's

---

[30] L. Pinkham, *William III and the Respectable Revolution* (1954).

claim to the throne. So far from displaying liberal constitutional attitudes, he had conspicuously protected such autocratic powers as he possessed in the Dutch Republic. He became concerned when he thought that James's English subjects would be so incensed at the perpetuation of the Catholic monarchy that they might rebel and set up a republic of their own, as they had done during the 1640s. It was as much to protect the monarchy as to rescue England from Catholicism that he invaded in November 1688.

The Whig interpretation of the Revolution Settlement has also been subjected to severe criticism. Of late, however, some historians have sprung to its defence, or at least a modified version of it.

The notion that the year 1689 saw the final triumph of Whig political theories over Tory notions of divine-right kingship has been challenged by several historians.[31] In particular the claim that John Locke's views were vindicated by the Revolution is now very much in question. Although Locke became the philosopher of the eighteenth century, his immediate impact was limited, despite the publication of his *Two Treatises of Government* in 1690. Indeed the arguments he advanced in them were far from typical of late-seventeenth-century thought. His attack on Robert Filmer's *Patriarcha* did not, as was once alleged, demolish divine-right theories of kingship. On the contrary, suitably modified to take into account the realities of what had happened in 1688, for instance by incorporating the idea of providential intervention in English politics, they survived as perhaps a majority view, being held by most Tories at least until the accession of the house of Hanover. Nor were Locke's notions of the formation of civil society by a social contract, and of government by a fiduciary trust, typical of Whig thought. Rather they were regarded as radical and even as verging on republicanism at the time.[32] Whig writers subscribed to a variety of views. Some mentioned a contract as the origin of government. Others, perhaps the more typical, took the

---

[31] See, for example, H. T. Dickinson, *Liberty and Property* (1977); J. P. Kenyon, *Revolution Principles* (1977).

[32] R. Ashcraft and M. Goldsmith, 'Locke, Revolution Principles and the Formation of Whig Ideology', *Historical Journal*, 26 (1983), 773–800.

historical view that England had always enjoyed in theory a balanced constitution.

The debates in the Convention do not document the clash of conflicting and coherent ideologies. Instead they reveal incoherence as men tried to grapple pragmatically with a crisis. Their confusion is reflected in the celebrated resolution and in the circumstances surrounding the Bill of Rights.

Close analysis of the resolution has led some scholars to stress the pragmatic rather than the ideological basis for its formulation. Professor Kenyon, for instance, argues that the references to the king's breaking the original contract and violating the fundamental laws were far less crucial than the assertion that he had withdrawn from the kingdom and had therefore abdicated, leaving the throne vacant. As for the Bill of Rights, no mention was made of the original contract in it.[33] Indeed, as Dr Frankle maintains, 'it was not, as is sometimes alleged, presented to [William and Mary] as a condition which they had to accept before receiving the crown. It was merely read to them as a reminder of the limitations on their newly acquired powers. No formal assent to the Declaration's provisions was either requested or received.' Moreover, none of its conditions imposed new limitations on the monarchy. The committee appointed to frame it did produce some twenty-three conditions, but the House of Commons separated those requiring fresh legislation from those which merely affirmed old laws. According to Frankle, the main reason why Whig plans to place further limitations on the powers of the Crown were thwarted was the refusal of the Prince of Orange to go along with them.[34]

These reinterpretations of the resolution and the Bill of Rights have not gone unchallenged. Dr T. P. Slaughter called in question the view that the references to the original contract and fundamental laws in the first had nothing to do with the throne being vacant, by pointing out that the verb 'to abdicate' could be used transitively in the seventeenth century, and that therefore the phrase 'abdicated the government' could not be isolated

[33] J. P. Kenyon, 'The Revolution of 1688: Resistance and Contract', in N. McKendrick (ed.), *Historical Perspectives: Studies in English Thought and Society in Honour of J. H. Plumb* (1974), 48–9.

[34] R. J. Frankle, 'The Formulation of the Declaration of Rights', *Historical Journal*, 17 (1974), 265–79.

from the rest of the resolution. In his view it was a crucial clause which caused the resolution taken altogether to add up to a statement that James had been deposed for breaking the original contract and violating the fundamental laws as well as for quitting the kingdom.[35] In reply Dr Miller has suggested that the resolution was ambiguous, and perhaps deliberately so to reconcile the divergent political views as to what had actually happened in 1688 which were held by the members of the Convention parliament. Thus Whigs who supported the wording might well have meant by it that they were deposing James for breaking the contract, while to Tories the main point was that James had deposed himself by abdicating, thereby leaving the throne vacant.[36]

Lois Schwoerer has devoted a whole monograph to the Declaration of Rights to argue that the Whig view triumphed in the Convention, and that the Revolution inaugurated not merely a new reign but a new kind of kingship.[37] As she rightly points out, the notion that the Declaration simply confirmed existing rights was a Whiggish version of the law. In fact, under the guise of affirming ancient liberties, it created new restrictions on the powers of the Crown. For example, the claims that the suspending and dispensing powers were illegal, and that the Crown could not maintain a standing army in peacetime without consent of parliament, were highly tendentious. By depriving the Crown of these powers, the Declaration of Rights did in effect limit the royal prerogative.

Perhaps the most ambitious attempt to rescue the Whig interpretation of the Revolution from its critics is by Angus McInnes.[38] He reasserts the claims of the late-seventeenth century to the concept, against those who have appropriated it for its central decades. So far from being a mere coda to the epic themes of the 1640s and 1650s, he argues, the reigns of James II and William III marked the real shift from absolute to mixed

---

[35] T. P. Slaughter, ' "Abdicate" and "Contract" in the Glorious Revolution', *Historical Journal*, 24 (1981), 327–37.

[36] J. Miller, 'The Glorious Revolution: "Contract" and "Abdication" reconsidered', *Historical Journal*, 25 (1982), 541–55.

[37] L. Schwoerer, *The Declaration of Rights* (1981).

[38] A. McInnes, 'When was the English Revolution?', *History*, 117 (1982), 377–92.

monarchy. Despite all the legislation of the Long Parliament and the subsequent establishment of a republic, the Crown was restored virtually unconditionally in 1660. During the 1680s it mounted a sustained campaign to build up its own authority and to break the resistance of any opposition. Thus the standing army was established and increased to a significant force. The judiciary was purged and brought under royal control. Parliament was evaded, while all the institutions of local government, the militia, the commissions of the peace, and the borough corporations, were systematically remodelled to make them subservient to the royal will. So far from previous events having made the creation of absolute monarchy impossible, under James II England was fast approaching that type of polity. The Revolution nipped these developments in the bud. Parliament became a permanent part of the constitution. The Declaration of Rights interrupted the hereditary succession to the throne and put limits on the royal prerogative. Above all the financial settlement made the king dependent upon parliament. The Convention determined not to repeat the mistake of the 1685 parliament by granting William and Mary sufficient revenues to rule without further parliamentary grants. It failed to vote the customs for life and undertook a rigorous scrutiny of the yields of the revenues. This set a precedent for future parliaments to keep a financial curb on the Crown.

Whether 1988 deserves to be marked as the tercentenary of a major turning-point in British history, or merely of a non-event, therefore, depends on which interpretation of the events which occurred in 1688 carries the most weight. Do they deserve the label 'revolution' or not?

This book seeks to answer that question. Before the events can be interpreted, however, they must first be established. The first part, therefore, consists of a narrative of the principal passages which culminated in the Dutch invasion, the flight of James II, and the Settlement of 1689. The second part seeks to assess their significance.

PART ONE

2

The Origins of the Revolution

❦

When we reflect on the calamities in the late unhappy time
of usurpation and rebellion and what desolation has been
made in this nation by former civil wars, we bless God for
our miraculous deliverance at this time.

(*The Address of the Grand Jury of Westmorland on the
Suppression of Monmouth's Rebellion*)

THE first problem posed by a narrative of the Revolution of
1688 is quite when to start. Traditionally accounts have begun
with the later years of the reign of Charles II. This is in sharp
contrast with traditional narratives of the causes of the English
civil war, which usually begin in James I's reign, and sometimes
in the Tudor age. Of late, however, such long views have been
criticized, and Clarendon's claim that he was not so sharp-
sighted as to see the origins of that conflict in the reign of
Elizabeth has been endorsed.[1] Such revisionism would make a
study of the Revolution starting in 1678, or even 1685, quite
fashionable.

Nevertheless, to treat the events of 1688 in isolation from the
upheaval of the civil wars would be absurd. Contemporaries
were deeply conscious of the parallels which could be drawn
between the experiences of their own times and those of their
fathers. Comparisons between the later Stuarts and Charles I
were constantly made, not least by the kings themselves.
James II was convinced that his father had lost first his throne
and then his head because of fatal compromises with his

[1] 'I am not so sharp-sighted as those who have discerned this rebellion
contriving from (if not before) the death of Queen Elizabeth' *Clarendon:
Selections from the History of the Rebellion*, ed. H. Trevor-Roper (Oxford, 1978),
iii. For a survey of the debate over the long- and short-term origins of the civil
war, see J. H. Hexter, 'The Early Stuarts and Parliament: Old Hat and *Nouvelle
Vague*', *Parliamentary History*, 1 (1982), 181–215.

enemies. The Tories were frequently compared with the supporters of Charles I and the Whigs with his opponents. Accounting for the rise of Whiggery in the late 1670s, Dryden could simply describe it as 'the good old cause revived'.[2] The 'good old cause' was the slogan for the radicals in the Interregnum. The fear of Catholicism in high places, on the other hand, could be traced to the charges brought by Pym against the 'malignant party' at Court in the Grand Remonstrance. Memories of the mid-century crisis could be invoked by any scare roused by the paranoia about popery. The Popish Plot was associated with the Irish rebellion of 1641 and the 'massacre' of Protestants that occurred with it. A generation which commemorated the anniversaries of Queen Elizabeth's accession day, the Gunpowder Plot, and the execution of Charles I as occasions for political demonstrations for or against the exclusion of a Catholic successor to the throne was steeped in highly partisan versions of the past. Fully to do justice to the participants in the drama that was acted out in 1688 would involve an Act I, Scene 1, set somewhere in the sixteenth century.

However, a more manageable start is another date in the contemporary political calendar, 29 May 1660. The Restoration of Charles II took place in a state of euphoria that a constitutional settlement which had eluded men for twenty years would finally be found. Twenty-eight years later the mechanism then employed, the summoning of a Convention not called by the king, was to be almost ritualistically followed. In 1660 the Convention invited Charles back to his realm. In 1689 its successor offered the Crown to William and Mary.

A major difference between the Restoration and Revolution Settlements, however, was their provision for those who could not conform to the Church of England. In 1689 the so-called Toleration Act granted immunity from prosecution to Protestant Dissenters who held their own separate religious services. In the 1660s legislation was enacted which added to the penalties for nonconformity. The Act of Uniformity of 1662 insisted upon subscription by clergymen to all Thirty-nine Articles of the Anglican Church. These had been a bone of contention

[2] J. Dryden, *Absalom and Achitophel*, ed. P. Roberts (1973), 27.

between Anglicans and Presbyterians over the century since they had been established as the orthodoxy of the established church. Those inclined towards Presbyterianism had scrupled at subscribing to some four which did not seem to them compatible with the Scriptures. Their notion that everything should be justified by the Bible came up against Anglican conviction that anything was justified which was not contrary to the word of God.

In the early stages of the Restoration it had seemed that their differences might be reconciled. Apart from the disagreement over the Articles, the others were relatively trivial. Presbyterians objected to episcopacy, and had scruples about episcopal ordination. They also disliked such Anglican practices as bowing at the name of Jesus, exchanging rings in marriage, and crossing an infant's head with water during baptism. To them those were relics of popery. Serious attempts were made in 1661 to get leading divines to negotiate a compromise on these issues in an attempt to keep the Presbyterian ministers within the restored Church of England. The conference called at the Savoy to achieve this, however, ended in deadlock.

So far from being comprehended within the established church, the Presbyterians were cast out of it by the Act of Uniformity. Nearly two thousand clergymen could not bring themselves to subscribe to all Thirty-nine Articles and, when the deadline for subscription was reached in August 1662, they left the Church of England. They were not allowed to depart in peace, for the Five Mile Act of 1665 severely curtailed their liberty. It forbade any ejected minister from living within five miles of his former parish, or any corporate town. The Conventicle Act of 1664 dealt harshly with those who attended any unofficial religious service involving more than five people. Fines of £5 for the first offence, £10 for the second, and £100 for the third were levied on offenders, with prison for failure to pay or even transportation for a third conviction. This Act expired in 1669, to be followed by a second Conventicle Act, which imposed even heavier fines on preachers or householders who allowed their premises to be used for illegal services. These fines could be levied by impounding possessions. Andrew Marvell called this Act 'the quintessence of arbitrary malice'.[3]

[3] Quoted in A. Fletcher, 'The enforcement of the Conventicle Acts,

There has been much debate as to why the Restoration religious settlement restored the Church of England on such a narrow basis.[4] On the surface this was the last thing one might have expected in May 1660. The established church under Archbishop Laud had been associated with a High Anglicanism regarded by many as crypto-Catholicism. Its extremism had done much to precipitate civil war. Since 1642 it had been submerged in a sea of rival sects, until it had seemed in danger of disappearing for ever. Then in the late 1650s the disillusionment of many Presbyterians with radical sectarians had led them to ally with their former Anglican opponents. Booth's rising in Cheshire in 1659 had seen such an alliance actually fighting to restore the king. It was widely expected that their new-found loyalty would be rewarded. Charles II had offered a 'liberty to tender consciences' in the Declaration of Breda, which heralded his Restoration. Instead of obtaining recognition by being kept within the communion of the Church of England, however, they had not even been granted toleration.

Why had the expectations of 1660 withered on the vine? Some historians have detected insincerity on the part of Charles II and his chief adviser, the earl of Clarendon. In this view, the offer of toleration in the Declaration of Breda was a cynical manœuvre to buy time until the Anglicans were firmly entrenched. It is hard to accept this interpretation. Charles's sincerity in making the offer seems to be substantiated by his Declaration of Indulgence in 1662, which attempted to relieve nonconformists of the penalties of their nonconformity. The Royal Edict of Toleration, however, was withdrawn when it was criticized in parliament. As for Clarendon although he was later happy to project the image of a narrow High Anglican, in 1660 he was anxious to engineer a restoration on the widest possible basis. Some sop to the Presbyterians seemed to make political sense, especially since they were strongly represented in the Convention.

1664–1679', in W. Sheils (ed.), *Persecution and Toleration* (Studies in Church History, 21; 1984), 246.

[4] See R. S. Bosher, *The Making of the Restoration Settlement* (1957); G. R. Abernathy, 'The English Presbyterians and the Stuart Restoration', *Transactions of the American Philosophical Society* (1965); I. M. Green, *The Re-establishment of the Church of England, 1660–1667* (Oxford, 1978); R. A. Beddard, 'The Restoration Church', in J. R. Jones (ed.), *The Restored Monarchy 1660–1688* (1979), 155–75.

He may have come to the conclusion that he had overestimated their numerical strength, and that they were politically expendable. Even so, he was not the architect of the religious legislation of the 1660s, which has falsely been dubbed the Clarendon Code.

There is more substance in the claim that the divines were responsible for the failure to reach agreement at the Savoy.[5] The Anglican hierarchy was by no means as intransigent as the term 'Laudian', which has been mistakenly applied to them, implies. Nevertheless they had survived the previous decades with difficulty, and their sufferings for their beliefs had not endeared them to their sectarian persecutors. Now that the boot was on the other foot they were not in a mood to compromise.

Nor did the Presbyterian representatives help their own cause. On the contrary, their leader, Richard Baxter, proved hopeless as a negotiator. Instead of agreeing to revise the Book of Common Prayer, he devised a whole new liturgy of his own. With such intransigent attitudes the conference was doomed to failure.

Yet the chief reason for the religious settlement resting on so narrow a basis was not the attitude of the king or Clarendon, nor the entrenched positions of the divines: it was the return to parliament in 1661 of a majority of ardent royalists. The Cavalier parliament was dominated by gentry who had endured the puritan excesses of the 1640s and 1650s. Now the moment had come for revenge, and they seized it. The legislation of the opening sessions of the parliament enacted their vengeance. Thus the Corporation Act of 1661 confined offices in borough corporations to communicating Anglicans by insisting that all those appointed or elected to them should have received communion in the Church of England in the year prior to their appointment or election. It also enforced oaths upon them declaring 'that it is not lawful upon any pretence whatsoever to take arms against the King'.

The Restoration religious settlement thus settled very little, ensuring that the dispute which had divided Englishmen for the past twenty years would be perpetuated into the new era. If the

[5] For the abortive attempts at comprehension, see R. Thomas, 'Comprehension and Indulgence', in G. F. Nuttall and O. Chadwick (eds.), *From Uniformity to Unity 1662–1962* (1962).

Anglicans could not accommodate the Presbyterians there was precious little hope for the Baptists, Fifth Monarchy men, Quakers, and other more extreme sects thrown up by the civil wars. Not even Charles II had held out hopes for tender consciences which disturbed the peace of the kingdom. The Fifth Monarchy men disturbed it within a year of his accession. Venner's rising in London in 1661 revived fears of the social radicalism of the Interregnum, and did much to assure a victory for the Cavaliers in the general election of that year. The king issued a proclamation banning meetings of 'Anabaptists, Quakers and Fifth Monarchy men'. The Quakers were singled out for special treatment in an Act of 1662, which penalized any meeting for worship of five or more of them. It has been estimated that some fifteen thousand Quakers were punished in varying degrees of severity under Charles II, 450 losing their lives for their convictions. Some 1,460 were in prison at the accession of James II.[6]

The euphoria associated with the Restoration, therefore, soon evaporated. 'Liberty of conscience' became a political slogan towards the end of the decade. It was even adopted by the rioters demonstrating against brothels in 1668, some of whom ominously carried green banners, the colour of the Levellers.[7] The same riot was accompanied by anti-Catholic propaganda. Hostility to popery was sparked off by the fire of London in 1666, which was attributed to the papists. 'How people do cry out in the streets,' Pepys noted in his diary 'that we are bought and sold and governed by papists.'[8] Already, a full decade before the Exclusion crisis, many of the ingredients to be found in it were present.

One that was lacking was the existence of political parties. The Cavalier parliament consisted for the most part of born back-benchers, who were notoriously difficult to organize.[9] They aligned themselves differently on different issues. The

---

[6] J. Besse, *A Collection of the Sufferings of the People called Quakers* (2 vols.; 1753), ii. p. xxxix.

[7] T. Harris, 'The Bawdy House Riots of 1668', *Historical Journal*, 29 (1986), 537–56.

[8] Quoted ibid. 542.

[9] D. T. Witcombe, *Charles II and the Cavalier House of Commons* (Manchester, 1966).

resulting kaleidoscope was partly due to the failure of the Court to provide organization. Clarendon indeed prided himself on this, refusing to involve himself in the necessary wheeling and dealing that building up a Court partly required. Junior ministers chafed at his aloofness from the sordid business, and undertook to do it themselves. One of the reasons for his fall was his failure to cultivate support in parliament. Yet, even after he fell, it proved difficult to get MPs to fall regularly into line.

Another ingredient missing in the 1660s was fear that there was a Catholic conspiracy at Court to suppress Protestantism. So far from seeking to stifle dissent, Charles II consistently sought to relieve Dissenters. After the fall of Clarendon there was even a renewed attempt at the comprehension of Presbyterians in the established church and the toleration of other Protestant sects. Bills to achieve both ends were drawn up with the approval of the Court. They came to grief because of the uncompromising Anglicanism of the Cavalier parliament. The Commons actually moved a resolution 'that if any people had a mind to bring any new laws into the House about religion, they might come as a proposer of new laws did in Athens, with ropes about their necks'.[10] Charles tried again in 1672 by issuing a second Declaration of Indulgence. Although many nonconformists took out licences to hold their own conventicles, their existence was threatened when the Commons declared illegal the suspending power on which the Declaration was founded. Charles reluctantly recalled the licences.

By then, however, fear of popery at Court had begun to replace fears of dissent. James, duke of York, brother and heir apparent of Charles II, had been converted to Catholicism in the late 1660s. By the early 1670s it had become common knowledge. There were also crypto-Catholics about the king, like Lord Clifford, while even Charles himself was suspected of being one. The Cavalier parliament reacted by passing the first Test Act in 1673, which obliged all office holders under the Crown to take communion in the Church of England within three months of their appointment. While this applied the principle of the Corporation Act to national government, it was aimed more particularly against Catholics than was the earlier

[10] Beddard, 'Restoration Church', p. 168.

measure. Thus those appointed to offices had to take an oath declaring their disbelief in the doctrine of transubstantiation. The Duke of York found himself unable to subscribe to this, and resigned the office of Lord Admiral. Later the same year he married Mary of Modena, a Catholic princess, despite parliamentary protests against the match.

Religion now began to polarize the Cavalier parliament into Court and Country parties. The Court party consisted mainly of those who still considered the danger from dissent to be paramount. The Country party united those who maintained that the chief threat was now posed by the resurgence of Catholicism.

During this period the king seems to have decided to drop his attempts at toleration for Dissenters and to have thrown in his lot with the earl of Danby, his Lord Treasurer, who organized the Court party in parliament. Danby stood on a platform of 'Church and king', drawing together the two chief objects of Cavalier allegiance. His exploitation of the patronage of the Crown and management of parliament proved extremely effective in the years 1674 to 1678.

In 1678, however, the Country party found an issue which was to undo all Danby's work almost overnight: the Popish Plot. At bottom the plot was a figment of the overheated imagination of Titus Oates. He claimed that he was privy to a Catholic conspiracy to kill the king. Although the account he gave was inconsistent with itself, it was widely believed. A witchhunt of papists ensued, in which several were executed. A second Test Act was put on the statute book, barring Catholics from sitting in either House of parliament. The duke of York's supporters, however, contrived to have him exempted from its provisions.

Danby, on the other hand, was brought down by the Country party. He was impeached for negotiating secretly with France. In an attempt to save his leading minister, Charles II agreed to the dissolution of parliament.

Whereas the previous general election had been held seventeen years previously, three now took place in the space of three years. The permanent state of electioneering acted as a pressure cooker on party development. During these years the Court party was metamorphosed into the Tory party, while the

Country party became the Whig party. The terms were originally used as words of abuse. Tory was an appellation used for Catholic bandits in Ireland, while Whig was an abbreviation for Whiggamore, the name for the extreme Presbyterian covenanters in Scotland. Of course the Tories were not Irish Catholics nor the Whigs Scottish Presbyterians. But the labels stuck. It is highly significant that they had a religious connotation. Tories were regarded as sympathizers with the Catholic duke of York and the Whigs as radical sectarians determined on his downfall.

Certainly the Whigs have been seen as a single-issue party, united in their objective of excluding James from the succession to the Crown.[11] Three exclusion bills were introduced into parliament between 1679 and 1681. The bills did not name a successor to the throne. They simply asserted that James should not succeed his brother but should go into exile on pain of a treason trial should he return. He was to suffer this fate for having 'been perverted from the Protestant to the popish religion, whereby . . . great encouragement hath been given to the popish party to enter into and carry on most devilish and horrid plots and conspiracies for the destruction of his Majesty's sacred person and government, and for the extirpation of the true Protestant religion'. Consequently, were he to succeed, 'nothing is more manifest than that a total change of religion within these kingdoms would ensure'.[12]

Although the bills were silent on the subject of who was to succeed, they invited speculation as to the successor. One candidate was the duke of Monmouth, Charles II's illegitimate son. Dryden accused the earl of Shaftesbury, leader of the first Whigs, of inveigling Monmouth into setting himself up as his father's heir in the influential poem *Absalom and Achitophel*. This, however, distorted Shaftesbury's relationship with the duke. The Whigs did not commit themselves to him until late in 1680 or early in 1681, and only then in desperation. Shaftesbury was fully aware that the king, though he was fond of his bastard, would not make him legitimate. He also knew that to push his pretensions would alienate the true successor, James's

[11] J. R. Jones, *The First Whigs* (1961).

[12] J. P. Kenyon (ed.), *The Stuart Constitution* (2nd edn., Cambridge, 1986), 387–9.

daughter Mary, and her husband William of Orange, whom she had married in 1677. He was too shrewd a politician to fall into that trap.

Charles II did not simply succumb to the Whig offensive. On the contrary, he exerted himself more vigorously than at any other time in his reign to resist the threat it posed to hereditary monarchy. He sent his brother out of the country, first to Brussels, then to Edinburgh. Monmouth too was sent into exile. He proposed limitations on the powers of a Catholic successor. He attempted to buy off the Whigs by bringing their leaders into an expanded Privy Council. When this failed to make them more amenable, he ended the experiment. He kept the parliament elected in the summer of 1679 prorogued until 1680.

Throughout these manœuvres, Shaftesbury remained firm to the principle of exclusion. He kept the Whig cause alive by remarkable feats of management. Thus, during the long prorogation of 1679, he organized the pope–burning processions of 5 and17 November. These were very elaborate and expensive ceremonies, requiring careful organization. Effigies of the pope and the College of Cardinals were carried on floats to bonfires in the City. These processions attracted huge followings. Shaftesbury has been accused of the basest demagogy in these demonstrations. Unlike Pym, however, he never unleashed the Whig mob on Westminster. Instead his rabble-rousing activities were confined to the City.

He was helped by the achievement of the Whigs in winning three successive general elections. This was the more remarkable following the long run of the ultra-royalist Cavalier parliament. However, by-elections for the ever-increasing number of vacancies brought about since 1661 had revealed a radical trend in the electorate. Successive by-elections tended to strengthen the Country party rather than the Court party. The Whig electoral successes did not come out of the blue. Nevertheless the party's ability to command majorities in parliament despite the opposition of the Court is an impressive tribute to its organization as well as to its popularity. After the general elections of 1679 and 1681 they outnumbered their opponents by a margin of three to two.[13]

[13] Henning, i. 46.

These elections took place in a very different context from those held earlier in the century. Professor Mark Kishlansky has shown how, under the Stuarts, the ideal of electoral consensus broke down, to be replaced by the concept of a campaign. Previously, candidates aspired to achieve unanimity among their constituents. Contests were regarded as breaches of the peace of local communities. The local magnates who formed their 'selectorates' strove to combine their efforts to select a single set of 'representatives'. This ideal survived in theory through the era of the unreformed parliament. In practice, however, it broke down in many constituencies during the Interregnum. 'A process of social distinction and community assent', he concludes, 'had given way to one of political power and electoral consent.'[14]

This process was exacerbated by the ideological divisions within the élite during the Exclusion crisis. At the first general election of the period, held early in 1679, there were contests in 19 counties and 90 boroughs. At the second, which took place later in the year, 16 shires and 67 boroughs went to the polls. There was a drop in the number of contests at the 1681 general election, to 9 counties and 48 boroughs. The fall was not due to a decline in the intensity of party conflict. On the contrary, Whigs and Tories finally emerged as irreconcilable rivals in the electoral campaign for the third Exclusion parliament. Further, candidates did not then stand in constituencies where their prospects were hopeless. If a canvass revealed little chance of success, they would withdraw. By 1681, after three general elections in two years, the strength of the rival parties was pretty well established in most counties and boroughs. What is surprising is the high number which still felt that the issue should be thrashed out to a poll.[15]

Parliamentary debates also revealed the collapse of consensus politics. Historians of early Stuart England have recently asserted that there was no fundamental conflict between Crown and parliament under James I or even in the early years of Charles I. Parliaments met in a spirit of consensus rather than confrontation. Clashes undoubtedly arose, but these were due

[14] M. Kishlansky, *Parliamentary Selection: Social and Political Choice in Early Modern England* (Cambridge, 1986), 225.

[15] Henning, i. 107–24.

to disputes at Court being carried over into the parliamentary arena as much as to a formed opposition. Even when the Crown was opposed directly, it was not over any struggle for sovereignty but over disagreements on practical matters, such as raising money for foreign adventures.

Although such revisionism has not yet been thoroughly applied to the relations between Charles II and his parliaments, some mileage could be made out of it during the Cavalier parliament. The moves against the earl of Clarendon in 1667, for instance, had their origin in the frustrated ambitions of fellow privy councillors like Henry Bennet.[16] During the period of the Cabal the faction fighting between those ill-suited ministers undoubtedly spilled over into parliament. Thus in 1673 the duke of Buckingham attempted to engineer the impeachment of the earl of Arlington.

The Popish Plot, however, polarized parliament along party lines. The issues to which it gave rise, above all the question of the succession, cannot be contained within the revisionist model. Debates on the exclusion of James, duke of York, were not fomented by factions at court. Indeed, when in 1679 Charles II tried to contain his brother's opponents by offering them places in a new Privy Council, it could be said that parliamentary battles spilled over into the Court.

The prevalent atmosphere of all three Exclusion parliaments was very much one of conflict rather than of consensus. Charles II himself provoked a confrontation at the outset of the first in March 1679, when he refused to accept the Commons' choice of a Speaker. In the last, many Whigs defied his Proclamation not to bear arms to parliament, going to Oxford armed to the teeth.

Above all, the friction between Crown and parliament was not over ephemeral matters but concerned basic constitutional issues. The exclusion of the duke of York from the succession to the throne raised fundamental principles, as his supporters pointed out. 'The propositions I have heard moved today', observed Secretary Coventry in the debate on the first bill, 'are the most ruinous to Law and the property of the subject imaginable. Will any man give the Duke of York less Law than

---

[16] C. Roberts, *Schemes and Undertakings: A Study of English Politics in the Seventeenth Century* (Columbus, Ohio, 1985), 57–77.

the worst felons here to banish and disinherit him without so much as hearing him?' 'This Bill, as it is drawn, does change the very essence and being of the monarchy', maintained Sir Leoline Jenkins in the debate on the second bill. 'Consider whether you do not reduce it to an Elective Monarchy'.[17]

Limitations, the Court's alternative to Exclusion, would also have changed the constitution. 'If you provide thus against the Duke of York,' another MP noted, 'you take away all Royal power and make the Government a commonwealth.' In the third Exclusion parliament the expedient of a regency during James's life was proposed, 'so as not to alter the constitution of the monarchy'. This was, however, rejected as impractical.[18]

How serious the issues at stake appeared to be to some members can be seen from the comments of a Court supporter in the debate on the second Exclusion Bill. 'The King, by passing the Bill, will involve the Nation in a civil War; and then the short question will be "Whether a civil War is more dangerous than a Popish successor"?' The Whigs faced up to this challenge. Colonel Birch replied, 'One said today, "It may be a civil war will ensue upon this Bill of Exclusion." We have no great reason to doubt that.' Sir Thomas Player riposted, 'I would let the world know that we are not afraid of war upon that occasion.'[19]

Others were, however, very much afraid that the Exclusion crisis would end in civil war. In April 1681 a correspondent in York informed Sir John Reresby:

As factious persons about the Town take upon them to speak treason and arraign the king's cabinet counsells, call in question dissolving as well as calling Parliaments; so likewise people of the same persuasion take the same liberty of speech intending thereby to incite and stir up the people to hatred or dislike of his Majesty's person and the established government hoping by this means to involve us into another unnatural civil war and thereby to root out monarchy and set up (their darling) a common wealth which is so apparently designed by the non con[formists] that he that runs may read.[20]

---

[17] Grey, vii. 242, 419.
[18] Ibid. 251; viii. 317.
[19] Ibid. vii. 402, 405–6.
[20] Leeds RO Mexborough MSS 18/12: J. Blythman to Reresby, 17 Apr. 1681.

Such fears led people to acquiesce in Charles II's suppression of Whig and dissenting activities.

The king dissolved the Oxford parliament within a week of its opening. Whether or not he intended ever to face another is questionable. He issued a Declaration, lamenting the deadlock reached in the two last parliaments, emphasizing his resolution to have 'frequent Parliaments' and hoping 'that a little time will so far open the eyes of all our good subjects that our next meeting in Parliament shall perfect all that settlement and peace which shall be found wanting either in Church or State'. Rumours began to circulate late in 1681 that a new parliament would be summoned for February 1682. Prospective candidates made their interests throughout the remaining years of the king's life, especially late in 1683 and early in 1684, before the third anniversary of the dissolution of the Oxford parliament occurred. Yet Charles continued to reign without calling a general election, in defiance of the Triennial Act of 1664. Despite the patent illegality of his action, there are few signs that anybody seriously resented it. By then the first Whig party had been smashed, and was in no position to complain, while the Tories were benefiting from the personal rule.

Charles began his attack on the Whigs by prosecuting those who turned up at Oxford armed in defiance of his Proclamation. The first earl of Shaftesbury survived the prosecution thanks to a Whiggish grand jury of Middlesex, who threw out the bill drawn up against him. He nevertheless thought it prudent to escape the king's wrath by fleeing to Holland, where he died the following year. Lesser men were less fortunate. Stephen College, the so-called 'Protestant Joiner', was indicted for treason in both London and Oxford. Again Whig jurymen in London found for him, but he failed to persuade the Tory jurymen of Oxford of his innocence. The evidence against him included a broadside, 'the Rary Show', which featured a print depicting the migration of a puppet show from London to Oxford, thus satirizing the circumstances attending the third Exclusion parliament. Charles chose to summon the Houses to the University town to get them to meet away from the radical capital in the most loyal city in the land. The print and the accompanying verse criticized the king's decision.[21] College,

[21] *Poems on Affairs of State*, ed. E. F. Mengel (New Haven, 1965), ii. 425–31.

one of the more accomplished Whig propagandists, thus became a victim of his own propaganda. He was found guilty of inviting Whig MPs to appear armed, and was executed for high treason.

Other leaders were implicated in the Rye House Plot in 1683. Whether or not there was a genuine conspiracy to assassinate the king as he returned from Newmarket that year has always been disputed. There appears to have been some treasonable talk, but little else. The duke of Monmouth turned king's evidence and was spared. Others, including Algernon Sidney and Lord Russell, were brought to trial, found guilty, and executed. The Whig leadership had been literally cut off.

Meanwhile the rank and file were ferreted out by purges of the corporations. *Quo warranto* proceedings were initiated against fifty-six boroughs, which surrendered their charters and were issued with new ones between April 1682 and Charles II's death in February 1685. More new charters gave the Crown the right to nominate previously elected borough officials such as mayors, aldermen and burgesses. Charles II employed these powers to purge corporations of Whigs and to replace them with Tories. It is usually held that these purges were undertaken with a view to obtaining a loyal parliament. However, as we have seen, there is some dispute as to whether Charles ever intended to hold another general election during his reign. Moreover, some of the boroughs subjected to *quo warranto* proceedings did not return MPs, for example, Chard, Kendal, Leeds, and Macclesfield.[22]

Charles was seeking not to pack parliament so much as to put municipal corporations in the hands of loyal men who would employ their authority to suppress Whigs and Dissenters.[23] It was notorious, for instance, that the Whig corporation of York

Mengel claims that no copies of the woodcut used to illustrate the poem survive (p. 425). However, one was published in M. D. George, *English Political Caricature to 1792* (Oxford, 1959), plate 16.

[22] R. J. Sinner, 'Charles II and Local Government: The Quo Warranto Proceedings, 1681–1685', unpublished Ph.D. thesis (Rutgers, 1976), fos. 316–22.

[23] R. G. Pickavance, 'The English Boroughs and the King's Government: a Study of the Tory Reaction, 1681–1685', unpublished D.Phil. thesis (Oxford, 1976).

was very lax in executing the laws against nonconformists, so much so that, in April 1682, 'the judge at the assizes told the mayor and aldermen upon the bench that if a Quo Warranto were brought against them he could not see but that their charter was forfeited for their misgovernment and for suffering conventicles to be so openly held (without any control) by their contrivance'.[24]

The last four years of Charles II's reign were marked by the rigorous enforcement of the laws against nonconformity. 'Never were meetings so universally broken in London, in all citys, towns, countreys,' lamented the nonconformist Oliver Heywood. 'Ministers driven into corners, it is a matter of great wonder how it is possible they have been so speedily and successfully suppressed. God hath set up the right hand of the enemy.'[25] The king himself, who had previously tried to restrain Anglican animosity towards Dissenters, now encouraged it. He announced in September 1681, 'that for his part he would put down popery but he would also have all the laws put in execution and none of the dissenters spared'.

How far Charles initiated the Tory reaction and how far he merely presided over it is hard to establish. Much of the initiative for the local purges undoubtedly came from the localities.[26] Moreover, even at the centre it is uncertain to what extent the king himself actively pursued the measures adopted. It seems possible that, following the unprecedented vigour with which he exerted himself during the Exclusion crisis, his natural lethargy and indolence reasserted themselves, and that he was content to leave much of the business of government to others, and particularly to his brother. According to Bishop Burnet, after his return from Scotland in 1682 James 'directed all our counsels with so absolute an authority, that the King seemed to have left the government wholly in his hands'. Sir John Reresby also claimed that he 'did now chiefly manage affairs'. 'It is well

---

[24] Leeds RO Mexborough MSS 20/14: T. Fairfax to Reresby, 8 Apr. 1682.
[25] *The Rev. Oliver Heywood 1630–1702: His Autobiography, Diaries, Anecdotes and Event Books*, ed. J. Horsfall Turner (4 vols.; 1882), ii. 223.
[26] J. Miller, 'The Crown and the Borough Charters in the Reign of Charles II', *English Historical Review*, 100 (1985), 70, stresses that 'the charters of 1682–5 were the products of the varying interactions between the Crown and the local Tories'.

known under whose influence the last years of the late reign were conducted,' observed a pamphleteer in 1688.[27]

Certainly James took over his old post as Lord Admiral, albeit without the official title, thus evading the Test Act. He also worked closely with the First Lord of the Treasury, Lawrence Hyde, earl of Rochester. Together they supervised appointments through the commission for ecclesiastical promotions, elevating High-Churchmen to the episcopal bench. They also encouraged, if they did not direct, the onslaught on borough autonomy and the suppression of dissent.[28]

Towards the very end of Charles II's reign, however, there are signs of a reaction against his brother. Rochester was demoted from the Treasury to the post of Lord-Lieutenant of Ireland. In November 1684 James himself was assigned to go to Scotland again as commissioner for the Scottish parliament. The same month Monmouth returned to England, and hopes were raised that he might be reconciled to his father.

Then, on the eve of James's departure for Scotland, Charles II suffered a stroke whilst shaving. He recovered sufficiently for alarm to be replaced by relief. However, on 6 February about noon he had another and this time fatal stroke. Had he died four years earlier there might well have been a civil war over the succession. But since then those who had claimed to be ready to fight to oppose the accession of his brother had been thoroughly crushed, while those who stood by the hereditary principle were entrenched in power. No king succeeded to a more powerful position than did James II.

[27] Burnet, iii. 5; Reresby, 329; *A Review of the Reflections on the Prince of Orange's Declaration* (1688), 2. Cf. below, p. 162.

[28] R. Beddard, 'The Commission for Ecclesiastical Promotions', 1681–1684: An Instrument of Tory Reaction', *Historical Journal*, 10 (1967), 11–40.

3

The Reign of James II

～∗～

Every thing is very happy here. Never king was proclaimed
with more applause than he that raignes under the name of
James the Second. He is courted by all men, and all orders
pay him ready Duty and Obedience . . . I doubt not but to
see a happy reign.

(The earl of Peterborough to Sir Justinian Isham, Feb. 1685)

This King's Interest is different from all other former
Kings since the Reformation. They always did what they
did by their Parliaments, by courting and suiting and
deceiving them. But this King's interest is otherwise, for
the body of the Nation is against his Religion, and he has
money and an army that is sufficient to enable him to
intimidate and force them, and otherwise they will not
comply with his pleasure.

(Roger Morrice, Entering Book, 1 Jan. 1687)

JAMES II succeeded peacefully. After all the bloodcurdling horror
stories which had circulated during the period of the Popish Plot
and the Exclusion crisis about what would happen when a
Catholic king came to the throne, there must have been a sense
of anti-climax. Fires were not kindled at Smithfield. Protestant
babies were not impaled on spits. English men were not
massacred nor their women raped by 'goatish monks'. Indeed
everything seemed reassuringly normal.[1]

James himself helped to produce this situation by reassuring
his Protestant and above all his Anglican subjects at the outset of
his reign. 'I have been reported to be a man fond of arbitrary
power,' he informed the Privy Council on the day of his
accession, 'but that is not the only falsehood which has been

---

[1] For some dire predictions of what would happen on James's accession, see
below, ch. 8.

reported of me: And I shall make it my endeavour to preserve this government both in church and state as it is now by law established'. Not only did he promise to defend and support the Church of England; he also undertook to abide by the law. 'I know, too,' he continued, 'that the laws of England are sufficient to make the King as great a monarch as I can wish: And, as I shall never depart from the just rights and prerogative of the crown, so I shall never invade any man's property.'[2] Sir John Reresby noted in his *Memoirs* that

That which in a great measure did quiet the minds and apprehensions of people was the declaration made by King James to the Privy Council immediately after the breath was out of the body of his brother, that he would defend the government of England both in Church and State as by law established; that he would follow the steps of the late King in kindness and lenity towards his people; and that as he would defend the just rights and prerogative of the Crown, soe [he] would invade noe man's property.[3]

All this was for public consumption. Privately the king told the French ambassador on 8 February

I have resolved to call a parliament immediately and to assemble it in the month of May. I shall publish at the same time a declaration that I am to maintain myself in the enjoyment of the same revenues the King my brother had. Without this proclamation for a parliament I should hazard too much by taking possession directly of the revenue which was established during the lifetime of my deceased brother. It is a decisive stroke for me to enter into possession and enjoyment. For hereafter it will be much more easy for me either to put off the assembling of parliament or to maintain myself by other means which may appear more convenient for me.

What the 'other means' were James indicated when he informed Barrillon in the same conversation that 'the least opposition on the part of those who refused to pay the duties would have engaged me in levying them by force'.[4]

The willingness to resort to forced levies of money was raised

---

[2] Dalrymple, i. 107.
[3] Reresby, p. 353; Sir John Lowther thought that James was 'att that time the most popular prince that had been known in England of a long time' (Lowther, 3).
[4] Dalrymple, i. II, 103–4.

again by three of the king's principal ministers in another
conversation with the French ambassador, which took place in
the middle of March. Rumours had been picked up that some
MPs were planning to recommend that James be granted
revenues for only three years, in order to ensure that he would
be obliged to summon parliament after they had elapsed. They
told Barrillon that the resolution had been taken to reject this,
on the grounds that it would change the form of government.
To avoid making the king dependent on parliament, it was
necessary to use the extreme remedies of dissolving parliament
and of maintaining him by naked force.[5] In the event, though a
resolution to that effect was mooted when the Houses met,
it failed to get sufficient support. Nevertheless, that James
should have contemplated the forcible collection of taxes which
had not been voted to him by parliament indicates that he was
not entirely frank with the Privy Council when he assured it
that he would never invade any man's property.

The general election of March 1685 was subject to more
pressure by the government to influence the outcome than
perhaps any elections ever held. It came after the massive
interference in the boroughs spearheaded by the *quo warranto*
investigations and the issue of new charters. Never before had
there been such blatant rigging of corporations with men loyal
to the Court. On top of this the Secretary of State, Lord
Sunderland, wrote letters to several constituencies informing
them of the king's preferred candidates. He leaned heavily on a
relative in his own county, Northamptonshire, to inform him
that his joining as a candidate with one of 'the faction' was 'very
prejudicial to his Majesty's service, which I question not will be
a sufficient argument to induce you . . . to join for the future
with none but men of undoubted loyalty in the elections of
members for that county'. In other counties the principal
nobility and gentry were instructed to meet to agree on loyal
candidates. Individual magnates were also commanded to make
their presence felt in county and borough elections. Thus the
marquis of Winchester undertook to do what he could 'for the
intended knights in Yorkshire . . . and for loyal persons to stand
for Richmond, Thirsk, Northallerton, Rippon, Aldborough

---

[5] Dalrymple, II. i. 147.

and others in my neighbourhood'. Electoral expenses were borne by the government for 'Official' candidates.[6]

At the end of the day, out of a total of 513 MPs for England and Wales, only 57 Whigs were elected. This was a few more than the forty James was alleged to have objected to, but a tiny minority after the majorities the party had commanded as a result of the Exclusion elections. Another sign of the thrashing they had received is that, whereas about a quarter of the MPs in the Exclusion parliaments had been Dissenters, only 5 per cent of those returned in 1685 were nonconformists.[7]

Yet the Whigs did not give up without a struggle. There were contests in 79 constituencies in 1685. This compares well with the numbers which went to the polls during the Exclusion elections, when 109 contests took place at the first in 1679, 83 at the second, and 57 in 1681.

Some of these contests occurred in boroughs which had received new charters specifically to smash the Whigs and build up Tories. In one of these, Buckingham, a candidate actually succeeded despite the opposition of no less a figure than Judge Jeffreys himself. Results in a tiny borough like Buckingham, where only the mayor and twelve aldermen could vote, were scarcely due to swings of public opinion. On the contrary, intrigue and wire-pulling of the most tortuous kind were resorted to in order to gain seven votes and thus a majority.[9]

In counties and large cities, however, the outcome of the polls was due more to the political preferences of freeholders and freemen than to pressure and manipulation. After the second and third Exclusion elections the Whigs held two-thirds of the 92 county seats in England and Wales. In 1685 15 counties were contested, compared with 16 in the summer of 1679 and 9 in 1681. Yet the Whig share of the seats dropped to a mere 8. This

[6] *CSPD, Feb.–Dec. 1685* (1960), 42, 115, and 42–124 *passim*. Sunderland also wrote to inform the earl of Gainsborough that the king 'would have you take great care of the Hampshire elections, so as to prevent all intrigues and disorders which ill-affected persons may endeavour to set on foot'. Interleaved copy of Lord Clarendon, *History of the Rebellion*, in the Pierpont Morgan Library, New York. I owe this reference to Professor John Kenyon. See also HMC *Rutland*, ii. 86: Sunderland to Rutland, 17 Feb. 1685.
[7] Henning, i. 13, 15.   [8] Ibid. 107–24.
[9] M. Kishlansky, *Parliamentary Selection: Social and Political Choice in Early Modern England* (Cambridge, 1986), 201–23.

was due to a genuine revulsion against the party which had seemed to threaten the country with civil war. In Nottinghamshire a black box was carried at the end of a long pole, together with a parchment banner proclaiming, 'Noe Black Box, Noe Bill of Exclusion, No Association'. After the Court candidates were returned unopposed, the box and parchment were burned in Newark market place 'before all the people'.[10] In Bedfordshire the Tories paraded with the decapitated heads of cocks impaled on sticks to symbolize their aversion to Lord Russell, executed for his involvement in the Rye House Plot, and to his brother, the second son of the duke of Bedford, who was standing for the county. Russell and his Whig partner were soundly beaten by the Tory candidates. As the Jacobite earl of Ailesbury observed in his *Memoirs*, 'the gentry were generally for us: a great mark of the eyes of the nation being well opened, and so it appeared by the choice throughout the kingdom'.[11]

Burnet was caustic about the parliament of 1685. He attributed the outcome of the elections entirely to the machinations of the Court, and claimed that the Commons was composed of men of neither parts nor estates. Yet Speaker Onslow noted in the eighteenth century, 'that was not so, for although very bad practices were used in the elections, yet the returns show they were in general men of fashion and fortune in the counties they were chosen for, but most of them indeed very high tories'.[12] Burnet's verdict rather than Onslow's has been endorsed by the most authoritative modern analysis.[13]

Burnet went on to claim that 'there was no hope left, either of working on their understandings, or of making them see their interest, in not giving the king all at once. Most of them were furious and violent, and seemed resolved to recommend themselves to the king by putting every thing in his power, and by ruining all those who had been for the exclusion.'[14] This view of James II's parliament being completely subservient to

[10] BL Althorp Papers, c.6: J. Millington to Halifax, 18 Mar. 1685.

[11] PRO 31/3/160: Barrillon to Louis XIV, 23 Mar., 2 Apr. 1685; Ailesbury, ii. 100.

[12] Burnet, iii. 17 and note m.

[13] Henning, i. 25; 10 per cent of MPs in 1685 had no taxable property in any county compared with only 3 per cent in 1689; cf. Reresby, p. 362; Ailesbury, ii. 98: 'such a landed parliament was never seen'.

[14] Burnet, iii. 17.

him at the outset of the reign has coloured most accounts since. Thus it is often stated that they voted the king £2,000,000 per annum, thereby making him financially independent when he chose to dispense with their services.

Professor Chandaman, however, has debunked the legend that this parliament was generous to a fault.[15] As Sir John Reresby recorded at the time, 'they voted him the same revenue for his life that the late king had for his life'.[16] This realized £1,300,000 in 1684–5. It was this which James had every reason to anticipate after 1685. The extra £700,000 or so which was also voted in that year was not ordinary revenue but was voted as extraordinary supply, partly to meet the cost of suppressing Monmouth's rebellion and partly to write off debts and recondition the navy. These were not voted for life. Some £400,000 earmarked for the rebellion was to be raised only over five years. The rest was granted for eight years, and could reasonably have been expected to raise £2,200,000 in that period. The debt James inherited from his brother fell not far short of that sum, which did not leave much for refitting the fleet. As Professor Chandaman concludes, the extraordinary supplies 'cannot be regarded as excessively generous, let alone as wildly extravagant'.[17]

The fact that James II was able to sustain a standing army without recourse to parliament for extraordinary supplies could not have been anticipated in 1685. In the event trade continued to expand which, coupled with the abandonment of farming the excise and the hearth tax, led to a considerably increased yield. Between 1685 and 1688 the ordinary revenue rose to an average of £1,600,000 a year. The yield from the extraordinary taxes granted for a limited period in 1685 also outstripped expectation, so that taken all together James's income came to about

[15] C. D. Chandaman, 'The Financial Settlement in the Parliament of 1685', in H. Hearder and H. R. Loyn (eds.), *British Government and Administration: Essays Presented to S. B. Chrimes* (Cardiff, 1974), 144–54.

[16] Reresby, p. 366.

[17] Chandaman, 'Financial Settlement', p. 150; there are signs that James found the cost of maintaining his army a significant strain. J. Childs, *The Army, James II and the Glorious Revolution* (Manchester, 1980), 6. By 1688 some regiments, including Cornbury's which went over to the Prince of Orange, were seriously in arrears of pay. Perhaps this was why James earmarked estates confiscated from rebels for his troops rather than for courtiers.

£2,000,000 per annum during his reign. As a frugal ruler, and also as a man of honour, he made every effort to pay off his brother's debts, probably spending £1,000,000 on this item alone. He also did give the navy a high priority, and increased expenditure on it. In the end, therefore, he depended almost entirely on his ordinary revenue, and he was lucky that economic circumstances led this to bring in £300,000 a year more than was anticipated in 1685. Thus the ordinary revenue rose to around £1,500,000 a year. It was this which enabled James to dispense with parliament, when the time came.

The time came sooner than might have been expected from this parliament, given its reputation for loyalty. There was criticism of James II's rule even in the first session. Sir Edward Seymour objected to the irregular methods used by the Court in elections, and proposed that consideration of supply should be delayed until they were investigated. Although nobody seconded him, he was supported by many who felt it imprudent to debate the issue at that time.[18] Amongst these was Sir John Lowther, member for Westmorland, who claimed that he was urged 'by men of great estates' to raise the question in parliament. He did so, stating that it 'was a matter of that importance, that it shaked the very constitutions of parliament', and moved for a committee to be appointed to consider applying to the king for a remedy. He was seconded by Sir Richard Middleton and Lord Willoughby, but, though 'the speech was heard very favorablie by the hous', the committee was never set up.[19]

Lowther also recorded how an attempt by the Court to make treasonable words actually treason was thwarted. In the committee on the bill two provisions were added. The first exempted preaching or teaching against Roman Catholicism. 'The second was, that all informations within that statute should be made within forty-eight houres. With these two provisoes the force of it was so mutilated that it was not thought worth having; and so it died.'[20]

---

[18] C. J. Fox, *A History of the Early Part of the Reign of James II* (1808), Appendix, pp. xc, xciii. According to Roger Morrice, Seymour claimed that the new charters had changed the method of election to 200 or even 300 seats, and moved that no MP elected for those seats whose return was controverted should sit on the committee of privileges and elections (Morrice MS P, 28 May 1685).   [19] Lowther, pp. 5–7.   [20] Ibid. 8–9.

A more ominous foreshadowing of the difficulties which were to develop in the second session on the subject of religion occurred early in the first. On 26 May, after voting the same revenues that Charles II had enjoyed, the Commons referred to the committee on religion a resolution that they should seek to preserve the Church of England. The committee, which consisted of about 330 members, drew up a recommendation that an address be made to the king to publish a proclamation for putting in execution the penal laws against all Dissenters. James, who had already indicated his intentions for Catholics by pardoning recusants who had suffered as royalists in the civil wars, took umbrage at this recommendation. He summoned the leaders of the Commons and prominent loyalists to his presence and gave them a severe dressing down for going along with it. He told them that, if the House persisted in making such an address, he would reject it in no uncertain terms. Next day the committee on religion reported to the House. Although there were not many more MPs in the Commons than were on the committee, the House rejected its recommendation on the grounds that it 'doth acquiesce, entirely rely and rest wholly satisfied in his Majesty's gracious word and repeated declaration, to support and defend the Religion of the church of England as it is now by Law established'. This was a reference to the king's speech to parliament at the opening of the session on 22 May, which repeated the assurances he had made to the Privy Council at his accession.[21]

It is difficult to detect how these criticisms were organized. This is partly due to the fact that no parliamentary diaries are known to survive from the first session of James II's parliament. Also the Commons was very inexperienced. The Whigs, who might have provided the nucleus of any formed opposition, were reduced to a tiny minority. There was also the fact that 273 members had never sat in parliament before. It was quite unique in the late-seventeenth century for over half the House to lack any experience of previous debates. Their attitudes were unpredictable to the Court as well as to the Whigs.

Certainly some of the manœuvrings were due to factional infighting. As in the early Stuart period, factions at Court can be

---

[21] Fox, *History*, pp xcv–xcvi; Morrice MS P, 4 June 1685.

detected fighting their battles in the parliamentary arena in 1685. Thus an apparently Tory proposition that those who had supported Exclusion should themselves be excluded from this parliament can be traced to the marquis of Halifax. So far from being aimed primarily at the Whigs, it was meant to embarrass ministers like Lords Godolphin and Sunderland, who had voted for the second Exclusion Bill. Halifax, who had been demoted from the post of Lord Privy Seal to that of Lord President, was struggling for survival, and saw this as a weapon against his enemies in the ministry.[22]

Similarly the Lord Treasurer, the earl of Rochester, might have been behind the controversial recommendation from the committee on religion that James should be addressed to enforce the penal laws against all Dissenters, including Catholics. He too was engaged in a struggle for power against the Secretary of State, Sunderland. Rochester was aware of a clique of Catholics, including Lords Arundel and Bellasis, who were looking to Sunderland to advance their cause. As a High-Church Tory he could well have seen the committee as a power base to oppose this group. It is interesting to note that, when James reprimanded the leaders of the Commons for not opposing the recommendation in the committee, he was particularly angry with his own servants who had supported it, either out of malice or ignorance. When disciplined by the king they were able to get the House to drop the recommendation and to resolve that it trusted the king's word. But the resolution had a sting in its tail. Of the Church of England the Commons declared that it 'is dearer to us than our lives'. These were not the sentiments of courtiers so much as back-bench Tories, and might have served as a warning to the king that the Commons would be prepared to oppose him if he appeared to be attacking the established church.[23]

That peers of the realm like Halifax and Rochester could influence proceedings of the Commons is a further indication of the importance of the Lords in the politics of the reign. Unfortunately the Upper House is even more poorly documented than the Lower in the first session of this parliament. James thanked them at the opening for undertaking to stand by

[22] Fox, *History*, p. xxv.
[23] Reresby, p. 369.

him as they had done when they 'withstood the violence of a Party which designed the overturning the monarchy'. The most important business of the session was to reverse the attainder of Viscount Stafford, who had been executed on perjured evidence during the Popish Plot. James hoped that this reversal would pave the way for restoring Catholic peers excluded by the second Test Act to the Upper House.[24]

The harmony that marked the first session of his parliament was to some extent produced by the fact that it took place against a background of rebellion. In his speech at the opening he had to acquaint them that he had just received news from Scotland that the earl of Argyll had landed there. Both Houses replied that they would stand by him with their lives. James thanked the Commons, telling them that he relied on their assurances 'which are the natural effects of you being monarchical and Church of England men. I will stand by all such: And, so supported, have no reason to fear any Rebels or Enemies I have, or may have.' On 13 June he had further to inform the Houses that the duke of Monmouth had landed in Lyme Regis. Again he was assured of their support. As long as they were threatened by a common danger, they were both wary about driving matters to extremes.[25]

Monmouth aimed his manifesto at both king and parliament. He accused James of seeking to establish 'an Absolute Tyrrany'. He also denounced parliament as a packed assembly which, so far from protecting the people against tyranny, had become the means of establishing it. He could hardly have expected sympathy from a body so denigrated, and he got none. A Bill of Attainder was rushed through both houses in a single day. The Commons also voted extraordinary supplies to deal with the rebellion. For good measure they put a price of £5,000 on his head.

Monmouth's rising has often been written off as a fiasco by historians taking their cue from Burnet, who wrote that it 'appeared a mad and desperate undertaking to the duke . . . himself'. Yet other contemporaries were impressed by the progress which he made. 'With 83 men and 200 guineas', claimed Sir John Lowther, 'he brought things to that passe, that

[24] CP(A) 155: Barrillion to Louis XIV, 12/22 June 1685.
[25] Grey, viii. 346, 348–9.

the success was much doubted by manie.' His assessment was much nearer the truth, as a recent account of 'the last popular rebellion' has shown.[26]

Monmouth landed in Lyme on 11 June, with only eighty-two supporters, but with rather more than two hundred guineas. His supporters quickly increased to a thousand, before he advanced north towards Taunton. Militia levies, deployed to intercept them, fled at their approach. Morale was boosted and there was talk of advancing to London. Yet the duke knew that he had not received the significant support he needed from the gentry. His advisers blamed this on his initial manifesto. Although this had attacked James, it had left Monmouth's title to be decided by a free parliament. This seemed to them to be too radical to appeal to the landed élite. He himself thought that 'it was a great obstruction to his affairs, and the only reason why the gentlemen of the country came not in to him, being all averse to a commonwealth'.[27] At Taunton, therefore, Monmouth was persuaded to put out a second manifesto claiming the throne. This proved to be his fatal mistake.

Meanwhile the flight of the local militias forced the king to send regular troops to the West Country under the earl of Feversham. They were reinforced by six regiments sent over by the Prince of Orange at James's request. William even offered to accompany them but was dissuaded. Knowing that a professional army was advancing from London, Monmouth abandoned any scheme to seize the capital in favour of taking Bristol. Unfortunately for him, regulars under Colonel Oglethorpe reached the city first, and intercepted the rebels at Keynsham. Although the skirmish there was indecisive, it put Monmouth off advancing towards Bristol. Thereafter his objective became less and less obvious. He kept his army in being largely through the incompetence of Feversham, who nearly came to grief in an ambush at Norton St Philip. But Monmouth's morale sank, especially when he learned of the defeat of Argyle's rebellion. He even contemplated abandoning the rebellion until his accomplice Lord Grey urged him that to do so would be an

[26] Burnet, iii. 25–6; Lowther, p. 10; R. Clifton, *The Last Popular Rebellion: The Western Rising of 1685* (1984).

[27] *Miscellaneous State Papers from 1501 to 1726*, ed. P. Yorke (2 vols.; 1778), ii. 323.

action 'so base that it could never be forgiven by the people'.[28]
The duke decided to stay, though what he hoped to salvage
from the exploit is hard to see. He retreated to Bridgwater,
which he entered on 3 July. There he made preparations to
advance north into the Midlands, when he learned that the
royalist army was encamped on Sedgemoor, 3 miles away.

Monmouth now decided that his one hope lay in a surprise
night attack on Feversham's position. The royalist commander
was actually surprised in his bed at 1.00 a.m. on 5 July by the
alarm raised that the rebels were about to strike his camp. The
regulars just had time to prepare for the attack. Grey's cavalry
first tried to disperse them, but the charge ended in confusion.
Then the rebel infantry advanced, to come up unexpectedly
against a ditch protecting the royalist position. Instead of
deploying to get round it, they stood and fired at their enemy.
The regulars withstood their wild and inaccurate firing and then
advanced. As dawn broke the rebels realized that they no longer
stood a chance, and fled, pursued by the royalist cavalry and
dragoons. With little or no cover, they were slaughtered by the
hundreds. Grey and Monmouth managed to escape from the
battlefield, only to be captured in Dorset.

Yet, although it ended in débâcle, Sedgemoor was not a
hopeless attack from the rebels' point of view. On the contrary,
Monmouth displayed great skill in it. According to the French
ambassador, everybody agreed that he had performed creditably
and that, if the cavalry had done its duty as well as the infantry,
he would have been able to win, in which case London would
perhaps have declared for him. Sir John Reresby also agreed that
Monmouth 'had showed the courage of a great captain' and 'had
he gott the day, it was to be feared that the disaffected were soe
numerous that they would have risen in other parts of England,
to the very hazard of the Crown'.[29]

After the suppression of the rebellion the judicial reaction was
swift. Monmouth himself was executed on 15 July, just ten days
after the battle of Sedgemoor. Two days after it the Lord Chief
Justice, Baron Jeffreys, was made president of a commission
appointed to try the rank and file of the rebel army. On
27 August Judge Jeffreys opened the first trial at Winchester. By

[28] Ibid. 327.
[29] CP(A) 155: Barrillon to Louis XIV, 9/19 July 1685; Reresby, 384–5.

22 September he was in Bristol, having held courts in Salisbury, Dorchester, Exeter, Taunton and Wells. Altogether he dealt with 1,336 cases in the space of just nine days in court. Most were found guilty. Those who had pleaded 'not guilty' were almost all hanged. In Dorchester the hangings took place immediately outside the court house while the other trials proceeded. Some 250 convicted rebels were suspended from the gallows and then had their quarters distributed throughout the West Country to be placed on public view as objects of terror to remind the king's subjects of their duty to him. When James himself visited the south-west a year later he was so revolted by the sight and stench of the rotting heads and decomposing limbs that he ordered them to be removed.[30]

Ever since the Revolution those proceedings have been known by the notorious name of 'the Bloody Assizes'. Burnet had harsh words to say of both Jeffreys and James. Of the judge he wrote that 'his behaviour was beyond any thing that was ever heard of in a civilised nation. He was perpetually either drunk or in a rage, liker a fury than the zeal of a judge.' Of the king he added that he took pleasure in relating the daily accounts he received of the trial, calling it 'Jeffreys' campaign'. After 1689, too, both tried to blame the other for the responsibility. Jeffreys claimed that he was not half bloody enough for the king. James accused the judge of 'imprudent zeal, or some said avarice, [which] carried him beyond the terms of moderation and mercy, and he drew great obloquy upon the king's clemency, not only in the number but in the manner too of several executions, and in shewing mercy to so few'.[31]

It has been claimed, however, that they were victims of hindsight. Strictly contemporary evidence, it is said, cast no aspersions on either. On the contrary, the House of Commons referred to the convictions as 'punishments rejoiced at by all good men'. James sent Jeffreys down to the West Country to 'inflict such punishments as the example of former reigns and the security of the present seem to require'. And in comparison with former reigns the repression was not particularly severe.

[30] P. Earle, *Monmouth's Rebels* (1977), 161–87.
[31] Burnet, iii. 59–66; J. S. Clarke, *The Life of James the Second* (2 vols.; 1816), ii. 43.

Some 450 men had been executed, for instance, after the rebellion of the Northern earls in 1569.[32]

And yet there are indications that the sentences meted out in the aftermath of the rebellion were regarded as savage even though overt criticism of them could not be made until after the Revolution. After riding the Western circuit in 1686, Lord Chief Justice Herbert complained about Jeffreys's conduct, 'and the rapine'. When assessing the possibility of a landing by the Dutch in the west, Herbert's brother, the Admiral, observed in September or October 1688 that it was 'a populeux [sic] county disafected to the present government, animated with great resentment for the cruelties exercised on their friends and relations'. Again, when Jeffreys was a prisoner in the Tower early in 1689 the clergyman who attended him advised him to expiate the guilt that must be on his conscience for his severity in the western trials, while a pamphleteer asked, 'how wou'd those poor wretches, whom he hang'd there by dozens, lament, if they had but liv'd to see this day? What an after slaughter was it, when the duumvirate of Tyrants, Kirk and his Lordship, went down to reap the gleanings of the bloody field; whose voice, like a two-edged sword, destroy'd more in cold blood than Absalom and all his host had done before?' On 14 May 1689 Sir Robert Cotton asserted in the House of Commons that 'those in the West did see such a shambles as made them think they had a Turk, rather than a Christian, to their King'.[33]

During the rebellion the French ambassador Barrillon observed that the king was very relieved to have a pretext to raise troops. And so it proved. Over the summer of 1685 James increased the army from the 8,565 he had inherited from his brother to 15,710. By December the total number of troops in England was 19,778. During July and August the army was encamped on Hounslow Heath 'to the astonishment of the people of England', as Sir John Lowther put it, 'who had not so much in historie heard of anie such thing in time of peace'. In September

[32] G. W. Keeton, *Lord Chancellor Jeffreys and the Stuart Cause* (1965).

[33] Ellis, i. 104; Japikse, II. i. 612; Burnet, iii. 66–7; *The Citizen's Lament for the Lord Chancellor's Loss of the Purse* (1688); Cobbett, v. 256–7. The appropriateness of Cotton's metaphor can be appreciated from the letters of Thomas Northmore on the subject of boiling, tarring and distributing quarters to 12 Devon towns (HMC Fifth Report, Appendix: *Pine Coffin*, p. 373).

they were dispersed throughout the country. Some went to garrison towns, but many were quartered on innkeepers, who were threatened with the loss of their licences should they refuse.[34]

The increased size of the army, and the fact that James had commissioned many Catholic officers despite the Test Act, was bound to provoke criticisms when parliament met on 9 November. The king met the critics head on in his speech at the opening. After thanking God for the successful suppression of Monmouth's rebellion, he continued.

But when we reflect, what an inconsiderable number of men began it, and how long they carried it on without any opposition, I hope every body will be convinced that the Militia, which hath hitherto been so much depended on, is not sufficient for such occasions; and that there is nothing but a good Force of well-disciplined Troops in constant pay, that can defend us from such, as, either at home or abroad, are disposed to disturb us.

He therefore asked for further supplies to maintain it on foot. As for the Catholics whom he had commissioned, James said, 'Let no man take exception that there are some officers in the Army, not qualified, according to the late Tests, for their Employments.'[35]

When the Commons adjourned to their own House, the Lords debated whether or not to thank the king for his speech. One peer moved ironically to give thanks to his Majesty since he had dealt so plainly with them, and 'warned them of what they might look out for'.[36] The irony was taken seriously and the thanks of the House recorded. Nevertheless, on the motion of the bishop of London, 23 November was set aside to consider the speech. In the event the sessions ended before that date.

Meanwhile the Commons had resolved to take the speech into consideration on 12 November before giving their thanks for it. It was then considered paragraph by paragraph, so that the augmentation of the army and the request for revenue to support it were debated before the controversial passage

[34] CP(A) 155: Barrillon to Louis XIV, 15/25 June 1685; Childs, *The Army, James II and the Glorious Revolution*, p. 2; Lowther, pp. 13–14.

[35] Grey, viii. 353.

[36] Burnet, iii. 88–9. The peer is variously identified as Devonshire or Halifax.

concerning Catholic officers. The debate on the increase in the armed forces revealed a division between those who accepted that the county militias had been useless in the rebellion, and therefore the necessity for a larger professional army, and those who preferred the militia, fearing a standing army as an instrument of absolutism. It was resolved to bring in a bill to improve the effectiveness of the militia. Supply was voted, but when it was moved that it be earmarked for 'the support of the additional forces' the resolution was defeated by 225 to 156.[37]

On Friday, 13 November, an unlucky day for James, a resolution was proposed that the House should go on with supply before proceeding to the next paragraph of the speech. This was defeated by the narrowest margin of 183 votes to 182. The following day, therefore, James's appointments of Catholic officers were taken into consideration. The upshot was that two resolutions were passed. One condemned the commissions as being contrary to the Test Act. The other was to bring in a bill to indemnify the officers concerned from retrospective prosecutions. An address to the king was then agreed, pointing out that the commissions were illegal, and requesting him 'to give such directions that no apprehensions or jealousies may remain in the hearts of his Majesty's good and faithful subjects'. Thereafter the Commons proceeded to debate supply, and after discussing sums ranging from £200,000 to £1,200,000 agreed to grant £700,000.[38]

James expressed his displeasure with the address of thanks for his speech, and on 18 November the Commons were informed of his answer. 'I did not expect such an Address from the House of Commons,' he told them, 'having so lately recommended to your consideration the great advantages a good understanding between us had produced in a very short time, and given you warning of Fears and Jealousies amongst ourselves.' This answer was received in a profound silence, which lasted for some time. It was broken by a motion that it be considered two days later. Seconding the motion, John Coke expressed some indignation, saying, 'I hope we are all Englishmen, and are not to be frighted out of our duty by a few high words.' The

[37] Grey, viii. 355–60.
[38] Ibid. 361–7.

reaction of the House was equally indignant, and Coke was sent to the Tower to reflect on his imprudent speech.[39]

On 20 November the king summoned the Houses into his presence. So far from the Commons being allowed to discuss his answer on that day, they were informed that 'for many weighty reasons' he had decided to prorogue parliament to 10 February. It never met again.

This short session, less than two weeks in duration, raises crucial questions about the relationship between Crown and parliament under the later Stuarts. Did it reveal a fundamental conflict over the location of sovereignty in the constitution, as traditional views of the reign maintain? Or can it be fitted into the pattern of politics which critics of the traditional view have detected in the early Stuart period? Was there a formed opposition to the Crown; or did the debates demonstrate the extension of Court factions into the parliamentary arena? These questions can only be given tentative answers in view of the scarcity of the evidence for the proceedings, especially in the House of Lords.

In the Commons the inexperience of many members was a vital consideration in organizing debates. Although most of them might have been labelled Tories, it seems inappropriate to talk about a Tory party in the House, at least as far as the majority of MPs were concerned. Rather they appear to have behaved as independent country gentlemen, anxious not to appear disloyal and yet at the same time deeply suspicious of the king's intentions, as they were revealed after Monmouth's rebellion. They were thus prone to be swayed alternately by the Crown's servants in the House appealing to their loyalty, and Country members, Tory as well as Whig, who aroused their anxieties about the Court. At the outset of the first session the Crown could count on their loyalty, as Thomas Bruce, MP for Wiltshire, found when he organized an enthusiastic meeting of Tory back-benchers in the Fountain Tavern in the Strand. By the second session, however, their suspicions had been aroused, making parliamentary management difficult.[40]

The Court's principal managers in the Commons were two Scottish peers, Lords Middleton and Preston. Charles, earl of

[39] Grey, viii. 369.
[40] Ailesbury, pp. 100–1.

Middleton, had risen in Charles II's reign from the colonelcy of a regiment via a diplomatic posting to the office of Secretary of State, in which James confirmed him on his accession. Although he had sat in the Scottish parliament, he had no experience of the English Commons before taking his seat as a member for Winchelsea in 1685. Richard Graham, Viscount Preston, had been envoy to Paris in the early 1680s, returning to England to become a privy counsellor in 1685. His family was resident in Cumberland, and he had sat for Cockermouth since 1675 before being returned for the county in James II's parliament. Despite his inexperience, Middleton was shrewd and hard-working, while Preston made up what he lacked.[41]

Sir John Bramston attributed the confused proceedings of this parliament to their incompetence. Yet their management was not as incompetent as Bramston believed, though they clearly ran into difficulties. Middleton tried to get the Commons to thank the king for his speech immediately, but had to accept a resolution to discuss it first. He nevertheless managed to get it discussed paragraph by paragraph, the intention being to get supply voted before the appointment of Catholic officers was debated. In this he was successful, for, though many complained about their commissions in the debate on 12 November, 'it were not then properly before them'. The division on 13 November, therefore, when a motion to this effect was defeated by one vote, was a crucial loss of control. Preston tried to retrieve it by putting the question that the paragraph in the king's speech about Catholic officers should be discussed, hoping that it too would be dropped. Although this was, as Bramston complained, procedurally irregular, and the Speaker, Sir John Trevor, called the division in such a way as to assist those who wished the motion to fail, it was nevertheless carried. Those who went against Preston's management on this occasion included 'the Sollicitor, Mr. Finch and Sir Christopher Musgrave in whom the Court confided more than in the Speaker'.[42] Other servants of the Crown also let it down that day. According to Sir Arthur Onslow, Middleton,

---

[41] G. H. Jones, *Charles Middleton: The Life and Times of a Restoration Politician* (1967); Henning, ii. 429–31.

[42] Bramston, pp. 199, 210–13; PRO 30/53/8, fo. 18: A. Newport to Lord Herbert, 12 Nov. 1685.

seeing many go out upon the division against the Court, who were in
the service of the government, went down to the bar, and as they were
told in, reproached them to their faces for the voting as they did; and a
captain Kendal being one of them, the earl said to him there, 'Sir, have
not you a troop of horse in his Majesty's service?' 'Yes, my lord', says
the other; 'but my brother died last night, and has left me 700*l.* a year.'

James himself was incensed at this breakdown of Court
discipline. He told Sir John Reresby, who arrived in London
just too late to participate in the debate, that the defeat by one
vote was hard, 'and the more soe bycause he lost it by his own
officers', which Sir John took as a reflection upon himself.
Among those who voted with the majority were Charles Fox,
paymaster general of the army, and John Darcy, an army
officer. Both were dismissed, shortly after the end of the
session.[43]

To some extent this breakdown of discipline may be traced to
factions at Court. Although his dismissal of the marquis of
Halifax from the Presidency of the Council on the eve of
the session was meant by James to signal that he wanted the
courtiers to speak with one voice, it clearly failed. One of the
most outspoken critics of the armed forces was Sir Thomas
Clarges, who actually moved 'that a standing army is destructive
to the country'. While Clarges was not a placeman, he sat for
Christchurch, Hampshire, through the influence of the earl of
Clarendon, who was lord of the manor. His opposition might
therefore be seen as a manoeuvre in the struggle for power
between the Hyde faction, presided over by Clarendon and his
brother the earl of Rochester, and the Sunderland faction.
Middleton, the inexperienced manager, was a protégé of Robert
Spencer, earl of Sunderland.

At the same time there was more to it than that. Clarges was a
friend of Halifax as well as a client of Clarendon. Other leading
lights among the opponents of the king's measures were Sir
Edmund Jennings, a creature of Danby's, and Sir William
Twysden, an adherent of the earl of Nottingham. So the
opposition in the second session of the 1685 parliament was

---

[43] Burnet, iii. 92 n.; Reresby, p. 395. Roger Morrice noted 10 MPs who
were dismissed after the session, including Kendal, whose legacy had
unexpectedly fallen to him not the night before but at the start of the session
(Morrice MS P, 19 Dec. 1685).

concerted by Tories both inside and outside the Court. They were joined by Whigs like Sir John Maynard, a veteran parliamentarian. His type was in very short supply in this House of Commons, though other members of former parliaments apparently advised the raw recruits of 1685.[44]

From their different viewpoints both Sir John Bramston and Sir John Reresby represented the divisions in the Commons as being between the Court on the one hand and the country gentlemen on the other. Reresby, as Governor of York, was clearly expected by James himself to vote for the Court. Yet in a crucial vote he opposed it. This was on a motion to join with the Lords to address the king to dismiss the Catholic officers from their commissions. 'The court party was against it', Reresby recalled, 'that the King might have a better excuse not to grant it when it came but from one of the two Houses; the country gentlemen thought it necessary to enforce it the more.' The motion was lost, but James was alarmed, dreading the two Houses joining forces on this issue.[45]

In fact the objections of the Upper House to the Catholic commissions led directly to the prorogation of parliament, despite Burnet's claim that 'as the scene lay in the House of Commons, so the debates there were more important'.[46] James, who regularly attended the debates in the House of Lords, clearly thought otherwise. He took exception to the speeches of Lords Anglesey, Devonshire, Halifax, and Mordaunt, and the bishop of London, against the appointment of Catholic officers. Jeffreys, who had been appointed Lord Chancellor on his return from the trials of the rebels, presided over these debates. He tried to browbeat the peers as he had cowed the rebels, but they were not to be silenced by his rough tongue. A growing number of lords came out against the court in this second session. Only the bishop of London among their leaders could be regarded as a dissident courtier, and after the prorogation he was struck off the Privy Council and dismissed from the Deanery of the Chapel Royal. The opposition in the Lords stemmed from deepseated beliefs that the king was acting in a fundamentally illegal manner. This view was shared by the

[44] PRO 31/3/162: Barrillon to Louis XIV, 16/26 Nov. 1685; Nottingham UL, Portland MSS PWA 2084.
[45] Reresby, p. 396.   [46] Burnet, iii. 91.

Commons. James's establishment of a standing army and his commissioning of Catholic officers were regarded as violations of his promise to govern according to law. At bottom it was a question of where the sovereign power lay: with the prerogative or with statute; in the king, or in the king and parliament?

The year following the prorogation of parliament was marked by the struggle between the Hyde and Sunderland factions, and the final triumph of the latter. Rochester found himself outmanoeuvred by a much tougher and shrewder politician. Sunderland got off on the right foot early in 1686 by siding with the queen and the Catholic cabal against James's mistress Catherine Sedley. He accused the Hyde faction of having procured the title of countess of Dorchester for Sedley, which outraged Mary of Modena. The Catholic cabal backed the queen and confronted James with the contradiction between his piety and his promiscuity. The king, taken aback, promised to break off his liaison with Sedley, and for a few months, during which she went to Ireland, kept his word.

In foreign affairs the Hyde faction leaned towards the Dutch republic, while Sunderland supported France. Rochester wished to maintain friendly relations with William of Orange, who was married to his niece, while Sunderland appreciated the strain between James II and his son-in-law. As a pensioner of France himself, he worked on the king's penchant for French money. An indication that Sunderland's influence was more persuasive than Rochester's was revealed in the Court's reaction to the revocation of the Edict of Nantes. When James proposed the burning of a book written by a French Protestant pastor, Chancellor Jeffreys, a prominent member of the Hyde faction, objected, on the grounds that it was extraordinary to burn a book printed in a foreign country which did not criticize England. James personally overruled his objections.

The Catholic cabal at Court was strengthened by the decision of the judges in the case of Godden versus Hales. This was a test case brought before all twelve justices of the common law courts of Common Pleas, King's Bench, and Exchequer in 1686. Before it was heard, James found he had to purge the judicial bench so that he could count on judges who would support his right to employ the dispensing power. The case involved Sir Edward Hales, a Catholic army officer who had not fulfilled the requirements of the Test Act that he should qualify for his commission by taking part in an Anglican communion service and abjuring transubstantiation. His own coachman brought the collusive action against him. Hales pleaded that he had letters patent authorizing him to keep his commission, notwithstanding the Act. The prosecution demurred, admitting Sir Edward's plea to be true in fact, but denying that it was a sufficient answer. Thus the trial brought up the question of the dispensing power, as the king had intended it should. Of the twelve judges, eleven found for the Crown. They defended their judgment on the grounds that the kings of England were sovereign princes, and that the laws of the land were the king's laws, so that he could dispense with them. Sir John Bramston commented caustically that he thought the judgment 'like which the Judges gave Cambises of old. He had a mind to marry his sister, and askt the judges if by the laws of Persia a King might not marry his sister. They answered they met with no such Law, but they had a law that the kinge might doe what he pleased.'[47] Armed with this verdict James had proceeded to appoint Catholics to offices under the Crown, by granting them dispensations from the Test Act. He also used the dispensing power to set aside many other statutes. Thus Obadiah Walker, master of University College, Oxford, was allowed to retain that post even when he became a Roman Catholic, notwithstanding nine acts of parliament of the reigns of Queen Elizabeth and James I. In July 1686 four Roman Catholics, Lords Arundel, Bellasis, Dover, and Powys, were admitted to the Privy Council, reinforcing the Sunderland faction.

Its influence was further consolidated by the appointment of the commission for ecclesiastical causes. James set up this tribunal to discipline the clergy following the bishop of London's failure to silence John Sharp, a clergyman who had disregarded a proclamation forbidding preaching against Catholicism by 'saying in a sermon that of all Christian religions the Popish was the last he would choose'.[48] Both factions were represented among the commissioners, which included the two leaders, Rochester and Sunderland, the archibishop of

[47] Bramston, p. 232. For the validity of this verdict, see below, pp. 149–50.
[48] Northants RO Isham Corr. 2252.

Canterbury, who refused to take his place on it, the bishops of Durham and Rochester, Lord Chancellor Jeffreys, and Lord Chief Justice Herbert. They became divided over the appropriate punishment for the bishop of London. Rochester would have preferred a lesser sentence than the deprivation of all his spiritual functions, whereas Sunderland thought it necessary to assert the royal authority over him. James was determined to crush Compton, so the harsher view prevailed.

The suspension of the bishop of London was seen as a sign that Rochester's days as Lord Treasurer were numbered. He clung to office during the last weeks of 1686 by the desperate expedient of expressing an interest in being converted to Catholicism. Two Catholic and two Protestant divines held a disputation in his presence. In late December, however, Rochester declared that he would never become a Catholic. James decided that the post of Treasurer was too important to be in the hands of a man who did not share his views and dismissed him on 6 January 1687. He was replaced by a commission composed of Bellasis as First Lord, Lords Dover and Godolphin, Sir John Ernle, and Sir Stephen Fox, a mixture of three Protestants and two Catholics. At the same time Rochester's brother, the earl of Clarendon, was recalled from Ireland, where Lord Tyrconnel, a Catholic, succeeded him as Lord-Lieutenant, while Lord Arundel, another Catholic, replaced him in England as Lord Privy Seal.

James was now determined to work only with men who would go along with his religious policies. To sound out who was for and who against him he interviewed office holders and members of both Houses of Parliament individually in the royal closet. Those who refused to co-operate with the king were dismissed. 'We doe hear every post of so many persons being out of their imployments', observed Lord Chesterfield in March 1687, 'that it seems like the account one has after a Battle of those who miscarried in the engagement.' Some placemen resigned their places rather than be subjected to the pressure of this closeting. When Admiral Herbert, a rake and libertine who owed everything to James, refused to agree to the repeal of the laws, the king despaired of obtaining that goal by persuasion.[49]

[49] BL Althorp Papers H1: Chesterfield to Halifax, 15 Mar. 1686. When James put it to Herbert 'that he had not been so regular a liver as to make the

In April, therefore, he prorogued parliament until November and issued a Declaration of Indulgence. The long prorogation was intended to accustom his subjects to religious toleration obtained by using the royal prerogative to suspend the penal laws. He hoped that the experience would allay their apprehensions sufficiently to persuade them to repeal the legislation when parliament met.

The king was prepared to take an even longer view of the prospects of achieving recognition for Catholics. He determined to force the Universities of Cambridge and Oxford to treat them on an equal basis with Anglicans. If the monopoly of the Church of England over these institutions could be relaxed, then a major obstacle to Catholic advancement would be removed. Consequently, when the vice-chancellor of Cambridge refused to admit a Catholic to the degree of MA, he was dismissed. James believed there were many men in both Universities who were Catholic at heart and who would declare themselves if they could with impunity. A few, like John Massey and Obadiah Walker in Oxford, did so. For the most part, however, the Universities stood out as bastions of uncompromising Anglicanism.

The most celebrated example of this was the refusal of Magdalen College, Oxford, to accept the royal nominee as its President. As G. V. Bennett has observed, 'Magdalen now provided a textbook case of passive obedience: the fellows asserted their legal rights, refused active obedience to an unlawful command, passively incurred deprivation and thus step by step pushed the Crown into action which was even more obviously illegal.' When the President died in March 1687 James ordered the Fellows to replace him with a Catholic convert, whom they considered to be unacceptable. Instead they chose one of their own Fellows, John Hough. James declared Hough deposed and appointed Samuel Parker, bishop of Oxford, but the college would not recognize the appointment. The king visited Oxford in September and in a great rage instructed the fellows to elect Parker. Upon their refusal the commission for ecclesiastical causes deprived twenty-five of their fellowships. As Bennett concludes,

Test a case of conscience' he replied 'every man has his failing' (PRO 30/53/8, fo. 42: to Lord Herbert, 11 Mar. 1687).

The ecclesiastical commissioners were committed to the perilous course of depriving men of their legal freeholds for refusing to act illegally. By March 1688 virtually all the Anglican members of the college had been ejected and the buildings were occupied by a set of Roman Catholic fellows and with a titular bishop, Bonaventure Gifford, as president. Anglican services in the chapel were discontinued and mass publicly celebrated. It is difficult to overestimate the shock and anger which these events caused.[50]

The dismissal of the Hyde brothers, the issue of the Declaration of Indulgence, and the attack on Magdalen College marked the final parting of the ways between James and the Anglican Tories. His experience of closeting Tory placemen and politicians had revealed that continued co-operation was out of the question. Yet the king must have wondered how next to proceed. It was apparently the earl of Sunderland who suggested a way ahead by allying with the Dissenters and Whigs against the Anglicans. At first sight this marked an astonishing about-turn on the part of the king. He had after all previously denounced them as republicans. Yet it made pragmatic sense. Both Catholics and Dissenters had been victims of the Church of England's monopoly of power and worship. An alliance between them against that monopoly could achieve the result James desired: a parliament which would repeal the laws which had created it.

In July 1687, therefore, James decided not to wait any longer to see if a long prorogation would change parliament's mind in the light of the experience of toleration. Instead he dissolved the parliament elected in 1685 and went all out to prepare the ground for an election which would return a majority pledged to repeal the Test Acts and penal laws. He sounded out the attitudes of justices of the peace and deputy-lieutenants of the militia, and dismissed those not in favour of repealing the legislation. He used his powers under the new charters to purge borough corporations of Tories and to replace them with Catholics, Dissenters, and Whig collaborators. In order to establish who would co-operate with him in the boroughs, he appointed regulators of corporations. In the summer of 1687 he himself went on an electioneering tour of the west, urging the choice of 'such parliament men as would concur with him in settling this liberty as firmly as the Magna Charta had been'.[51] 'In all the King's progress very few of the gentry waited on his majesty,' the Prince of Orange was informed. 'Yet the King is still assured that by his power in the corporations he shall have a House of Commons to his liking.'[52] By April 1688 he felt sufficiently confident that these methods would work to decide on a general election for the following November.

James chose to publicize his intentions by reissuing the Declaration of Indulgence, appending to it the information that parliament was to be summoned in November to enact it. In order to give this news maximum publicity, an order in Council of May 1688 ordered the clergy to read the Declaration 'in the usual time of divine service upon the 20th and 27th day of May, in all churches and chapels within the cities of London and Westminster, and ten miles thereabout: and upon the 3rd and 10th of June in all other churches and chapels throughout the kingdom'. The bishops were also instructed to distribute the Declaration throughout their dioceses.

The archbishop of Canterbury and six bishops signed a petition asking James not to insist upon their distributing and reading the Declaration. They justified their action by referring to the fact that 'the Declaration is founded upon such a dispensing power as hath been often declared illegal in Parliament and particularly in the years 1662 and 1672'. James, who had relied upon the Church's constant preaching of passive obedience and non-resistance to keep it loyal to the Crown, was completely taken aback when he was presented with the petition on 18 May 1688. 'This is a great surprise to me,' he was reported as saying. 'Here are strange words. I did not expect this from you. This is a standard of rebellion.' The lead taken by the seven

---

[51] Burnet, iii. 190. As men presented addresses to him, James bade them to return MPs who would repeal the Test Act and penal laws 'and make this liberty of contions a Magnay Cartay' [*sic*] (Leeds RO Mexborough MSS 50/42: T. Oglethorpe to Reresby, 24 Sept. 1688). In Oct. James urged the Lord Mayor and Aldermen of London to return MPs who would 'make his declaration for liberty of conscience as firmly law as Magna Charta' (NLS Yester MSS 7053, fo. 70).

[52] *CSPD 1687–9* (1972), 66: J. Fitzpatrick to the Prince of Orange, 1 Sept. 1687.

bishops was followed by an overwhelming majority of the clergy both in London and in the provinces who disobeyed the proclamation.

James blamed the bishops for this widespread defiance and determined to punish them. It was decided to cite them before the Court of King's Bench on a charge of seditious libel. Because they refused to give recognisances, they were imprisoned in the Tower, where they spent a week before being bailed by twenty-one peers. After their appearance in King's Bench on 29 June, the jury found them not guilty. Macaulay's description of the outcome has never been surpassed.

As the words were uttered, Halifax sprang up and waved his hat. At that signal benches and galleries raised a shout. In a moment ten thousand persons who crowded the great hall replied with a still louder shout, which made the old oaken roof crack; and in another moment the innumerable throng without set up a third huzza which was heard at Temple Bar. The boats which covered the Thames gave an answering cheer. A peal of gunpowder was heard on the water, and another, and another; and so in a few moments the glad tidings went flying past the Savoy and the Friars to London Bridge and to the forest of masts below.[53]

They were not glad tidings for James. Nevertheless he was encouraged to press on with his plans by the birth of a son to his queen while the bishops were in the Tower. Even after the acquittal, the commission for ecclesiastical causes required archdeacons to send in lists of those clergymen who had failed to read the Declaration in order that they might be disciplined.

It is not clear who advised the reading of the Declaration by the clergy, the subsequent prosecution, and the continued pressure on Anglicans after the acquittal of the bishops. Following the fall of Clarendon and Rochester, Sunderland was virtual prime minister. But since then he had been obliged to accept adjustments in the government to accommodate the Catholic cabal. The most notorious appointment had been that of Father Petre, a Jesuit priest, to the Privy Council in November 1687. Petre had appeared to be admitted 'in his Jesuits habit, to wit a Long cloak a cassock and a little band'.[54] By 1688, according to Burnet, 'Father Petre had gained such an

[53] Macaulay, ii. 1030.   [54] Morrice MS Q, p. 259.

ascendent that he was considered as the first minister of State.'[55] He was alleged to have said that the members of the Church of England 'should be made to eat their own dung'.[56] Petre had the reputation of 'a man of strong passions, very positive and rash, a great contemner and neglecter of others, perfectly ignorant of our constitution and very little understanding men or things with us, feared by some and loved by none'. Certainly there can have been little love lost between him and Sunderland by then. It seems that James followed the lead of the Catholics in his Council at this time, while the Anglicans counselled more moderate measures.[57]

In a desperate attempt to regain the king's confidence, Sunderland announced his conversion to Catholicism. This seems to have worked. In mid-July a Scottish observer wrote from London that Sunderland 'is certainly the premier minister and tho' in truth the King is not governed by any body I believe he hath more power with his Majesty than anybody'.[58] His renewed influence was felt when the commission for ecclesiastical causes postponed its next meeting from August until December. This postponement effectively killed the inquiry into the failure to read the Declaration of Indulgence, which had threatened to wreck the commission. Thus the bishop of Rochester had resigned from it rather than punish clergymen for obeying their consciences.[59] It was a small concession compared

---

[55] Burnet, iii. 221, 228.   [56] NLW Ottley MSS 1467.

[57] Morrice MS Q, p. 259. The Lord Chancellor denied any part in the decision to prosecute the bishops, 'but said there was no remedy; some men would hurry the king to his destruction' (Clarendon, ii. 177). He was presumably referring not only to Petre and the Catholic advisers but also to Dissenters like Penn and Stephen Lob who were close to James in these weeks. There was a report that Lob advised the reading of the Declaration, and that when the clergy refused James asked him what he should do next (PRO 30/53/8, fo. 64:—to Lord Herbert, 16 June 1688).

[58] NLS Yester MSS 7011, fo. 56: James Hays to Tweeddale, 14 July 1688. One of the symptoms of the struggle for power between the two factions at Court in the summer of 1688 was a significant increase in the size of the Privy Council. Four new Counsellors were admitted in July, and it was rumoured that another fifteen were to be added. These rumours caused one wit to run through Whitehall 'in great haste and being asked the reason he said he feared to be seized on for a Privy Counsellor' (PRO 30/53/8, fo. 66:—to Lord Herbert, 14 July 1688); Morrice MS Q, pp. 281–2.

[59] The bishop of Rochester not only resigned but published his reasons for

with those which James was to make a month later when he realized that the Dutch really were planning to invade his kingdom.

doing so, saying that 'the safety of the Church of England seeming to be exceedingly concern'd in this prosecution I must declare I cannot with a safe conscience sit a judge in this cause upon so many pious and excellent men'. The chancellors and archdeacons concerned were prepared to defy the commissioners, and consulted civil lawyers at Doctors Commons, who advised them not to court a charge of contempt but to give reasons why they could not present lists of those who had and had not read the Declaration, since the order they had received to do so could not be complied with at the usual times of visitation. Their defiance was successful. Before adjourning the commissioners ordered a visitation in November (BL Add. MSS 34487, fos. 23, 25, 27).

4

The Dutch Invasion

〜⚜〜

> I cannot forbear remarking, how wonderfullie this thing
> succeeded in opposition to so many visible and apparent
> accidents, anie one whereof had they happened, the whole
> design must certainly have miscarried.
>
> (*Sir John Lowther, Memoirs of the Reign of James II*)

ON 27 August 1688 the earl of Sunderland, James II's chief
adviser, informed the English envoy in France, 'I believe there
never was in England less thought of rebellion.'[1] Within four
months both the minister and his master had fled the country,
the government had collapsed, and the Glorious Revolution was
in full spate.

Was the regime hopelessly out of touch with reality for a
leading minister to make such an apparently total error of
judgement in his prediction? Certainly Sunderland's biographer
sees definite signs of the nervous strain which was to lead to
blind panic and breakdown within weeks.[2] James, too, was
displaying traits of mental instability. His temper, never even at
the best of times, more frequently exploded in violent outbursts
of fury. He refused to look facts in the face, totally disbelieving,
for example, reports that his son-in-law was preparing to invade
England. His wishful thinking was partly due to an incompetent
intelligence service. Whereas Louis XIV and William of Orange
were probably the best informed rulers in Europe, James's
ambassador at the Hague from December 1686 to the end of the
reign, the marquis d'Albeville, retailed the most trivial tittle-
tattle.[3]

---

[1] Quoted in J. P. Kenyon, 'The Earl of Sunderland and the Revolution of
1688', *Cambridge Historical Journal* (1953), 281.

[2] J. P. Kenyon, *Robert Spencer, Second Earl of Sunderland* (1958), 205, 215.

[3] A comparison of d'Albeville's dispatches for the year 1688 (BL Add. MSS
41816) with those of van Citters (Algemeen Rijksarchief, The Hague, States

Yet Sunderland's prediction cannot be brushed aside on the grounds that he was losing his nerve while his master was losing touch with reality. Despite the fact that the Immortal Seven had already sent their invitation to William of Orange,[4] promising overwhelming support for him should he come over, the statement 'there never was in England less thought of rebellion' was not an unreasonable assessment of the situation. Resistance to James could be expected from two quarters: Anglican Tories alienated by his pro-Catholic policies; and Whigs and Dissenters not convinced that he was sincerely committed to toleration. There were valid reasons for assuming that neither would resist to the point of rebellion.

The king himself attributed the revolution to 'the groundless apprehensions of the Church of England, blown up by the Prince of Orange's emissaries, and the blackest calumnies of angry and implacable men, [which] made the most zealous members of that Church quite forget their so much preached up doctrine of passive obedience to their lawful Prince'.[5] Although he may have been disingenuous in saying that Anglican apprehensions were groundless, he was absolutely right to claim that the Church of England preached passive obedience and non-resistance. Sermon after sermon, especially those preached on 30 January, the anniversary of Charles I's execution, dwelt

General 5915; transcripts in BL Add. MSS 17677HH), Barrillon (CP(A); transcripts for Jan. to June in PRO 31/3/175–77), and above all of d'Avaux (CP(H) 155–7; edited extracts in *Négociations de Monsieur le comte d'Avaux en Hollande depuis 1684 jusqu'en 1688*, ed. E. Mallet (6 vols.; Paris, 1752–3), vol. vi) reveals the English ambassador's incompetence. Not only are the Dutch and French ambassadors' dispatches more voluminous, they are also better informed. D'Avaux was convinced much sooner than d'Albeville that William planned to invade England. In May 1688, when the English ambassador was regaling Secretary Middleton with trivia about the drinking habits of the Prince of Orange and the elector of Saxony (BL Add. MSS 41816, fo. 10), d'Avaux was informing Louis XIV of a secret expedition by the Secretary of the Amsterdam Admiralty to equip 12 large ships to be ready to sail at short notice, which could only be intended against England (*Négociations*, vi. 146–7). I was harsh, however, to criticize d'Albeville for spending much of Aug. 1688 in England ('The Orangist Conspiracy against James II', *Historical Journal*, 30 (1987), 457) without pointing out that van Citters was absent from England in Holland from 6 July to 7 September!

[4] See below, p. 220.
[5] J. S. Clarke, *Life of James the Second* (2 vols.; 1816), ii. 18.

on the sinfulness of resisting the Lord's anointed upon any pretext whatsoever. Nor was the doctrine cited in a purely hypothetical or abstract way. It found concrete expression in the Act of Uniformity of 1662, which obliged Anglican clergymen to 'declare and believe that it is not lawful upon any pretence whatsoever to take arms against the King'. James was therefore not being naïve when he told the bishops, on the presentation of their petition, 'this is a standard of rebellion. I did not expect this from you.'

Even those who had not taken the declaration against resistance, and did not subscribe to the High Anglican position, might have been given pause by the experience of the civil wars. Those had driven home the view that civil war and anarchy were the worst evils which could occur to any society, and that even the rule of a tyrant was to be preferred. The most rigorous exposition of this argument had been expressed by Thomas Hobbes in *Leviathan*. Although Hobbes was denounced by most writers who mentioned him in the late-seventeenth century, he still exerted a powerful influence. One prominent politician influenced by him was the marquis of Halifax. The opening lines of his *Character of a Trimmer*, that laws are 'the chains that tie up our unruly passions, which else, like wild beasts let loose, would reduce the world into its first state of barbarism and hostility', are pure Hobbism. Not that one needed to have read either Hobbes or Halifax to have held back from resisting James II on the grounds that his rule was preferable to what had happened during the Interregnum.

The bulk of those whom James had alienated were not converted to theories of resistance. Only a minority of radical Whigs took seriously the notion that it was legitimate to resist a tyrant. The king had lost the allegiance of most of his subjects, but only this minority subscribed to the view that they should actively oppose him. Even those who invited William to come over did not hold out the offer of the Crown. They merely asked him to intervene to put pressure on the king to summon a free parliament. Their reassurances that nineteen out of twenty of the people were so desirous of a change that they would assist the invasion, given adequate protection, were in the event to prove wildly optimistic. Sunderland's assessment of the situation was more realistic than theirs.

William's acceptance of their offer was therefore fraught with risk. There has been endless speculation as to the motives behind his colossal gamble. In Whig mythology, of course, he was hailed as 'our Great Deliverer'. William took it upon himself to come to England to rescue Englishmen from absolute power and to restore their liberties. It was an act of pure altruism. He did not even hint that he sought the Crown himself. His manifestos simply proclaimed that he came to rid James of his evil counsellors and to secure the election of a free parliament.

Thus his Declaration, issued from the Hague on 20 September, announced the loftiest motives for intervention in England's affairs. It began with a general statement of principle.

It is both certain and evident to all men, that the public peace and happiness of any state or kingdom cannot be preserved, where the Laws, Liberties, and Customs, established by the lawful authority in it, are openly transgressed and annulled; more especially where the alteration of Religion is endeavoured, and that a religion, which is contrary to law, is endeavoured to be introduced; upon which those who are most immediately concerned in it are indispensably bound to endeavour to preserve and maintain the established Laws, Liberties and Customs, and, above all, the Religion and Worship of God, that is established among them; and to take such an effectual care, that the inhabitants of the said state or kingdom may neither be deprived of their Religion, nor of their Civil Rights.

The Declaration went on to accuse James II's chief advisers of overturning the religion, laws, and liberties of England, Scotland, and Ireland. As instances of this it cited the employment of the suspending and dispensing powers, the erection of the commission for ecclesiastical causes, which was 'manifestly illegal', and its use to suspend the bishop of London and to eject the Fellows of Magdalen College, Oxford. It condemned the attempt to repeal the penal laws and Test Act by pressurizing individuals and waging an assault upon parliamentary boroughs. The purging of the judiciary was singled out for special condemnation. Legal remedies, such as petitioning the king, had been harshly suppressed. The attempt to pack parliament threatened to remove 'the last and great remedy for all those evils': 'Therefore it is, that we have thought fit to go over to England, and to carry over with us a force sufficient, by the blessing of God, to defend us from the violence of those evil Counsellors . . . this our Expedition is intended for no other design, but to have, a free and lawful Parliament assembled as soon as is possible.'[6]

In reaction to Whig hagiography, historians have insisted that William had his sights set on the Crown all along. His manifestos merely reveal that he was a consummate politician. A cold and calculating man, he certainly was not going to make the same mistake as Monmouth did by proclaiming himself king. That had ensured the duke's downfall and death. William was being far more subtle; but basically he sought the same prize. There can be no doubt that he did. A spy in the Modenese entourage advised him to make no mention of the Crown but to stress that he came to rescue Protestantism and Liberty, and then he would accomplish his ends.[7]

Quite when he decided to risk all for the throne, however, has been the subject of some dispute. Hostile contemporaries claimed that it had been his ambition since the Exclusion crisis. The late Professor Lucille Pinkham dated his determination to oust his father-in-law from the summer of 1686, but her reading of the evidence has not been generally accepted.[8] Most now accept that he made the decision to intervene in England some time during the early months of 1688. Until then he was simply anxious to preserve his wife's patrimony intact until the time, which they thought was imminent, when James would die and Mary would inherit it. There was no need to anticipate an event which was expected to occur naturally in the near future. By the winter of 1687, however, it was widely known that Mary of Modena was pregnant, and that if, as Catholics confidently predicted, she gave birth to a son, then James's daughter would be disinherited. When Admiral Edward Russell visited William in Holland during April 1688 he asked the prince what he

[6] Cobbett, v. 1, 10.

[7] Algemeen Rijksarchief, The Hague, Fagel Archive 1:10:19:2019; anon. to Fagel, 23 Oct. 1688. Bentinck's remonstrating with Clarendon on 4 Dec. that 'there are not ill men wanting, who give it out that the Prince aspires at the Crown, which is the most wicked insinuation that could be invented' was probably sincere, but gave William more credit than he deserved (Clarendon, ii. 215).

[8] L. Pinkham, *William III and the Respectable Revolution* (Cambridge, Mass., 1954), 3.

intended to do. According to Burnet, he 'answered that, if he was invited by some men of the best interest and the most valued in the nation, who should both in their own name and in the name of those who trusted them, invite him to come and rescue the nation and their religion, he believed he could be ready by the end of September to come over'.[9] The consequence of this interview was the invitation from the Immortal Seven in June.

Even if the earl of Sunderland had been aware of the contents of the invitation, he might still have remained confident that England was never further from a rebellion than in the summer of 1688. The very conspirators accepted that a rising could only take place if the Dutch launched a successful invasion. Sunderland had every reason at the time to ignore the threat as not being remotely feasible.

The assumption that the Dutch would not invade was based on the premise that any move they made against James II would be countered by France. It seemed to be totally against Louis XIV's interests to allow William of Orange to launch an invasion. Although the two kings were not formally allied for purposes of mutual defence, they were in close enough collaboration for the Dutch to be wary about denuding their country of troops, which might well be needed to resist detachments from the French army directed against the Republic in the event of war breaking out between it and England. Then in September Louis unexpectedly destroyed the basis of Sunderland's calculations by ordering his commander, the duc d'Humières, to attack Phillipsburg, a fortress on the Rhine about 300 kilometres from the Dutch border. William, who had earlier in the month seen d'Humières's army as a threat to his design, now realized that he could carry it out without risk of French reprisals.

Why the French king left James in the lurch has been the subject of much speculation ever since. Certainly he was well aware that William was completing the final preparations for a descent on England, so it cannot be attributed to ignorance of the prince's intentions, though he might have felt that it was too late in the year for them to be put into effect until the following

---

[9] Burnet, iii. 240–1.

spring. On the other hand, Louis was planning a major war in Europe in the summer of 1688, and might well have cynically welcomed a diversion of the Dutch forces from the Rhineland to England. He possibly counted on the invasion precipitating a civil war in the British Isles, which would tie up the Dutch indefinitely. There was no way he could have predicted that in the event James II would give up without even striking a blow.

Louis XIV's intentions also featured in William's plans for more long-term reasons. All his adult life the prince had been convinced that the French king sought to impose his regime on the rest of Europe. He had been made dramatically aware of the threat posed by France to his own country at the age of 21, when Holland had only been saved from invasion by the deperate expedient of breaching the dykes. Ever since William had worked hard to bring about a conjunction of forces which would be able to withstand French aggression. His marriage to Mary in 1677 fitted this strategic pattern, since he hoped it would bring England out of a French system of alliances into a coalition against France. He welcomed the formation of the League of Augsburg between the Holy Roman Empire, Spain, Sweden, and a number of German states in the summer of 1686 to resist any further eastwards expansion by France after its acquisition of Strasburg and Luxemburg had been recognized in 1684. The French attack on Phillipsburg, which removed the pressure on William, was a pre-emptive strike against this alliance and thus precipitated the war of the League of Augsburg, which was to last until 1697. By invading England William hoped not merely to obtain the Crown but also to commit the country to that war and exploit English resources for the fight against Louis XIV. His success ensured that the most serious miscalculation of all was made by the French king in 1688.

Louis XIV assisted the Dutch invasion indirectly also by failing to station a French fleet in the Channel. Ships which might have intercepted William were kept in the Mediterranean during that fateful summer. It is possible that they were intended for use against the papal states in the event of the cold war between Louis and the pope breaking out into open hostilities. Relations between the French king and the papacy had been strained for years. Louis XIV's determination to appropriate ecclesiastical revenues for the French Crown was one bone of contention. Another was his insistence on extending diplomatic immunity for his ambassador in Rome. More immediately he had been on the opposite side to the pope in the election of the archbishop elector of Cologne. The chapter had voted for the rival candidates in July 1688, but the vote had ended in deadlock and was referred to Rome. Although Louis put pressure on Pope Innocent XI to decide for his candidate, the decision went in favour of the other, who was backed by the Emperor. Within a week French troops invaded the Rhineland.

Although it cannot be maintained that the Dutch expedition had papal approval, James II's support of Louis XIV's disputes with the papacy left him ironically isolated in 1688. His own relations with Rome were singularly frustrating for a monarch who hoped to bring England back into the Catholic fold. He renewed diplomatic relations with the Vatican for the first time since the Reformation, despite sixteenth-century legislation making it treason to correspond with the pope. The embassy, however, conducted by the earl of Castlemaine, whose main claim to fame was that he had been the cuckolded husband of one of Charles II's mistresses, was not a resounding success. He had failed to get a cardinal's hat for Father Petre, for example, on which James had set his heart. And in the crisis of his reign James was virtually ignored by Innocent XI. Indeed he obtained no foreign help at all when William launched his expedition.

While William had no serious European adversaries, he still had to deal with potential opposition from within the Dutch Republic. The House of Orange could by no means count on the automatic support of all or even of most Dutchmen to support its ambitions. On the contrary, the political history of the United Provinces had revolved around a struggle between the Orangists and their republican opponents. In 1650, on the sudden death of William's father just before his own birth, the republican party had triumphed to the extent of stripping the House of Orange of the monarchical trappings of the office of Stadtholder, or Governor. Although this post existed in all seven provinces, each had bestowed it upon the head of the house until it was regarded as quasi-hereditary. The years which elapsed until the collapse of the republic under the shock of French invasion in 1672 were known as the Stadtholderless period. In that crisis a popular uprising removed the leaders of the republican party and turned to William for salvation. His popularity led to the rapid restoration of the Stadtholdership, which was made hereditary by the two principal provinces, Holland and Zeeland, and his promotion to the positions of Admiral General and Captain General of the United Provinces. Even so he was by no means monarch of the Dutch. The constitution was almost anarchic in its federal structure. Power was diffused upwards through urban oligarchies to the States, or representative assemblies of the provinces, to the States General, who were collectively known as their 'High Mightinesses'. These exercised far more than legislative authority, for example appointing ambassadors who reported directly to them. They were, however, dominated by the Province of Holland. Historically the oligarchs of the great towns of Holland, and the chief official of the provincial States, the Grand Pensionary, were not friendly towards the House of Orange. Fortunately for William he contrived to get upon good terms with the Regents, or bourgeois élite of Amsterdam, while in Gaspar Fagel he had a Pensionary with whom he worked well until that official's premature death in December 1688.

With the co-operation of the Dutch authorities, both federal and provincial, William was able to assemble an invasion force remarkably quickly. Over the summer of 1688 an army of between 14,000 and 15,000 was mobilized. They were not only Dutchmen but Germans, Swedes, and Swiss, while about a fifth were exiled British. Provisions for these men and some 3,660 horses for the cavalry were loaded on to 400 transport ships under the command of Admiral Herbert.[10]

These preparations could scarcely be kept secret. Yet as late as the end of August there was speculation about their intentions. The English consul in Amsterdam informed Lord Middleton on the 17th of that month how some were 'affirming that it is to land somewhere in England about the time that a parliament is to sit, but others say that it is to oppose France'. Eleven days later he wrote, 'the discourse of, and reasons for, this equipage

---

[10] H. H. Towen, 'Neither Fish nor Fowl: The Stadholderate in the Dutch Republic', in H. H. Towen and A. Lassley (eds.) *Political Ideas and Institutions in the Dutch Republic* (Los Angeles, 1985), 21–2; J. Childs, *The Army, James II and the Glorious Revolution* (Manchester, 1980), 175.

are very various. One day they say they will demand reason of France, another that they will go and cause a rebellion in England.'[11]

James remained unconvinced that they were aimed against him until well into September. It seems that, despite the warnings he received from foreign sources, he could not bring himself to believe that his own son-in-law was seeking his downfall.[12] Their relationship, although it was occasionally strained, was reasonably cordial for most of the reign. He kept up a correspondence with the Prince of Orange from the moment of his own accession. While his own letters tended to be brief, they were far from curt. On the contrary, with their frequent references to such subjects as the weather, hunting, and the health of close relatives, they document the kind of intimacy one might expect between a father and his son-in-law. The occasional jarring note, such as the harbouring of disaffected subjects in the Dutch Republic, and William's defence of the Test Acts, only temporarily interrupted their normal cordiality. The first serious cause of friction occurred early in 1688 when

[11] BL Add. MSS 41816, fos. 159, 167. D'Avaux, the French ambassador at the Hague, came close to stumbling on the conspiracy involving the Prince of Orange and the signatories of the invitation to him when a French officer living in exile in Holland, one Tellières, turned spy in the hope of being granted a pardon to return to France despite crimes he had committed there. Tellières at first passed on information about the Huguenot refugees whose confidence he had gained. These contacts eventually got him involved with go-betweens passing intelligence between the English and Dutch conspirators. Just as he was about to learn something substantial, however, he was killed, allegedly whilst resisting being arrested by armed men sent from the Court of Justice to answer charges of betraying the Huguenots (Speck, 'Orangist Conspiracy', pp. 457–9). The circumstances were so strange, that rumours began to spread that he had been involved in a plot to assassinate the Prince (HMC *Rutland*, ii. 121; Newsletter, 25 Aug. 1688; Morrice MS Q, p. 289).

[12] In addition to d'Avaux and Barrillon, the very experienced and astute diplomat Usson de Bonrepos made a special visit to England late in Aug. in which he warned James about his danger, and urged him to make contingent plans to meet it, in an interview with the king on 25 Aug./4 Sept. (Archives Nationales, Paris, K 1351 no. 4). Besides the French, others alerted James to the imminence of a Dutch invasion, among them the papal envoy who told him of William's intentions on 31 Aug., but the king chose not to believe him (BL Add. MSS 15397, fos. 239–40). I owe these references to Professor John Kenyon.

James recalled the Anglo-Dutch brigade to England.[13] Whereas at the time of Monmouth's rebellion William had encouraged the States General to dispatch it, now he put pressure on them to resist its recall. Only officers were allowed to leave if they wished. Those willing to stay, and all the lower ranks, were to remain in the Republic. The correspondence survived this crisis, but it became noticeably cooler thereafter. James changed his customary concluding remark, 'you shall find me as kind to you as you can desire', to the rather more ambiguous, 'you shall find me as kind to you as you can expect'. The cool response in Holland to the birth of James's son in June scarcely improved relations. Yet James continued to correspond until 17 September, when he wrote his last private letter to William, endorsing it as usual, 'for my sonne, the Prince of Orange'.[14] Soon after sending it he must have received d'Albeville's dispatches of 18 and 21 September warning him that 'their goeing for England is no more a secret in these parts'.[15] The destination of the Dutch task force could no longer be doubted, even by the king of England.

Notwithstanding the efficiency with which the armada was equipped, William still ran an enormous risk. It was perilously late in the year for a major naval expedition to be launched. Even when James finally accepted that it was directed against himself, he still took comfort in the belief that no commander would risk an invasion until the following spring, by which time he could have his defences in much better order to repel the invaders. The fleet had already been put into a state of readiness to resist the Dutch armada early in August, and later that month the army was mobilized for action. Garrisons were reinforced, especially those at Hull and Portsmouth. Troops were brought to England from Ireland and Scotland, while regiments hastily

[13] G. Hilton Jones, 'The Recall of the British from the Dutch Service', *Historical Journal*, 25 (1982), 423–35.

[14] Dalrymple, II, ii. 290, 294–5. When James next wrote to William it was a formal letter signed by himself and Secretary Middleton, dated 1 Dec. 1688 (Japikse, II, i. 22–3). The fact that it was also in French upset the prince, since the king had been used to writing to him in English (Clarendon, ii. 219–20).

[15] BL Add. MSS 41816, fos. 202, 209. It was on 24 Sept. that James told Clarendon that the Dutch were going to invade in earnest. When the earl asked him if he really believed it, the king replied with warmth 'do I see you my Lord?' (Clarendon, ii. 189).

recruited extra men to increase the forces available to do battle with the Dutch should they land. By the end of September the arrangements were still not complete, for as late as 18 October a Scottish officer could write that the king was 'in a much better posture to receive him [William] than he was twenty days ago'. John Childs sums up James's final plans as being 'to man the garrisons, secure London, and then concentrate the remainder of his forces into a mobile field army which would assemble within a twenty-mile radius of London, ready to respond in the direction of William's invasion'.[16]

The Prince of Orange hoped to counter these preparations by going ahead with his scheme as quickly as possible, even though this involved setting out into the treacherous North Sea at a season when it was likely to be at its roughest. He also counted on conspiracies in the English army and navy to incapacitate them from offering him serious resistance. The leaders of the military and naval conspirators were all veterans who had served in Tangiers under Charles II. Among army officers, the most important were John Lord Churchill, the future duke of Marlborough, Percy Kirk, and Charles Trelawney. These co-ordinated the efforts of the so-called Treason Club and the Association of Protestant Officers. The naval officers had for the most part benefited from the patronage of Arthur Herbert, who went over to the prince in the summer of 1688 and was the English commander of the Dutch task force. He had previously commanded the Straits fleet in the Mediterranean, a tour of duty in which he had promoted men like Matthew Aylmer, Wolfran Cornwall, George Churchill, and Cloudesley Shovell. These were ready, along with four others, Edward Russell informed Herbert, 'to salute my Ld Dartmouth and come over to us'. They resented the disgrace of their former patron, his replacement by Roger Strickland, and the latter's promotion of Catholics in the fleet after his own conversion to Catholicism in 1686. Although, as in the army, the proportion of Catholic naval officers never became more than 10 per cent, and although James replaced Strickland with Lord Dartmouth in the final crisis, the damage had been done. Like their military colleagues, these men were prepared to join in an Orangist conspiracy

[16] NLS Yester MSS 14405, fo. 177: John Hays to Lord Tweeddale, York, 18 Oct. 1688; Childs, *The Army, James II and the Glorious Revolution*, p. 174.

against James II. Indeed the two conspiracies were intimately connected, for many of the conspirators had commissions in both services.[17]

His assumption that the conspiracies were significant enough to ensure that he would meet with no serious resistance from either the navy or the army of James II was the most calculated of all the many risks which William of Orange ran in 1688. He anticipated that many officers would actually go over to him, and counted on defections from the English fleet above all for the success of his expedition. He and Herbert even appealed to the navy in print. His own manifesto 'to all commanders of ships and all seamen that are now employed in the English fleet' was an open invitation to mutiny.

You are only made use of as instruments to bring both yourselves and your country under Popery and Slavery by means both of the Irish and the foreigners who are preparing to compleat your destruction. And therefore we hope that God will put it in your hearts at this time to redeem yourselves, your country and your religion from these miseries.

This in all human appearance can only be done by your coming now to assist us, who are labouring for your deliverance. And we do assure you that we will be ever mindful of the services that you shall now do us; and we promise to you that we will place particular marks of our favour on all those who will upon this occasion deserve well of us and of the nation.[18]

In the event he did not have to rely on their good offices, since Dartmouth was unable to get the English fleet out of the Thames estuary to engage his. Had the two met, William might well have been disappointed in his expectations, as he was to be in those he entertained of the army officers.

In addition to making naval and military preparations, James also made political concessions amounting to what would

---

[17] Childs, *The Army, James II and the Glorious Revolution*, p. 148; P. LeFevre, 'Tangier, the Navy and its Connection with the Glorious Revolution of 1688', *Mariner's Mirror*, 75 (1987), 127–90; BL Egerton MSS 2621, fo. 47: Russell to Herbert, Exeter, 13 Nov. 1688; D. Davies, 'The Seagoing Personnel of the Navy, 1660–89', unpublished D.Phil. thesis (Oxford, 1986), ch. 7. I am grateful to Dr Davies for a copy of this chapter.

[18] Speck, 'Orangist Conspiracy', p. 461; BL Egerton MSS 2621, fo. 13. For an earlier draft of the manifesto see Japikse, i. 59–60.

nowadays be called a U-turn to try to deal with the situation. These, as the marquis of Albeville predicted, forced William of Orange to change his Declaration, and to publish a supplement on 14 October asserting that 'the imperfect redress that is now offered is a plain confession of those violations of the Government that we have set forth'. The king's advisers continued to claim 'an arbitrary and despotic power'. The prince therefore still justified his intervention, insisting that 'a declaration of the rights of the subjects . . . not by any pretended acts of grace to which the extremity of their affairs has driven them', but in a free and lawful parliament was as essential as ever.[19]

When the Declaration appeared in England James was mortified by its claim that the Prince of Wales was a supposititious child and that William had been invited by both temporal and spiritual lords. He promptly summoned a meeting of peers and bishops to demand which of them approved of the invitation, but was reassured that none did, even though one of those present was the bishop of London. He also convened an assembly on 22 October of peers, bishops, judges, the Lord Mayor and aldermen of London, and several lawyers to assert the legitimacy of the Prince of Wales. Some forty people swore on oath that the birth had been authentic. Their depositions and those of the king and the dowager Queen Catherine of Braganza were then enrolled in Chancery.

Notwithstanding these attempts to refute his justification for his invasion, William went ahead with it. His first attempt, however, in mid-October, ran into ferocious storms and had to be abandoned. Many supplies were lost, including over a thousand horses, which suffocated when the hatches had to be shut. The return to port and being kept on board ship did little to boost the morale or fitness of the troops. The gales which nearly wrecked his fleet blew obstinately from the west, pinning the task force in Dutch harbours for weeks. Then, late in October, they changed direction to the east, blocking the English fleet in the Thames estuary and allowing the Orange armada to make its way unhindered down the English Channel to Torbay. Today we would say that William was incredibly

[19] BL Add. MSS 41816, fo. 251; Cobbett, v. 12. For the concessions, see below, p. 136.

lucky. At the time they attributed his successful landing on English soil to Providence.

The gales which blew from the west and prevented him from getting to England until November were known as 'the Popish wind'. People prayed for an easterly wind throughout October, during which 'the common Question was every Morning, Where is the Wind to-day?' When the weather vanes eventually turned through 180 degrees, they signalled the eagerly antici-pated arrival of the 'Protestant Wind'.[20]

It is often claimed that the easterly gale force drove William down the English Channel to Torbay when he had intended to land in the north of England. However, it has recently been established that Roger Morrice was right when he noted 'the Prince landed neere Exeter by designe from the beginning'. The notion of a Yorkshire landing was a feint meant to deceive the government's supporters. It certainly succeeded in mislead-ing the earl of Bath, who wrote from Plymouth that 'the landing in the West was a great surprise after so many rumours of their intentions to land in the North'.[21]

It has even been suggested that the western invasion misled the prince's own supporters, who expected him to land in the north. According to Burnet, those who invited William

advised his landing in the North, either in Burlington Bay, or a little below Hull; Yorkshire abounded in horse; and the gentry were generally well affected, even to zeal, for the design; the country was plentiful, and the roads were good till within fifty miles of London. The earl of Danby was earnest for this, hoping to have had a share in the whole management by the interest he believed he had in that country.[22]

The fact that in the event William landed almost as far away from the coast of Holderness as he possibly could has been attributed to his determination not to be beholden to Danby and his northern associates. But William did not leave them in the

[20] C. Jones, 'The Protestant Wind of 1688: Myth and Reality', *European Studies Review*, 3 (1973), 202–3.

[21] Ibid. 201–21; S. Lindgren and J. Neumann, 'Great Historical Events that were Significantly Affected by the Weather: "Protestant wind"—"Popish wind": The Revolution of 1688 in England', *Bulletin of the American Meteorological Society*, 106 (1985), 634–44; Morrice MS Q, 17 Nov. 1688.

[22] Burnet, iii. 303.

dark about his intentions. In September Jacob van Leeuwen was
sent over to England to make contact with the English
conspirators. He got in touch with Edward Russell, Lord
Lumley, and Danby. They gave him details of the king's
military and naval preparations, and asked him where it was
proposed to land. When van Leeuwen claimed he did not know,
they themselves advised the west of England. The marquis
d'Albeville got wind of this, writing from the Hague on
6 November, 'he [the Prince] was advised from England to land
in the West, where he might be assured towns and men
sufficiently would declare for him, and surprise the Court,
being not expected to land there'.[23]

By then it was too late, for William had landed in Brixham on
5 November. His troops then marched through the pouring rain
along the muddy Devon lanes through Newton Abbot to
Exeter, arriving there on the 9th. Here the Prince set up his
headquarters, staying until the 21st. The long sojourn there was
necessary, according to one member of the expedition, 'to
refresh the army after it had been so long on shipboard, and to
recover the horses to their former strength, as also for the
gentlemen of the country thereabout to come and joyn his
Highness there'. William himself was concerned to recruit not
the local country gentry but the professional soldiers whom the
invitation had assured him would desert James and join him in
significant numbers. Indeed he expected 'the most part' of the
King's army to come over.[24] A few deserters came in while he
remained at Exeter, including Lord Cornbury, the earl of
Clarendon's son. But the response initially was quite small, and
many of the rank and file of the mutinous regiments actually
returned to the royal camp. The prince must have been
concerned about the military prospects facing him. The king's
army was superior in numbers, some 25,000 to his own 14,000
or so, who had scarcely recovered from the voyage. Retreat
became a real possibility. Before he hazarded a major advance,
therefore, he took care to safeguard his rear, negotiating the
surrender of Plymouth from its commander, the earl of Bath,

[23] Speck, 'Orangist conspiracy', p. 460; HMC 7th Report Appendix,
Graham papers, p. 422.

[24] *Graham Papers*, p. 417; J. Whittle, *An Exact Diary of the Late Expedition of
his Illustrious Highness the Prince of Orange into England* (1689), 48.

on 18 November. Only when he was assured that the port and
its citadel were secure did he himself advance eastwards.

Although the numbers of deserters from his army were not
great, while the news that many men actually returned to their
posts cheered him up, James was sufficiently concerned about
the breakdown of discipline to seek to reassert his authority.
Where previously he had decided that the best plan for him was
to stay in London, he now resolved to join his forces at
Salisbury, where they were under the rather ineffective earl of
Feversham. The king arrived at the camp on Salisbury Plain on
19 November. Unfortunately he succumbed to severe nose-
bleeds, which incapacitated him from giving a firm lead. These
are often assumed to have been psychosomatic. No doubt
James's nerves were frayed in these weeks. But according to
some accounts, almost certainly by eyewitnesses, he was 'very
ill in his health and bleeds upon every occasion at the nose and
mouth and much purulent matter comes out'.[25] The king was a
sick man at Salisbury. Instead of inspiring his army to march
west against the enemy, he agreed at a council of war on
23 November to retreat to London. This fateful decision gave
William the military advantage.

Indeed, from a military point of view the king's position was
now quite desperate. After his decision to retreat, more
deserters left his army, including Lord Churchill, who went
over to William the very night following the council of war.
Thereafter Feversham would have had the utmost difficulty
impeding the Dutch advance, even if he had tried to do so. In
fact William showed himself to be in no great hurry to follow
James to the capital. He grouped his army together at Sherborne
and then moved slowly towards Hungerford, arriving there on
7 December. Meanwhile his supporters had responded to his
invasion with sympathetic uprisings in the Midlands and the
north, taking Derby on 17 November, Nottingham on the
20th, York on the 22nd, Hull on 3 December, and Durham on
the 5th.

Having lost the initiative militarily, James tried to seize it
politically. On his return to London from Salisbury on
27 November he invited all the peers in town to give him their

[25] BL Egerton MSS 2621, fo. 67: Burnet to Herbert, Sherborne, 29 Nov.
1688.

advice. Lord Rochester advised him that calling parliament was
'the only remedy in our present circumstances'.[26] He was also
urged to pardon the prince and his supporters, and to dismiss all
Roman Catholics from his employment. Next day writs were
issued for a parliament to meet on 15 January. James then
appointed Lords Halifax, Godolphin, and Nottingham to go to
William's headquarters and negotiate terms with him. He also
proclaimed a general pardon.

When the king's commissioners made contact with William at
Hungerford on 8 December, he met them not in private but
in the presence of the English lords and gentlemen who
accompanied him. Indeed he was so anxious to involve them
that he allowed them to discuss the king's proposals. Thus the
proposition that parliament should be elected on the writs
which James had issued was formally debated, with a chairman,
and put to the vote. Some of the English gentry were against the
impending elections, on the grounds that they had not been able
to make their interests in their own localities. They actually
carried a motion to ask the king to recall the writs. This decision
disconcerted the prince, who overruled it. As he explained, 'we
may drive away the King; but, perhaps, we may not know how
easily to come by a Parliament'. The majority who had carried
the clause were furious, and reinstated it.[27] But William insisted
that it should not be presented to the king. Instead he informed
the commissioners that he wanted all Catholics dismissed, both
armies to be stationed 40 miles from London, and the garrisons
of the Tower, Tilbury, and Portsmouth to be placed in trusty
hands.

Ironically, James obliged the majority who wanted the writs
to be recalled by abandoning the general election when he fled
from London on 11 December, just before the commissioners
returned. The news was a relief to William. When Halifax had
asked Burnet what the reaction would be if the king went away,
the reply, which the prince approved, was that 'nothing was so
much to be wished for'. The earl of Clarendon saw William at
Wallingford the next day, and the prince 'could not conceal his
satisfaction at the king's being gone'.[28] Unfortunately for both
prince and king, James only got as far as Faversham, where he

---

[26] Clarendon, ii. 209.   [27] Ibid. 221.
[28] Burnet, iii. 341; Clarendon, ii. 224.

was detained by fishermen. Instead of escaping to France, where he had already sent his wife and their infant son, he was escorted back to London by guards dispatched to Kent to rescue him from his predicament. He arrived back in his capital on 16 December, cheered by welcoming crowds.[29]

During his brief absence there had been incredible confusion. James left almost total chaos behind him. His own bastard son, the duke of Berwick, wrote pathetically to Lord Dartmouth, 'the King being gone and I left without orders I desire you will let me know whether you have received any for me. I beg likewise you will be pleased to give me your advice what I shall do.'[30] Law and order broke down. Mobs roamed the streets of London, looking for Catholic targets. Amongst those they found to attack and destroy was the Spanish ambassador's residence. Nor was the army able to assert order, for the king left a message with Lord Feversham to disband it, which was done. The demobilized soldiers added to the chaos, wild rumours being circulated that many were Irish who were on the rampage. Fortunately the earl of Rochester and the bishop of Ely had anticipated that James would withdraw, and taken it upon themselves to summon a meeting of peers with the Lord Mayor and aldermen at the Guildhall 'and take upon them the Government for the preservation of the Kingdom and this great City'. As the bishop himself observed, 'we had otherwise been a state of banditi, and London had certainly been the spoil of the rabble'. He and Rochester hoped to use the council of peers to reconcile the Prince of Orange and the king, but they found themselves outmatched by those who were now exasperated at James's attempted flight and sought 'effectual securities for our Religion and laws' in a free parliament to be presided over by William. They issued several orders, but stopped short of inviting the prince to enter London, a courtesy which was extended to him by the mayor and aldermen.[31]

[29] According to most commentators, including Burnet, who observed 'so slight and unstable a thing is a multitude, and so soon altered' (Burnet, iii. 353). One eyewitness, however, who 'saw him in Fleet Street', also saw 'much gaping but no rejoicing' (*The Diary and Autobiography of Edmund Bohun*, ed. S. Wilton Rix (Beccles, 1853), 81).   [30] Staffs RO DW/1778/Ii/1678.

[31] R. A. Beddard, 'The Loyalist Opposition in the Interregnum: A Letter of Dr. Francis Turner, Bishop of Ely, on the Revolution of 1688', *Bulletin of the Institute of Historical Research*, 40 (1967), 106; *CSPD 1687–9* (1972), 379.

William did not actually enter London until 18 December. Meanwhile, James had attempted to resume government, and had even presided over a council. But his heart was not in it, and when he received a request from the prince to remove from the capital he accepted it, only changing the destination from Ham to Rochester. Soon after James's second departure for Kent, this time with a Dutch guard, William entered St James's. It was observed that he was not welcomed as rapturously as the king had been the day before.

On 20 December all the peers in London were summoned to meet the prince the next day. When they met, he left the settlement of affairs entirely to them, and then withdrew. They agreed to meet daily in their own House. On 22 December they published an order 'requiring all papists and reputed papists to leave London within five days for their respective habitations, from which they are not to remove about five miles distance'. It was also reported that they had ordered the seizure of all Irish officers as hostages, in case Lord Tyrconnel should instigate reprisals against Protestants in Ireland, 'that whatsoever protestants he should destroy in that kingdom so many of the papists here should be destroyed for them'. If such terrorist measures were envisaged, it seems hardly likely that a third reported resolution was passed with any hope of success, namely 'that the king shall be sent too [*sic*] to desire his concurrence and for calling a new parliament'.[32]

Even if it was hoped that James would collaborate in the summoning of a parliament, there was no chance of that, for he escaped from his captors at Rochester on 23 December and fled to France, this time successfully. His final departure brought the question of the kingship to the fore. Already some lawyers had advised William to assume the Crown and to summon parliament by virtue of being king, but he had refused on the grounds that it violated his Declaration that a free parliament should resolve the country's constitutional difficulties. On 24 December the peers debated the situation created by the king's flight. Lord Paget moved that his withdrawal was tantamount to a legal death, and that Princess Mary should be declared queen. He was seconded by the bishop of London, but

---

[32] Bodleian Ballard MSS 45, fo. 22: J. Jones to A. Charlett, 22 Dec. 1688.

they failed to carry a majority. Instead William was addressed to take the administration of the government into his own hands, and 'to write circular letters to all the counties, cities and universities, and cinqu-ports, to choose Representatives to meet in a Convention at Westminster on the 22nd of January next'. The prince replied 'that he could not give an answer to these addresses, till he had spoken with the gentlemen who had been formerly in the House of Commons'. On 26 December, therefore, he met such members of the Exclusion parliaments as were in town, together with the Lord Mayor of London, aldermen, and about fifty common councillors. They agreed to make the same addresses to him as the Lords had done. William then reconvened the peers on 28 December and accepted the addresses. The circular letters for the Convention were accordingly issued.

5

The Convention

⟨decorative ornament⟩

Munday is the grand day for settling the Government . . . .
The beginning was serene and their actions unanimous.
God grant it may so continue.
(*Richard Lapthorne to Richard Coffin, 26 Jan. 1689*)

THE elections for the Convention were held in January 1689.
Traditionally they have been represented as relatively tranquil
after the turbulence of the Exclusion contests and before the
bitter campaigning of the reigns of William and Anne. This
tranquillity was attributed to a consensus behind the Revolution
which ensured that it was 'not necessary to arouse the electorate
over the niceties of the constitutional issues involved'.[1] Of late,
however, this view has been called in question.[2] Several
constituencies were contested, and in some of them the dynastic
issue was undoubtedly raised. William Sacheverell's defeat in
Derbyshire, for instance, was attributed to 'his not appearing
for the prince'.[3] Even where there were no actual contests, there
were clearly disputes. In Newcastle upon Tyne some Tories
alleged that no legal choice could be made without the king's
writ.[4] The press not only reported electioneering but also
exhorted the electorate. Thus *Considerations Proposed to the
Electors of the Ensuing Convention* in London admonished them
not to choose those who 'did what in them lay to surrender your
charter or which is all one submit to the king's regulation of it'.[5]

---

[1] J. H. Plumb, 'The Elections to the Convention Parliament of 1689',
Cambridge Historical Journal, 5 (1937), 254.

[2] H. Horwitz, 'Parliament and the Glorious Revolution', *Bulletin of the
Institute of Historical Research*, 47 (1974), 40–2.

[3] BL Add. MSS 40621, fo. 3: Sir Edward Harley to Robert Harley, 19 Jan.
1689.   [4] *London Mercury: or, The Orange Intelligencer*, 3–7 Jan. 1689.

[5] The copy in Cambridge University Library (Sel.3.235) is endorsed in
manuscript 'January the 9th 1688/9 spread by a soldier who came over with the
Prince of Orange who knew nothing about it'.

Yet, despite some evidence of campaigning by rival candidates, the elections do seem to have been less contentious than those immediately before and after. There were apparently only 60 contests, 19 fewer than had taken place in 1685, while 106 occurred in 1690.[6] One reason for this was that the abortive election called by James II had seen electioneering in many places which had tested the strength of the rival interests only a month before, making another test unnecessary. Thus the earl of Danby wrote to the mayor of Pontefract on 16 December, 'I hope you will make such distinction in the elections of parliament men to serve for your borough that you will not choose any who have only looked on while others have ventured their all to preserve you.'[7] Sir John Lowther solicited support from the freeholders of Cumberland to elect him for the county to parliament, 'the only probable means of cureing all the miseries of this nation', and recommending Thomas Wharton as his partner, 'son to my Lord Wharton whose antient and noble estate in this and other countys and zealous asserting the Protestant religion at the dangerous time doth very well deserve from us all that return'.[8]

The king, who had only issued the writs half-heartedly, countermanded them when he fled, dropping the Great Seal into the Thames for good measure, thus bringing the electoral process to a grinding halt. Nevertheless some writs got down into the provinces and elections were held in some constituencies in Yorkshire. For example, knights of the shire were returned for the county, and burgesses for Beverley, Hedon, Scarborough, and York. It is significant that both Yorkshire and York, where elections were held under the auspices of the earl of Danby, each returned a Whig and a Tory without contests.[9]

Yorkshire was in some respects a microcosm of the country as a whole, both in these abortive elections and in those held to choose members of the Convention. In January 1689 sixteen Whigs and fourteen Tories were returned. This marked a huge

[6] Henning, i. 107–24; H. Horwitz, *Parliament, Policy and Politics in the Reign of William III* (Manchester, 1977), 329–34.

[7] A. Browning, *Thomas Osborne, Earl of Danby* (3 vols.; Glasgow, 1944–51), ii. 155.

[8] Cumbria RO Kendal, DD/F 3372: Sir John Lowther to 'Sir', 5 Dec. 1688.

[9] Henning, i. 469, 491.

swing to the Whigs over the 1685 result, when only four had been returned. The outcome was not as decisive as the results of the 1681 election had been, however, when only eight Tories had been elected. In 1689 the county was much more evenly divided—if divided is the right word. For, as in December, there is evidence of the parties agreeing to share the representation. No fewer than six of the county's fifteen constituencies sent one Tory and one Whig to Westminster, apparently without contests.[10] The elections to the Convention differed from others in the late-seventeenth century by being marked more by consensus than by conflict.

The Convention met on 22 January 1689. The consensus which had marked the elections to the Commons can be discerned in the deliberations of that House during the crucial debates which occupied them until 13 February, when William and Mary were declared king and queen. On the other hand, the proceedings of the peers were marked by bitter divisions.

There was undoubtedly a Whig majority in the Lower House. This was revealed at the outset by the choice of a Whig Speaker, Henry Powle. Sir Edward Seymour, who had occupied the chair in Charles II's reign, thought he stood a chance with Tory support on this occasion, but was quite discountenanced to be repudiated with cries of 'No Seymour, no Seymour'.[11] Yet it was a majority of moderate Whigs. Significantly Powle, who had chaired the informal sessions of MPs and London councillors in December, had been in favour of expedients rather than of exclusion.

The moderation of most members can be detected in their

[10] Yorkshire, Beverley, Boroughbridge, Hull, Richmond, and York (Henning, i. 468–91). Suffolk by contrast witnessed contests in five of its eight boroughs. In that county those Whigs who had collaborated with James II were trounced at the polls, 'the former regulation having made all people sick of the folly and madness of the phanatique administration when they were in the saddle' (Cambridge University Library Add. MSS 4403, M.W. to E. Bohun, 15 Jan. 1689). Suffolk was, however, exceptional in this election. See P. E. Murrell, 'Suffolk: The Political Behaviour of the County and its Parliamentary Boroughs from the Exclusion crisis to the Accession of the House of Hanover', unpublished Ph.D. thesis (Newcastle upon Tyne, 1982), fo. 57.

[11] 'Journaal van Constantyn Huygens den zoon van 21 October 1688 tot 2 September 1696', *Werken Witgegeven door het Historische Genootschaap*, NS 23 (Utrecht, 1876–8), 72.

response to the warning William of Orange gave them in his letter, which was read out in their opening session: 'next to the danger of unseasonable divisions amongst yourselves, nothing can be so fatal as too great delay in your consultations.'[12] Sir Henry Capel, brother of the Rye House plotter Lord Essex, who had committed suicide in the Tower, and himself an exclusionist Whig, asserted 'we are a full House', and urged them to consider the state of the nation more or less immediately. Sir Thomas Clarges protested that there were many absentees, and 'would have this affair debated in a full House'.[13] He therefore moved that the following Monday, 28 January, should be set aside for the debate. Although Clarges was a Tory, he carried the House with him. Sir Edward Harley, Whig member for Radnor, wrote that night 'many of the returns being not yet come in there can be no perfect list of the members'. He saw no sinister design behind Clarges's motion, concluding that 'the transactions of this day gives hope of unity and agreement'.[14] Another observer saw no unreasonable delay in the postponement of the discussion for nearly a week when he observed that 'the prince sent them a letter to speed affairs upon which the Commons appointed Monday next to consider of the great affairs of the nation'.[15]

Clarges nevertheless did have a partisan motive. He had concerted with the Tory leader Lord Nottingham to delay a debate on the state of the nation by the Commons to enable the Lords to initiate discussion of the settlement. They had picked up rumours before the Convention assembled that a plan was afoot to make William and Mary king and queen, and conspired to try to avert this outcome. They hoped that loyalists in the Lords would rally to the exiled James, and thus set the agenda for the Convention's debates on the situation which the king had left behind him when he fled to France. These hopes were thwarted, however, by the marquis of Halifax, Speaker of the Upper House, who persuaded some Whig peers to move the postponement of their own discussion of the state of the nation

---

[12] Grey, ix. 3.   [13] Ibid. 5.
[14] BL Add. MSS 40621, fo. 5: Sir Edward Harley to Robert Harley, 22 Jan. 1689; by 26 Jan. there were 417 MPs present (Horwitz, *Parliament, Policy and Politics*, p. 9).
[15] Bodleian Ballard MSS 45, fo. 24: J. Jones to A. Charlett, 21 Jan. 1689.

until 29 January, the day after that set aside by the Commons.[16] This proposal was successful, even though it was 'opposed with great warmth by the Lords Nottingham, Chesterfield, Clarendon, Rochester, Abingdon and others; with great reflection upon the . . . motion, as if the Lords were only to take aim from the Gentlemen below'.[17]

When the Commons met on the morning of 28 January, they appointed a committee of the whole House to consider the constitutional position. Some Whigs thought that to go into such a committee would in itself prolong the proceedings unduly, since members could speak more than once in it, unlike in a debate in the House. Although the Tories were most insistent that the Speaker should leave the chair, their votes alone cannot have resolved the question. Otherwise the chairman they appointed, after abortive attempts to chair Seymour and Sir William Pultney, would hardly have been the Presbyterian Whig, Richard Hampden.[18] At the end of the day this committee agreed the celebrated resolution 'that king James the second, having endeavoured to subvert the constitution of the kingdom, by breaking the original contract, between king and people, and by the advice of Jesuits and other wicked persons having violated the fundamental laws, and having withdrawn himself out of this kingdom, has abdicated the government; and that the throne is thereby vacant'. This elaborate and complex wording was a composite of arguments used by both Tories and Whigs during the debate.

The first wording of the resolution was suggested 'after a great pause' by a Tory, Gilbert Dolben, who argued 'that the king is demised, and that James the second is not king of England', and moved 'that king James the second having voluntarily forsaken the government, and abandoned and forsaken the kingdom, it is a voluntary demise in him'.[19] It has been suggested that the notion of a voluntary demise, a sort of constitutional suicide, was much more in line with Tory than with Whig thinking.[20] Certainly some Whigs saw it as a trap to

---

[16] Clarendon, ii. 252–4.

[17] A. Simpson, 'Notes of a Noble Lord, 22 January to 12 February 1688/9', *English Historical Review*, 53 (1937), 92 (hereafter 'Notes of a Noble Lord').

[18] Morrice MS Q, p. 444.   [19] Grey, ix. 7, 9.

[20] Horwitz, *Parliament, Policy and Politics*, p. 10.

raise immediately the problem of the succession, though Dolben protested that none was intended. Sir Robert Howard thereupon proposed an alternative motion, 'that James II has abdicated the Government by breaking the original contract', and was seconded 'angrily' by Sir John Morton.[21] However, Dolben's original motion was seconded by the Whig, John Arnold, 'after another long pause'.[22] Moreover a Tory, Sir Robert Sawyer, indicated his own preference for 'abdicated' rather than 'demise'. Though he objected to the Whiggish notion of an original contract, he accepted that 'wee have indeed a kind of interregnum at present' and by implication that the throne was vacant. The Whig Boscawen urged the House to 'declare "that the throne is void" and fill it'. He even gave a strong hint who its occupant should be, maintaining that France was likely to declare war, 'and we have reason to make use of our best weapon, to chuse a king to go before us and fight our battells (which was the first occasion of kingly government) and that a woman cannot so well do'.[23] This was the first overt preference for William to be expressed in the Convention.

Some Tories baulked at this proposal. It seemed to them that to fill the vacancy was tantamount to making the Crown elective. They argued that it amounted to deposing the king, and asked the lawyers in the House to give their opinions whether or not kings could be deposed. A Tory alternative to deposition was a regency, justifiable on the grounds that James should be treated as a minor or a lunatic, incapable of exercising kingly power. Some Whigs made their hostility to such a notion very clear. When one was rebuked by the chairman of the committee for reflecting on the lawyers' arguments, another 'angrily' observed, 'if the question be whether you have power to depose the king, that may tend to calling him back again and then we are all ruined'. Other Whigs, however, were just as concerned as Hampden that the debate should not become

---

[21] Grey, ix. 20; John Somers, 'Notes of Debate, January 28, January 29, 1689', in *Miscellaneous State Papers from 1501 to 1726*, ed. Philip Yorke, second earl of Hardwicke (2 vols.; 1778), ii. 403 (hereafter Somers); 'A Jornall of the Convention at Westminster Begun the 22 of January 1688/9', ed. L. G. Schwoerer, *Bulletin of the Institute of Historical Research*, 49 (1976), 251 (hereafter 'Jornall').

[22] 'Jornall', p. 249.   [23] Grey, ix. 21, 23; Jornall, p. 255.

heated. Clearly the advocates of a regency had broken the
consensus. Equally clearly, however, they were a minority even
among the Tories, for, when the chairman put the whole
resolution to the committee, 'most of the House' agreed to it
'very loudly'. Only five members actually opposed it.[24]

The final resolution as it emerged from the debate reflected
the prevailing consensus. Nobody had had a good word to say
about James II. Tories as well as Whigs could agree that he had
'endeavoured to subvert the constitution of the kingdom'.
Though they might disagree that he had broken 'the original
contract', they could accept that he had acted 'by the advice of
Jesuits and other wicked persons', had 'violated the fundamental
laws', and had 'withdrawn himself out of this kingdom'. Some
Tories would have preferred the word 'demise' to 'abdicate',
while most might have had reservations about the vacancy of
the throne. It was a Whig lawyer, Sir George Treby, who
bluntly pointed out to them that 'we have found the crown
vacant, and are to supply that defect. We found it so, we have
not made it so.'[25]

The questions of reporting from the grand committee to the
House, and then of conveying the resolution to the Lords,
further revealed a split between those who urged dispatch and a
group willing to delay the Convention's deliberations. While
those who spoke urging speed were mainly Whigs, and those
who tried to prolong business were for the most part Tories, the
two groups were not divided exclusively along party lines.
Thus Sir William Williams, a Whig, albeit one who had
collaborated with James II, was among those who thought that
'we have done enough for this day'. On the other hand, Sir
Richard Temple, a Tory, first moved that Hampden should
report the resolution immediately to the House. His motion
seems to have been supported by the overwhelming majority of
members, for the only words heard by a parliamentary diarist
were the approving ones 'Ay ay'. The House also expressed
impatience with members who hindered the putting of the
resolution and the motion to convey it to the Lords that very
day.[26]

[24] Jornall, pp. 258–61.   [25] Grey, ix. 13.
[26] 'Jornall', pp. 261–2. Sir Richard Temple played a key part in the
Convention. Only two MPs, Hampden and Maynard, made more than his

Apart from a handful of Tories, who sought to impede the progress of the settlement, much the greater part of the Commons seems to have been intent on agreeing a formula to the effect that James was no longer king and that the Convention should replace him. Even most of those who resisted that conclusion were not necessarily deliberate wreckers intent on destroying any alternative to the king's recall, but held genuine doubts about its validity. They were not convinced that James could be declared to be no longer king, since that seemed to make the kingship elective rather than hereditary. They would have preferred a regency as being more consistent with constitutional precedents. Some of those who advocated a regency, however, undoubtedly did so because it was in the best interests of James II. Aware that advocacy of his return would receive short shrift, the next best tactic was to avoid his deposition by setting up regents to administer the country until such time as he could be reinstated. Although this was a minority view in the Commons, it had much more substantial support in the Lords. As in the Commons, its supporters comprised two elements. One, led by the earl of Nottingham, entertained genuine misgivings about the legality of proceeding by declaring that James had forfeited the right to rule altogether. The other, amongst whom the earl of Clarendon and the bishop of Ely were prominent, remained loyal to him and sought as best they could to keep open the option of his restoration.[27]

On 29 January the resolution of the House of Commons was debated in a committee chaired by the earl of Danby. The more extreme loyalists denied the charges against James. Clarendon maintained that the king 'can do no wrong', while the bishop of Ely denounced the resolution as 'accumulative treason'. Nottingham was more cautious. Whilst prepared to concede that the king might have done what the Commons alleged, he insisted that it did not follow that he had forfeited the throne,

eleven recorded speeches. He is often considered to have been a Whig. Yet, though he was undoubtedly a careerist and an opportunist with a consequently chequered voting record, contemporaries called him a Tory: Godfrey Davies, 'The Political Career of Sir Richard Temple, 1634–1697', *Huntington Library Quarterly*, 4 (1946), 47–84.

[27] A. Simpson, 'The Convention Parliament, 1688–1689', D.Phil. thesis (Oxford, 1939), fos. 52–82.

much less that the Convention could depose him. The earl of Rochester criticized the implication that the monarchy was elective, and first proposed a regency. Halifax objected that a regency would be an even greater change in the constitution than the proposal that the throne was vacant. Nottingham denied this, urging that it was 'the best remedy which comes nearest to the forms of our law'.[28] This view commanded enough support for the Commons' resolution to be postponed until the question was put to the vote 'whether a Regency with the administration of regal power under the style of king James the second during the life of the said king James be the best and safest way to preserve the Protestant religion and the laws of the kingdom'. This motion was lost by only three votes, 51 to 48.

The debate was spun out until eight at night, so discussion of the resolution was put off to the following day, 30 January.[29] The decision to reconvene the committee as soon as possible was a victory for those who were anxious to reach a settlement. For 30 January was the anniversary of the execution of Charles I, and some Tories tried to use that as an excuse to postpone the debate further. Although they were unsuccessful, they did manage to persuade the peers to amend the resolution by changing the word 'abdicated' to 'deserted'. The close result of the previous day's division revealed that their lordships were far less concerned to reach a consensus than were the Commons. Quite the contrary, their debate on the resolution revealed deep divisions and was characterized by angry exchanges. Clarendon recorded that in it 'several peevish and angry things were said of the king'. Thus Lord Montague 'did declare that from this day he looked upon himself to be absolved from all allegiance to King James. Lord Delamere said it was long since he thought himself absolved from his allegiance to king James . . . and if king James came again, he was resolved to fight against him, and would die single with his sword in his hand, rather than pay him any obedience.'[30] Roger Morrice also noted that the debates on the regency and the resolution of the Commons were

[28] H. Horwitz, 'Parliament and the Glorious Revolution', pp. 50–2.
[29] The earl of Winchilsea accused 'the Regency Lords' of filibustering (Bodleian Ballard MSS 45, fo. 25).
[30] Clarendon, ii. 257.

conducted 'with the greatest passion and violence'.[31] The fact that almost all the bishops sullenly sided with the loyalists gave rise to particularly deep resentment.

The substitution of the word 'abdicated' with 'deserted' by the peers raised the question of the ultimate meaning of the Commons' resolution. As we have seen, the various clauses of it made it a composite of Tory and Whig indictments of the king. How far it represented a compromise whereby Tories could accept some and Whigs other parts of it, and how far it was meant to be a coherent whole, has caused some dispute.[32] In the joint committees convened to try to resolve the disagreement between the two Houses, the Commons made it clear that the resolution was meant to cohere. They disliked the word 'deserted', they insisted, since that merely referred to James's withdrawing himself from the kingdom, whereas the word 'abdicated' 'respects the whole for which purpose the Commons made a choice of it'. Thus the king had not abdicated simply by leaving the country but by 'having endeavoured to subvert the constitution' and by 'having violated the fundamental laws' as well. Though this undoubtedly made the king's political actions as well as his flight responsible for his forfeiture of power, it still left it open as to which of his activities was more to blame. Whigs might well have stressed his subversion of the constitution 'by breaking the original contract between king and people', and Tories his violation of the fundamental laws 'by the advice of Jesuits and other wicked persons'. The Lords expressed their dislike of 'abdicated', partly because it was not a term known to English law, and partly because it implied a conscious renunciation on the part of the king, which James manifestly had not done. As the earl of Pembroke put it, his quitting the kingdom 'was no more than a man's running out of his house when on fire, or a seaman's throwing his goods overboard in a storm, to save his life, which could never be understood as a renunciation

[31] Morrice MS Q, p. 450: At one stage 'Lord Wharton desired my lord Clarendon might be called to the bar for calling the civil war a rebellion' (Bodleian Ballard MSS 45, fo. 25).

[32] T. P. Slaughter, '"Abdicate" and "Contract" in the Glorious Revolution', *Historical Journal*, 24 (1981), 323–37; J. Miller, 'The Glorious Revolution: "Contract" and "Abdication" Reconsidered', *Historical Journal*, 25 (1982), 541–55.

of his house or goods'.[33] Since, in the view of the peers, James
had not abdicated, it followed that the throne was not vacant.
On 31 January, therefore, they amended the resolution again,
deleting the reference to the vacancy in the last clause. There
was an attempt to replace it with the words that 'the Prince and
Princess of Orange should be declared King and Queen', but
this was defeated by 52 votes to 41. Then the motion to delete
the expression 'and that the throne is thereby vacant' was carried
by 55 to 41.

The outcome of the three divisions in the Lords on 30 and
31 January 1689 has been attributed to the behaviour of a group
of peers led by the earl of Danby, who allegedly favoured the
succession of Mary to her father's throne. While the voting on
the motion for a regency was sufficiently narrow to be
determined by a group of three or four, the divisions on the
offer of the Crown to William and Mary and on the vacancy of
the throne were too decisive to be attributed to the manoeuvres
of Danby's supporters, who anyway voted for the motion to
make William and Mary king and queen. The majorities on
31 January consisted overwhelmingly of loyalists, although a
few Maryites may have joined them.[34]

If the claims that the monarchy was hereditary and not
elective, and that the throne was not vacant, could both be
upheld, then Mary's supporters were convinced that she should
logically succeed. The trouble with this logic was the birth of a
son to Mary of Modena the previous June. Although most peers
and MPs seem to have preferred to ignore his existence or
assumed, in a paradigm case of what psychologists call
dissonance reduction, that he was supposititious, he clearly
complicated the issue. It is significant that the Convention never
investigated the circumstances of his birth, even though William
had referred the matter to parliament in his Declaration. An
inquiry was started, but was dropped on the grounds that the
child being in France made it impossible to establish the truth.[35]

---

[33] Burnet, iii. 385–6: Dartmouth's note.

[34] H. Horwitz, 'Parliament and the Glorious Revolution', pp. 44–5; E.
Cruickshanks, D. Hayton, and C. Jones, 'Divisions in the House of Lords on
the Transfer of the Crown', *Bulletin of the Institute of Historical Research*, 53
(1980), 159–61.

[35] 'There's no room for the examination of the little gents title which

However, he was referred to during the debates. Boscawen observed that there was not only the question of James II to consider, 'but a little one beyond the sea too, that will pretend'. Sir Richard Temple referred to 'a pretended Brat beyond the sea, whom you cannot set aside'. Sir Thomas Clarges noted that 'James has taken away the child, if it be his, into another kingdom'. 'Of the Prince of Wales', commented Sir Joseph Tredenham, "tis the opinion of the House that there is a legal incapacity as well as a natural.'[36] He was referring to a resolution passed by the Commons on 29 January 'that it hath been found, by experience, to be inconsistent with the safety and welfare of this Protestant kingdom to be governed by a Popish Prince'. The Lords had agreed with this, which set aside the claims of both James and his son.

Indeed the agreement of both Houses to disinherit Catholic kings was the single most radical act of the Convention. It was also a striking indication of a pragmatic consensus which normally distinguished debates on the constitutional problem in the Commons, and on this occasion at least informed discussion in the Lords as well. Yet the concurrence of the Upper House with the resolution seemed at odds with the difficulties experienced by many of the peers in accepting that the throne was vacant. The main problem, as far as the opponents of a vacancy were concerned, was that it also set aside the claims of James II's Protestant daughters.[37]

If only Protestants could succeed, however, then the case for Mary could not be gainsaid. Hence the Maryites opposed the notion that the throne was vacant. Her supporters in the Commons rallied to the Lords' amendments. On 5 February Sir Thomas Clarges claimed that, 'These reasons of the Lords seem to me to be so cogent, that they deserve to be seriously

---

perhaps will be hereafter the best proof he has of his title that after 'twas in their power to examine his birth they durst not refer it to a free parliament as was pretended', a Tory wrote to Oxford, 7 Feb. 1689 (Bodleian Ballard MS 45, fo. 27).

[36] Grey, ix. 23, 55–6, 62. 'A Paper humbly offered to the ensuing Parliament' giving reasons for believing that the Prince was a supposititious child was never read (Nottingham University Library: Portland MSS PWA: 2186).

[37] H. Horwitz, '1689 (and all that)', *Parliamentary History*, 6 (1987), 23–32.

weighed. I take the Crown to be hereditary and that king James has "abdicated" the Crown, and the pretended Prince of Wales being in the power of the French King and the throne vacant, the Crown ought to proceed to the next Protestant successor.' This proposition that the throne was not vacant since the succession had passed to Mary produced the first real breakdown of consensus in the Commons. A motion to agree with the Lords' amendment to the vacancy clause was defeated by 282 votes to 151. Some Whigs apparently went along with the question up to the appointment of tellers for the division in order to flush out Tories to vote for it. Yet, though the minority was immediately disgraced and blacklisted as being opposed to the abdication, most of them were not Jacobites but Maryites. They were not seeking to restore James II.[38]

Their basic commitment to undoing the damage which James had wrought was demonstrated in the progress of the document initially known as the Heads of Grievances and ultimately immortalized as the Declaration of Rights. The first positive proposal for it was made in the Commons on 29 January, the day after the throne had been declared vacant. A Whig, Thomas Wharton, moved that it be filled by the Prince and Princess of Orange. He was seconded by a Tory, Sir Dunscombe Colchester.[39] Then another Tory, Lord Falkland, made a crucial intervention.

It concerns us to take such care, that, as the Prince of Orange has secured us from Popery, we may secure ourselves from Arbitrary Government. The Prince's Declaration is for a lasting foundation of the Government. I would know what our foundation is. Before the question be put, who shall be set upon the Throne, I would consider

[38] Grey, ix. 54; E. Cruickshanks, J. Ferris, and D. Hayton, 'The House of Commons vote on the Transfer of the Crown, 5 Feb. 1689', *Bulletin of the Institute of Historical Research*, 52 (1979), 37–41.

[39] Somers, p. 414: Dr Lois Schwoerer identifies the seconder of Wharton's motion as the Whig Lord Colchester, even though she acknowledges that 'Sir Duncombe Colchester's name appears in Somers's notes of the debate, but it is more likely that Wharton's friend Lord Colchester seconded the motion' (L. G. Schwoerer, *The Declaration of Rights* (1981), 884, 350 n. 3). It is only 'more likely' if one is determined to make it 'a Whig motion to declare William and Mary King and Queen' (ibid. 186). There is no other reason to suspect that Somers, who was present at the debate and presumably knew how to distinguish Lord Colchester from Sir Dunscombe, got it wrong.

what powers we ought to give the Crown, to satisfy them that sent us hither.[40]

Falkland's role in this debate has given rise to speculation. While it is not denied that Tories genuinely wished 'to prevent a recurrence of those royal measures under which they had suffered during the reign of James II', it has been maintained that the proposal was made for tactical reasons also. The Tories allegedly tried to postpone the filling of the vacancy by this move. 'Party strategy' has been adduced in explanation of the initiation of so vital a discussion by Falkland, an inexperienced member of the Commons. It has been seen as a tactic concerted beforehand with the Tory leadership, and particularly with Sir Edward Seymour, from whom Falkland had bought the treasurership of the navy in 1681. The contributions of other Tories are also cited as being suggestive of a conspiracy to prolong the debate. Above all, their failure to oppose the proposal on principle is taken to indicate party discipline. In Dr Lois Schwoerer's words,

It is incredible that no Tory should have felt that the proposal was theoretically repugnant or that some of the proposed restrictions were unacceptable. Is it possible that the backbenchers were brought into line by the Tory leadership? If that did not happen, then one must grant unanimity of opinion between Tories and radical Whigs on limiting the English Crown. That kind of unanimity is not credible.[41]

Yet why is it not credible, especially if the Convention considered that it was not limiting the Crown but declaring its lawful bounds? Few Tories believed in unlimited royal power. Many had gone along with limitations as a solution to the problem posed by a Catholic successor during the Exclusion crisis. They shared with fellow Englishmen the view that there should be a rule of law. It was generally agreed that James had broken that rule. Moreover, the ways in which he had done so were more injurious to Tory than to Whig interests. The commission for ecclesiastical causes, the suspension of the bishop of London, the ejection of the Fellows of Magdalen College, Oxford, and the trial of the seven bishops had all hit the privileges of the Church of England, which were much more dear to Tory than they were to Whig hearts.

[40] Grey, ix. 29–30.   [41] Schwoerer, *Declaration of Rights*, pp. 185–90.

Furthermore Falkland was not an inexperienced politician. He had sat in James II's parliament and contributed twice to debates on 29 January 1689 before making his proposal. When a member suggested that William should deploy ships to cruise upon the Irish coast, 'to give encouragement to Protestants there', Falkland, presumably acting in his capacity as treasurer of the navy, replied that this had already been done. Again, when it was proposed that it was against the law to be governed by a popish prince, he objected that it contradicted the resolution passed on the 28th, and the House agreed to resolve that it was 'inconsistent with the safety and welfare of this Protestant kingdom', not that it was illegal. Falkland had therefore played a significant role in the House before he rose to propose consideration of the powers of the Crown.[42] He was seconded by the Whig William Garway. Sir William Williams then stressed the consensual nature of the proposal by saying, 'I now speak for all England.' As he pointed out, 'The Prince's Declaration has given us a fair platform.'[43] It had indeed. William's second Declaration of 14 October contained the expression, 'it is plain that there can be no redress nor remedy offered but in parliament by a Declaration of the Rights of the Subjects that have been invaded'.[44] William could not object if the Convention took him at his word. It could even be that he himself welcomed a debate which would at least cloak his ambition for the Crown by fulfilling his ostensible motives for invading England.

Of course William also wanted a speedy settlement. His supporters in the Commons were uncomfortably aware that a major constitutional debate on the rights of the subject could be protracted indefinitely. References to the ancient constitution and to Magna Carta made them nervous. Serjeant Maynard expressed the fear that they might sit five years 'and would not delay to supply the throne lest instead of an arbitrary govern-

---

[42] Grey, ix. 26, 29: in so far as Falkland might have been put up to propose to declare the rights of the subject, it is possible that it was in consultation with Prince George of Denmark, for whom he acted as groom of the stole, rather than with the Tory leaders. George could have been looking after the interests of his wife, Princess Anne, who favoured her sister Mary rather than William.

[43] Ibid. 30.

[44] Cobbett, v. 12.

ment we should have none'.[45] 'I am as much afraid of losing time as any body', commented Colonel Birch, and advocated filling the throne first before presenting a list of grievances, which 'will not take you a day's time'.[46] Despite these doubts about delay, a committee was duly appointed under the chairmanship of Sir George Treby, which managed to produce a document to present to the House by six in the evening of 30 January.

Treby's committee consisted of thirty-nine members, twelve of whom were Tories. Roger Morrice noted that 'the committee is very justly and equally chosen'. He distinguished 'the men of art of great ability and craft', for whom the exercise was 'specious', from 'the men of ability and prospect that are for the common interest of the kingdom so that the intreaguers cannot possibly delude the committee'.[47] It has been claimed that its work was done by an even more adverse ratio of Whigs to Tories than in the full membership. Fifteen 'active' members have been identified, of whom only one, Lord Falkland, was a consistent Tory. In the absence of any minutes or other detailed record of their proceedings, however, this can only be conjectural.[48] On the other hand, the document which they produced was undoubtedly radical. It consisted of no fewer than twenty-three 'Heads of Grievances'. In addition to the clauses which were eventually to be incorporated in the Declaration of Rights, they included provisions for preventing the Crown from curtailing or perpetuating sessions of parliament, for religious toleration, and for appointing judges on good behaviour rather than at pleasure.[49]

These Heads were reported to the House on 2 February. Unfortunately we do not know how the first twenty-one were received, since Anchitel Grey, our only full source of debates in this session, was clearly not present in the Commons until discussion of the twenty-second.[50] It cannot therefore be

---

[45] Grey, ix. 32; Somers, 417.   [46] Grey, ix. 35.
[47] Morrice MS Q, p. 445.
[48] Schwoerer, *Declaration of Rights*, 200.
[49] They are listed in Schwoerer, *Declaration of Rights*, pp. 299–300. They were also published in 1689 as *The Public Grievances of the Nation Adjudged Necessary by the Honourable the House of Commons to be Redressed*.
[50] Grey, ix. 42.

inferred from silence that Tories did not contribute to the debate and consequently that their earlier contributions had been largely tactical. Indeed, it was a leading Tory, none other than Sir Edward Seymour, who originally suggested a decision, eventually taken on 4 February, which expedited the progress of the Declaration considerably. On 29 January he had warned that attempting too ambitious a document would make them suffer 'more than by reason of not doing at all'. He was 'not for making new laws but declaring old'.[51] This distinction was adopted in the drafting of the Declaration, when the committee was instructed to separate clauses declaratory of old laws from those requiring new legislation. The former were made the basis of the Declaration of Rights.

The way forward to present the Declaration to a new monarch was cleared on 6 February, when the Lords finally backed down and accepted the full resolution which the Commons had passed on 28 January. Their objections to the word 'abdicated', and the vacancy of the throne, were removed when William himself bluntly let it be known that he would settle for nothing less than the Crown. On or about 3 February he summoned a meeting of leading politicians, including Lords Halifax and Danby, and told them that, were a regency to be agreed, he would not undertake to be regent; if Mary were declared queen, 'he could not think of holding any thing by apron strings'. Unless he were offered the Crown, 'he would go back to Holland, and meddle no more in their affairs'.[52] This concentrated minds wonderfully, for, as Halifax had told the prince earlier, 'as nobody knew what to do with him, so nobody knew what to do without him'.[53] Thus the announcement 'helped not a little to bring the debates at Westminster to a speedy determination'.[54] What clinched it was Mary's own wish, conveyed by Burnet, to rule jointly with her husband. Lord Dartmouth, who was present, observed that the peers finally agreed to the full wording of the resolution, 'by some Lords being prevailed upon to absent themselves, from an apprehension that if they had insisted it must have ended in a civil war'.[55] Even then some peers defiantly divided the House.

[51] Grey, ix. 35; Somers, 419.
[53] Ibid. 396: Dartmouth's note.
[55] Ibid. 398: Dartmouth's note.

[52] Burnet, iii. 395.
[54] Ibid. 396.

However, 'deserters and absentees reduced the loyalist strength from their over-all majority of earlier in the week to a minority of forty-six, while the Williamites, swelled by new recruits, former loyalists and Danby's group, now numbered sixty-four.'[56]

Having at last agreed that the throne was vacant, the Lords now proceeded immediately to the question of filling it. Morrice recorded how the marquis of Winchester moved that

they would make it a day to be remembered with all gratitude by all ages to come if they would go on to set upon the throne that person that was likely to be an Instrument to do as much for the securing our Religion Liberty and Property as the late King had done to destroy them, etc. Therefore he desired the Prince and Princess of Orange might be declared King and Queen of England, etc.[57]

Even at this late stage the earl of Nottingham led a rally of Tories who still could not bring themselves to accept the transfer of the Crown on constitutional grounds. Only conquest, they argued, could justify such a usurpation. It made the kingship elective and violated their oaths of allegiance. Moreover, the usual title was 'king of England, Scotland, Ireland, etc.' But the Convention had no more right to declare kings of Scotland than the Scots had to choose kings of England. 'Herein Halifax presence of mind', commented Morrice '(as it was in many other great occurrents this day in this debate) was very serviceable and he offered this expedient, that they might crown the Prince and Princess of Orange King and Queen of England with all the appurtenances thereunto belonging etc. and afterwards consult with Scotland.'[58]

Notwithstanding the last-ditch stand by some Tory peers, the resolution was passed without a division. Clarendon thought that, had there been one, then forty would have voted against the motion, though Morrice claimed that it was 'generally thought there would have been about 25 Not Contents'.[59] The last ditchers then capitulated. Clarendon tried to persuade them

---

[56] Cruickshanks *et al.*, 'Divisions in the House of Lords', p. 65. Their analysis of the division list corrects Clarendon's account in Clarendon, ii. 261–2.

[57] Morrice MS Q, p. 460.   [58] Ibid. 461.

[59] Ibid.; Clarendon, ii. 261. In 'Notes of a Noble Lord', p. 95, Clarendon noted, 'I verily believe there were above 30 negatives.'

and their supporters in the Commons to secede from the Convention, but Nottingham repudiated this suggestion, saying 'we must support the government as well as we can'. Having objected that removing James and replacing him with William and Mary violated the oaths of allegiance, Nottingham agreed to chair a committee to draw up a new oath of fidelity to the incoming rulers, which dropped the traditional phrase 'rightful and lawful'. The revised phrasing allowed many to accept them as ruling *de facto* (in fact) who, like Nottingham himself, could not be persuaded that they ruled *de jure* (by right).[60]

On 7 February the Lords' acceptance of the Commons' resolution about the vacancy of the throne and their recommendations for filling it together with the revised oaths were reported to the Lower House. Some Whig members were eager to accept all the proposals immediately. Others, however, including the Speaker, counselled caution until the committee dealing with the Heads of Grievances had reported. The resolution concerning the offer of the Crown was consequently postponed to the following day. Meanwhile the House heard a report from Sir George Treby, chairman of the committee on grievances, that afternoon. The debate lasted until 'pretty late that night' and became quite 'tumultuous'.[61] Nevertheless, although personal insults were exchanged, party rancour does not appear to have marked the proceedings. On the contrary, Danby's son, Lord Dumblain, actually apologised for having voted against the vacancy of the throne on 5 February, saying, 'I have great obligation to [the prince] and have showed my duty to him.'[62] Moreover, despite the noisy scenes, some progress was made. The House agreed without a division that 'no Papist may succeed' to the Crown, 'nor any person that hath made or shall make profession of being a Papist'. The members also discussed the question of the exact powers of William in the proposition that he should be joint ruler with Mary, and of the succession to them, with Anne's claim in mind. These topics were debated on the following day, when a committee was

---

[60] 'Notes of a Noble Lord', p. 97. Nottingham was seconded by Danby. When Halifax objected to the proposition on the grounds that it ridiculed the title, Danby rounded on him and 'schooled him so shamefully that my Lord Halifax did not open his mouth' (Bodleian Ballard MSS 45, fo. 27).

[61] Morrice MS Q, p. 461.   [62] Grey, ix. 73.

appointed to clarify them and to offer amendments to the Lords'
resolution about the settlement of the Crown. Accordingly this
committee, chaired by the Whig John Somers, recommended
that William should have the sole administration of the
government, and that the Crown should descend to children of
William and Mary, then of Mary, then of Anne, and finally 'for
default of such issue to the heirs of the body of the said Prince of
Orange'.

The question of the relationship between the settlement of the
Crown and the Declaration of Rights then arose. 'You will not
go up with your vote to the Lords, to declare the Prince and
Princess King and Queen, and nothing with it', urged Sir
Richard Temple. 'If you will give the committee leave, they will
connect it all at once.'[63] A Whig objection that the Lords should
not be involved in the Declaration, but that it should be
presented directly to William, was overruled by the Speaker.
Somers's committee accordingly adjourned to draw together
those Heads which it deemed did not require new legislation
and the Lords' resolution on the settlement of the Crown as
amended by the Commons.[64]

It has been maintained that connecting the Declaration of
Rights and the resolutions for filling the throne represented the
triumph of radical Whig tactics. William and Mary were not
simply to be proclaimed king and queen. They were also to
accept conditions on their royal authority, as stipulated in the
Declaration. In a sense the document was quasi-contractual.[65]
This interpretation goes to the very heart of the Revolution

---

[63] Ibid. 79.

[64] According to Dr Schwoerer, it is 'of paramount importance that the
committee was overwhelmingly Whig' (*Declaration of Rights*, p. 229). Yet the
ratio of Tories to Whigs on Somers's committee, 6:21, was almost the same as
that on Treby's committee, 12:40. Moreover, one member, admittedly a
Whig, recommended the appointment of a committee since 'we are all of one
mind' (Grey, ix. 79). Assuming the silence of Tories from the record of the
debate in Anchitel Grey's diary, and concluding that 'if the preservation of
the statement of rights had depended on Tories in the House of Commons, the
document would have been lost' (Schwoerer, *Declaration of Rights*, p. 229), is
very dubious. Grey only recorded six speeches, one of which was by Sir
Richard Temple, whom Schwoerer regards as Whig but who is taken here to
have been a Tory.

[65] Schwoerer, *Declaration of Rights*, p. 231.

Settlement. Did it merely change rulers? Or did it alter the nature of the kingship?

When Treby's committee first began to draw together the Heads of Grievances, it was reported that they intended to present them to the new ruler as conditions for the acceptance of the Crown. Thus Roger Morrice noted that they were drawing up 'heads containing what the Kings of England by law and what the subjects may claim; and that the king or queen is to swear and sign before he or she be crowned'.[66] It seems likely that this intention was incorporated in the final version of the Heads which was sent up to the Lords late in the evening of Friday, 7 February. Otherwise it is hard to explain why some Tory peers, led by the bishops, could use them as a handle to try to alienate the Prince of Orange from the Whigs.[67] Certainly William expressed dissatisfaction with the document at this late juncture. His displeasure can scarcely have been due to any particular clauses denouncing James II's use of the royal prerogative and declaring it illegal. After all, he had himself denounced many of James's actions as unconstitutional in his own Declaration, and had invited a free parliament to declare the rights of the subject. He was surely kept informed of the contents of the Heads from 19 January onwards, when they were under discussion in the Commons. There is no way that he could have been taken by surprise about them ten days later.

But he might well object to them being offered to him as 'stipulations'. He had not come to England to establish contractual kingship. Such conditions would indeed place 'fetters' on the Crown.[68] The knowledge that William would object to terms encouraged the Tories to exploit the situation for their own ends. 'Great art has been used to prejudice the Prince against the men that were for redressing the grievances,' Sir Edward Harley informed his son Robert. They 'told him they had taken away all his power and left nothing but a name . . . the Prince was highly incensed against these men that were

---

[66] Morrice MS Q, p. 445; cf. Reresby, p. 546: 'before any person was named to fill the throne they would frame conditions upon which only he should be accepted as King'.

[67] Morrice MS Q, p. 463.

[68] Ibid.

for restraining his power and that he would not take the crown upon conditions'.[69]

A crisis was averted when the framers of the Heads explained their status to the prince. First they insisted that they were not changing the law but declaring old laws. Although technically this was highly debatable, there seems no reason to doubt that they genuinely believed this to be so. They were convinced that the Heads were not 'stipulations' but statements of fact. In this sense they were not 'conditions' at all. Secondly, and more importantly, they were prepared to accept a crucial amendment to the Heads, surely at William's insistence. The document which went up to the House of Lords on 8 February stated that he was to exercise the 'administration of the Government'. This was altered in the Upper House the following day to read that he was to enjoy the 'sole and full exercise of the regal power'.[70] While both clauses made it clear that, during their joint lives, William alone was to wield power and not share it with his wife, the change in wording was highly symbolic. The 'administration of the Government' was no more than he had been asked to take upon himself by the peers on 24 December 1688 and by the Convention on 22 January 1689. He had been chief executive at the request of those who had invited him to assume responsibility for the government. Entrenched in the Heads of Grievances, this formula could be taken to imply that his status had not been significantly changed by his acceptance of the Crown, and that he was still the servant of those who framed the document. It could even be construed as a contract. By substituting the words 'sole and full exercise of the regal power', the final version of the Declaration removed any ambiguity on that score.

Just in case any survived, it was made crystal clear that the Declaration was in no sense a new Magna Carta in the ceremony held in the Banqueting House on 13 February. For the Declaration to be a condition of his acceptance of the Crown, William would have had to acknowledge it first and then accept the offer of the kingship. In fact his speech was carefully worded to make it unequivocal that he and Mary accepted the proffered crowns

[69] BL Add. MSS 40621, fo. 22: Sir Edward Harley to Robert Harley, 9 Feb. 1689.
[70] *Lords Journals*, xiv. 122.

first and then that he undertook 'to preserve your religion laws and liberties', that is, acceptance of the Crown preceded their acknowledgement of the Declaration of Rights.[71]

[71] Cf. H. Nenner, 'Constitutional Uncertainty and the Declaration of Rights', in B. Malament (ed.), *After the Reformation: Essays in Honour of J. H. Hexter* (1980), 291–308.

PART TWO

6

James II and the Revolution

❧❀❧

Seldom do we find a precedent of any Prince that laboured, against all the common rule of policy, so industriously to lose a Crown as James II.

(*Quadriennium Jacobi: Or, the History of the Reign of King James II from his First Coming to the Crown to his Desertion*)

ON the night of 11 December 1688 James II found himself at Faversham in Kent, in the company of two close friends and about fifty of his subjects, most of them sailors who lived in that town. They met on board a customs vessel, which the seamen boarded searching for fugitives fleeing illegally to France. Not knowing they had encountered the king, they took him for what they were pleased to call an 'old rogue, ugly, lean-jaw'd hatchet-fac't Jesuite' and subjected him to several indignities. Thus he was very closely searched; according to a contemporary account, his 'very breeches were undone and examin'd for secret weapons so undecently as even to the discoveries of his nudities. This the King afterw'ds much resented, as not fit to be offer'd to a gentleman or any other person.'

The next day James was conveyed by his captors to the Queen's Arms in Faversham, where his true identity was revealed. So far from the revelation earning him the respect of his captors, however, he was subjected to fresh humiliations. James asked them to obtain a boat so that he could escape, but they refused. Although they agreed to send for the earl of Winchelsea to come to the king's assistance, and even allowed him to transfer from the inn to a private house, they still insisted on guarding him very closely. It was said that 'they follow'd him to his devocons, nay, and were so indecent as to press near him in his retirem' for nature'. On 15 December, four days after his capture, James was rescued by a company of guards' sent from London to escort him back to the capital. Upon being rescued 'his spirit seem'd to revive, and he became as it were anothr man, as being glad to be rid of such guards, whose rudeness none could justify and what would be the consequences at last none could guess'.[1]

What had brought the king to such a curious rendezvous with the men of Faversham? He might well have asked himself the same question, ruefully adding another: has it come to this? For he was trying to get to France, where he had already sent his wife and infant son. He was fleeing from William of Orange, who was invited to enter London the day after James left. Characteristically James bungled it, and returned to the capital with his armed escort. This was a grave embarrassment both to the king and to the Prince of Orange. William would much have preferred his father-in-law to have been successful in his bid to leave England. Indeed he made quite sure that the king's next attempt would not end in fiasco. James was allowed to reside in Rochester, technically under house arrest. But the guards were tipped off to be lax in their duties, and on 23 December the king escaped them, getting away on board a waiting boat. This time his bid to reach France was successful.

Had James stayed to face his critics it is impossible to envisage that the Revolution would have taken the course it did. There was a significant party of loyalists who, while they were critical of what the king had tried to bring about during his reign, were prepared to come to terms with him. The king's presence would immeasurably have strengthened their hands. As it was, his departure took the ground from under their feet, leaving those with alternatives to his continued kingship almost a clear field. A key question of 1688, therefore, is, why did James go?

The answer must be sought in the king's mental state. It seem clear that he was undergoing some kind of physical and nervous breakdown during the closing weeks of his reign. The nose-bleed which incapacitated him at Salisbury continued to debilitate him considerably. ''Tis generally thought that his Matie is very ill', reported a newsletter of 16 December, '(and has been reported to be dead) of an imposthume which is

---

[1] *Notes and Queries*, 3rd series, 5 (1864), 391, 392; James had clearly been unnerved by his ordeal. BL Althorp Papers; H 4 (13): 'concerning K. James his being taken.'

inward from his nose and up into his head.' At Faversham an eyewitness 'observed a smile in his face of an extraordinary size & sort; so forced, awkward and unpleasant to look upon, that I can truly say I never saw anything like it'. The king said quite wild things about why he wished to leave the country. Thus he asserted that 'he was certain the P[rince] of O[range] on his coming design'd his life and that he thought there was but one step between his prison and his grave'.[2]

Some historians have sought the explanation of James's mentality in his sexual intrigues. His promiscuity was so notorious that people joked about its incompatibility with his Catholic piety. Charles II was alleged to have said of Catherine Sedley, a mistress not celebrated for her beauty, that she must have been recommended to his brother by a priest for a penance. Bishop Burnet related how his queen got her revenge on Sedley by getting the priests to point out the inconsistency between James's professions of faith and practice of adultery. According to Charles Carlton, the psychological strain became intolerable. As he puts it,

concubine and confessor are an uncomfortable combination, and as James oscillated between absolution and illicit orgasm, penance and promiscuity, his guilt grew and he tried to absolve it by increasingly drastic and dangerous acts of faith. . . . In psychological terms James's superego tried to compensate for its inability to control his libido by developing an exaggerated concern with religion . . . the conflicts within James's psyche became unbearable and, perhaps from a desire to punish himself by bringing about his own defeat, James broke down during the crisis of his reign when England was invaded.[3]

James's biographer F. C. Turner also detected a connection between the king's mental state and his sexual activities. 'At the time of his accession James was suffering from premature mental decline' he observed.

He had never been given credit for superior mental equipment, but he would probably not have been noticeably inferior to his neighbours if

---

[2] BL Add. MSS 34487, fo. 50; P. C. Vellacott, 'The Diary of a Country Gentleman in 1688', *Cambridge Historical Journal*, 2 (1926–8), 62; *Notes and Queries* 3rd series, 5 (1864), 393.

[3] Burnet, iii. 121; C. Carlton, 'Three British Revolutions and the Personality of Kingship', in J. G. A. Pocock (ed.), *Three British Revolutions: 1641, 1688, 1776* (1980), 196–7.

he had lived as a country gentleman—the nickname 'Squire James' which he acquired at about the age of forty reflects the popular view of his abilities—but he had declined even from that low standard. In February 1685 he was little more than fifty-one years of age, and should have been at the height of his mental powers; and it is difficult to avoid a suggestion that in the sexual excesses of his youth he had incurred infection which had resulted in a fairly common mental disease.[4]

It is possible that James had contracted syphilis. At least one lady, Madame Bellène, declined the offer of his bed despite all its other advantages, because she feared he might infect her.[5] On the other hand, his physical health does not seem to have suffered. He did not succumb to any serious illness until 1695. He was still hunting at the age of sixty-five, and lived to be sixty-eight, which was not a bad record for the time. His wife Mary of Modena and his son James Edward—who lived to be seventy-eight—do not appear to have contracted venereal disease from him. The only evidence Turner cited is his 'extreme haughtiness and arrogance, an exaggeration in his kingly office . . . a total absence of misgiving, amounting to foolhardiness in regard to the consequences of his action'. A man can display all these attributes without suffering from 'a fairly common mental disease'.

Yet the fact that in 1688 'his spirits sunk extremely' requires some explanation, even if we are not to find it in his sex life.[6] For James does not appear to have been prone to depression or to have lacked confidence before then. On the contrary, his public manner was assured to the point of arrogance. Any uncertainty he might have felt about his security at the outset of his reign vanished after the suppression of Monmouth's rebellion. He treated his only parliament at the opening of its second session to a blunt and brusque speech, telling them forthrightly that there was no way he would part with his Catholic officers. He browbeat the Fellows of Magdalen College when he visited Oxford in the summer of 1687 in a display of high-handed bad temper, which revealed to the world

[4] F. C. Turner, *James II* (1948), 234.
[5] PRO 31/3/172: Bonrepos to Seignelay, 11/21 Aug. 1687.
[6] Burnet, iii. 333.

that he was not a man to cross: 'Get ye gone; know I am your King and I command you to be gone.'[7]

It is true that in private he could show some insecurity. He wept throughout an interview with the earl of Rochester in which he was trying to convert his lordship to Catholicism. The incident is highly revealing of the man. He needed to feel secure, and found security in the support of his old friends the High-Church Tories and in Catholicism. Unfortunately for him these became incompatible. Having to choose between them was as much a strain for him as the choice between loyalty to the Crown or the Church was for them. The abruptness with which he jettisoned his new allies and turned to his old friends in September 1688 bespeaks a psychological as well as a political necessity. Yet he was still torn between his need for familiar friendship and his dependence on his creed. Hence the tortured vacillation which people noticed when for a few days he kept drawing back from the consequences of his decision. Lord Chancellor Jeffreys despaired at one time that 'all was nought; some rogues had changed the king's mind . . . that the Virgin Mary was to do all'.[8]

This typically crude assertion of Jeffreys contained a glimmer of the truth about the king's dilemma. James ultimately put a lot of faith in divine Providence. One major cause of his personal crisis was that he concluded that Providence had turned against him, where previously he had been convinced that it was on his side. As he put it in the Declarations of Indulgence, it had 'pleased Almighty God not only to bring us to the imperial crown of these kingdoms through the greatest difficulties, but to preserve us by a more than ordinary providence upon the throne'. The awful realization that he had been weighed in the balance and found wanting proved too much for him.

Looking back over his past up to the summer of 1688, James can be forgiven for thinking that Providence had saved him in order to fulfil some divine plan. In 1648, when he was only fourteen years old, he had been forced to leave England disguised as a lady in order to escape from the custody of the

---

[7] *CSPD 1687–9* (1972), 70. James concluded his harangue with the warning 'immediately repair to your chapel and elect the Bishop of Oxon or else you must expect to feel the heavy hand of an angry King'.

[8] Clarendon, iii. 117, 191.

Long Parliament. He had not been many months in exile when his father Charles I was executed. His father's death when he himself was only fifteen left a permanent mark on James. He attributed Charles I's fate to his making too many concessions to his opponents, and learned from this that kings should never compromise. It was a maxim which made him so inflexible as a king that ironically it helped to lose him his throne.

He spent twelve years abroad. Until 1656 he lived mostly in France, home of his mother Henrietta Maria. When he became eighteen he enlisted as an officer in the French army, then led by the Vicomte de Turenne. Here James found his true *métier*. He had a boundless admiration for Turenne and enthusiasm for the military career. Indeed it has been said of him that 'his personality was that of an efficient but not very intelligent army officer'. James also became fond of France during his exile there. Years later, when he was king, he told the French ambassador 'that he had been brought up in France and . . . that his heart was French'. This might be taken with a pinch of salt, as he was anxious to please the ambassador, or rather through him the French king Louis XIV. On the other hand, the fact that he instinctively fled to France rather than stay to fight for his throne in 1688 indicates that he preferred exile there to humiliation at home.[9]

Unfortunately circumstances made him leave his adopted country and go into exile again, this time from France to the Spanish Netherlands. In 1655 France allied with the English Republic, so James had to quit Turenne's service, and enlisted instead with the Spanish forces based in Brussels. In 1659 he fought for Spain at the battle of the Dunes, when they lost Dunkirk to a combined Anglo-French army. It was clear, though, that his heart was not with his Spanish employers.

Then in 1660 the first intervention of Providence in his favour occurred with his brother's Restoration to the throne of England. During Charles II's reign James channelled his martial energies into naval affairs. As Lord Admiral, with Samuel Pepys as his Secretary, he ensured that the fleet was properly manned and equipped. He even commanded at sea in 1665 and 1672, directing the fleet in the battles of Lowestoft and Southwold

[9] J. R. Western, *Monarchy and Revolution* (1972), 83; C. J. Fox, *A History of the Early Part of the Reign of James II* (1808), appendix, p. cix.

Bay. However, he had to resign from the Admiralty in 1673 when the Test Act debarred Catholics from holding office under the Crown.

Quite when James was converted to Catholicism is uncertain. During his exile in France he had actually quarrelled with his mother when she had attempted his conversion from Anglicanism to her own Catholic faith. For some time after the Restoration he behaved like a High Anglican. The conversion of his idol Turenne from Protestantism to Roman Catholicism in 1668, which astounded contemporary Europe, possibly influenced James too. It has been argued that his military cast of mind responded sympathetically to an authoritarian creed, and that he came to regard the Reformation as a form of insubordination. Certainly he was distressed by religious diversity and sought an infallible judge to decide controversy. At all events, by 1669 he had persuaded himself that only the Roman Catholic faith could secure salvation. Even then his complete commitment to it was gradual. He was received into the Catholic Church in 1672, which cost him his post as Lord Admiral the following year. But he did not stop attending Anglican services until 1676. It was only then that the pope accepted that he was fully converted, and removed objections to his marriage to a Catholic princess, Mary of Modena, which had taken place in 1673. After 1676 James's devotion to his new church was complete. Hilaire Belloc, who as a Catholic himself admired James's conversion, wrote that,

He concluded the Catholic church to be the sole authoritative voice on earth, and thenceforward his integrity, his immoveable resolve, are the most remarkable political features of his age. . . . Through all [his] successive trials he not only stood firm against surrender but on no single occasion contemplated the least compromise or by a word would modify the impression made. It is like a rod of steel running through thirty years.[10]

Such rigidity alarmed Protestants, whose fears reached fever pitch in the Popish Plot. During the ensuring Exclusion crisis the Whigs tried to prevent his accession. Moreover, had the Exclusion Bill passed into law, James would not only have been

---

[10] H. Belloc, *James the Second* (2nd edn.; 1928), 27–8. For an account of James's conversion, see Bodleian Tanner MSS 29, fo. 130.

debarred from the throne but sentenced to perpetual banishment. The second bill stated 'that if the said James, Duke of York, shall at any time from and after the fifth day of November . . . 1680 return or come into or within any of the kingdoms or dominions [i.e. England and Ireland] he . . . shall be deemed and adjudged guilty of high treason'.[11] As it was, Charles thought his brother's presence in England too politically sensitive and ordered him out of the country. He spent almost three years, from 1679 to 1682, in exile, first in Brussels, then in Edinburgh. This second enforced absence from his native land strengthened his convictions. 'If occasion were,' he wrote to a friend urging him to renounce Rome, 'I hope God would give me his grace to suffer death for the true Catholic religion as well as banishment.'[12] That Providence was protecting him during these years seemed to be demonstrated by his escape from shipwreck *en route* to Scotland in 1682, when many seamen drowned.

James was convinced that the Whigs aimed not just at limiting the Crown but at eliminating the monarchy altogether. As he reminded loyalists, 'remember Edward 2, Richard 2 and the King my father'. He even thought that the duke of Monmouth had 'got it into his head to drive things if he can to a republick hoping then to make his self their general and stadholder as the Prince of Orange is in Holland'. James regarded their failure to achieve their aims as providential. When the Tory reaction began with the trial of Edward Fitzharris, who *inter alia* had accused him of plotting to kill his brother, he saw in it 'the hand of God'.[13]

James might also have detected the hand of God in his own accession. As he later wrote, 'it had never entered into his heart or imagination that he should outlive the late king, for though he was three years and about four months younger, yet he always looked upon him as of a much stronger constitution, and consequently never had the least fancy he should come to the crown'.[14] He was by no means alone in this view, for one of the arguments used against the Exclusion Bill had been that it was

[11] J. P. Kenyon (ed.), *The Stuart Constitution* (2nd edn.; Cambridge, 1986), 388.

[12] HMC *Dartmouth*, i. 36.   [13] Ibid. 34, 39, 57.

[14] J. S. Clarke, *The Life of James the Second* (2 vols.; 1816), i. 5.

an unnecessary measure, since James was unlikely to outlive Charles II.

The transition from one reign to another was not only sudden and unexpected, but in image at least a sharp and significant break. The lazy, pleasure-seeking Charles was replaced on 6 February 1685 by a hard-working, serious-minded, and pious James. Laziness and diligence are of course relative terms. James, who went fox-hunting whenever possible, usually twice a week, could scarcely be called a workaholic. Indeed his devotion to the chase has been seen as a sublimation of his martial instincts, when he could no longer command armies in the field. Yet, compared to the legendary indolence of his brother, he did apply himself to business. Even the hostile Burnet admitted that 'he sat many hours a day about business with the Council, the Treasury and the Admiralty'.[15] He also projected a more regal image. Unlike Charles, who used to receive foreign representatives in his own bedchamber with his hat in his hand, he received them seated in a special room, with his hat firmly on his head. He was determined to make the Crown appear in a more dignified light, one which borrowed the rays of the Sun King Louis XIV.

He sought to emulate the king of France in other ways too. The French model of absolute kingship appealed to him. The notion that all he really sought was religious toleration for Catholics, and that he only resorted to the increase of royal authority as a means to that end, and not as an end in itself, is ultimately unconvincing. He told the French ambassador at the outset of his reign that, if parliament did not grant him sufficient funds, he would cashier it and resort to raising revenues by force. Of course one must be sceptical about what he told Barrillon, and it could be that he was boasting about his intention to emulate Louis XIV. But he was deadly serious when he tried to repeal the Habeas Corpus Amendment Act of 1679 as well as the Test and penal laws. This Act, passed by the first Exclusion parliament, was subtitled, 'For the better securing the liberty of the subject and for prevention of imprisonment beyond seas'. It established that even men

[15] Burnet, iii. 13. Lord Burlington, a more sympathetic observer, claimed that 'the king is the most indefatiguable Prince in his business that ever wore the Crown' (Leeds RO Mexborough MSS 31/21).

accused of high treason were entitled to be released upon bail after a writ of habeas corpus had been issued, unless they were brought immediately to trial. Nor could they be held in prison outside the jurisdiction of parliament. James was determined to repeal it, since he considered it to be destructive of royal authority. Barrillon thought his effort would be resisted as firmly as his attempts to repeal the penal laws, because the English believed the Act guaranteed their security. Sir Edward Seymour raised this issue in parliament, declaring that habeas corpus was the firmest foundation of the liberties of England, and that, if it were abolished, arbitrary government would soon be established.[16]

Moreover James did not simply want to obtain toleration for Roman Catholicism. He repeatedly stated that he wanted to establish the Catholic religion. While he was not so sanguine as to hope to replace the established church with the Church of Rome, he sought to put them on an equal footing.[17]

It must be stressed that these were James's own aims, and not those of the 'divers evil councillors, judges, ministers, jesuits, and other wicked persons' later condemned in the Bill of Rights for giving him advice. James was no puppet king, but was determined to rule as well as to reign. He made it quite clear from the outset that he judged any minister who was not wholeheartedly in sympathy with his aspirations as being against him when he dismissed the marquis of Halifax from the post of Lord President of the Council in October 1685. He told Barrillon that he was aware of the inconvenience of having divided counsels and of allowing ministers to have sentiments opposed to his own.[18]

Not that it was completely a one-man show. At his accession James relied principally on the advice of the earls of Rochester and Sunderland. Lawrence Hyde, earl of Rochester, was the brother of the king's first wife, and closely attached to his own

[16] Fox, *History*, appendix, pp. xv–xxiv, xciv.

[17] He told Barrillon that he wished to establish Catholicism on 16/26 Feb. 1685: (ibid. pp. xxix–xxvii). Sir John Bramston observed that 'the Roman religion he resolved to establish, maugre all the laws' (Bramston, *Autobiography*, p. 343).

[18] PRO 31/3/161: Barrillon to Louis XIV, 19/29 Oct. 1685.

niece Princess Mary and her husband the Prince of Orange. His competence as Lord Treasurer had done much to bring solvency to Charles II's financial affairs, but towards the end of his reign that king had cooled towards Rochester and proposed to demote him. James, who had worked closely with the earl and his elder brother the second earl of Clarendon during the early 1680s, reinstated him as Lord Treasurer when he succeeded to the throne. Rochester was regarded as the leader of the High Anglicans and as such was suspected by the new king's Catholic confidants, Lords Arundel, Bellasis, and Dover, and Father Petre. They looked for support to the cynical and wordly earl of Sunderland, whom James appointed as principal Secretary of State, to which post was added that of President of the Council when Halifax was dismissed. During the first two years of the reign Sunderland slowly gained ground over Rochester, whose conceit about his indispensibility made him overconfident, until he found himself forced to resign in January 1687. Rochester had carried out a rearguard action to limit the damage to the Church of England wrought by the king's efforts on behalf of the Catholics. Sunderland outmanœuvred him by encouraging the king's endeavours.

When James failed to persuade High-Church Tories like Clarendon and Rochester to uphold his measures, he was at a loss how to proceed. They after all were the mainstays of monarchy, while the Whigs and their dissenting allies he associated with rebellion and republicanism. It was apparently Sunderland who persuaded him that, on the contrary, he could forge an alliance with them on the basis of their mutual interest in religious toleration.

Despite the fact that he failed to persuade the Tory parliament to support the repeal of anti-Catholic legislation, James was utterly convinced that Providence was on his side and that he would achieve his goals. He even told the French ambassador that God had ordained that the very laws which had established the Protestant religion in England could be used to re-establish the Catholic faith. The Act of Supremacy, which ironically led to a Roman Catholic king becoming Supreme Governor of the Church of England, certainly gave James extensive powers over matters ecclesiastical, which could indeed be employed to help his co-religionists. Thus it was by virtue of the royal supremacy that he set up the commission for ecclesiastical causes.[19]

When the archbishop of Canterbury declined attending the commission, pleading old age and illness, he was struck off the Privy Council, ostensibly for the same reasons. His exclusion, however, was generally taken as yet another sign that James would not suffer anybody to hold office under the Crown who was not entirely in his interests. After Rochester's dismissal he became more and more committed to this principle, even closeting courtiers who were members of parliament to sound out their attitudes to the repeal of the penal laws. Those who would not agree to it were dismissed. To James's surprise, most preferred to lose office rather than pledge their support for his policies.

James thus parted with the Stuarts' best friends in Church and state. The churchmen and politicians, led by Archbishop Sancroft and Lord Rochester, had co-operated in the Tory reaction following the Exclusion crisis to make the monarchy as strong as it ever became by the time of his accession. Now James turned to others for support. When bishoprics fell vacant, he ignored the advice of Sancroft and his colleagues to appoint sound High-Churchmen like themselves, and instead preferred time-serving bishops who were not averse to his flirtations with Catholicism. Thus Thomas Cartwright was promoted to Chester and Samuel Parker to Oxford in 1686. Cartwright was said to have gone down on his knees before one of the Roman Catholic bishops sent to England in 1687, which caused one disgruntled Cheshire man to write to another, 'if the Church of England had no better men in it than he, we should before now have been heathens and worshipped the Devil'. The news of Parker's death in March 1688 prompted the uncharitable remark from Bishop Nicholson of Carlisle, 'and great pity it is he dyed not a little sooner'. Rochester's fall was acknowledged to be a major break with 'the Church of England party', for he was 'the visible head and cement of it'.[20] As it became clear that the king could not expect the continued co-operation of Tories,

[19] PRO 31/3/166: same to same, 12/22 July 1686.
[20] Cheshire RO DCH/K/3/7: Thomas Slater to William Adams, 6 Oct. 1687; Cumbria RO Kendal Fleming MSS 3186; Morrice MS Q, 1 Jan. 1687.

he concluded that there was no point in reconvening the parliament elected in 1685.

He therefore embarked on a campaign to procure a new parliament which would do his bidding. He was prepared to make enough peers to give him a majority in the House of Lords. According to a breakdown of the peerage on their attitude towards the repeal of the Test Act, there were some 86 against, 32 in favour, and 20 undecided. Since most of those who had not declared were almost certain to have been against, there was a majority of about seventy opposed to repealing the Act. Had the twenty-five or so Catholic peers been able to take their seats, then James would still have had to ennoble about fifty supporters to be sure of a majority. However, Catholics were effectively debarred from both Houses of Parliament by the second Test Act of 1678. James had not ventured to issue dispensations from that, having obtained legal advice that the dispensing power could not extend to a statute which regulated the membership of parliament itself. Consequently he was faced with a massive creation of peers in order to pack the Upper House. Nevertheless by September 1688 he was prepared to do it.[21]

Although alterations to obtain a majority of peers were directly within the king's control, the extent to which he could manipulate the returns of members to the House of Commons to achieve his ends was more problematical. The opinion poll which the king conducted was not very encouraging. This was organized in the closing months of 1687, and lasted well into 1688. The Lord-Lieutenants were instructed to put three questions to the magistrates in their counties: Would you, if elected to parliament, vote for repeal of the Test Act and penal laws? Would you vote for candidates pledged to repeal them? Will you suport the Declaration of Indulgence by living friendly with those of several persuasions as subjects of the same prince and as good Christians ought to do? Only the third question produced an overwhelmingly positive response. By contrast

---

[21] PRO 31/3/174: Bonrepos to Seignelay, 24 Nov./4 Dec. 1687; BL Add. MSS 15397, fos. 252–4; Adda's dispatch, 14/24 Sept. 1688; CP(A) 166: Barrillon to Louis XIV, 8/18 Sept. 1688. There was a rumour in May that James had 'determined to make 60 new peers' (Bodleian Ballard MSS 21, fo. 18).

about a quarter of those consulted consented to the first two questions. Between a quarter and a third replied negatively to them. Although this seemed to leave a substantial proportion of doubtfuls, James would have been unwise to have put much faith in them. On the contrary, as John Carswell concluded from his analysis of the replies, 'although James had a not inconsiderable body of support, he had something like two-thirds of the landowning classes against him, and half of these were not afraid to say so'.[22]

However, as Professor J. R. Jones observes, it was primarily a poll of gentry opinion.[23] Although this revealed that the counties would not support the king's measures, it did not necessarily indicate the attitude of the parliamentary boroughs, which returned 421 members to the Commons compared with only 92 knights of the shire. Regulating many of their corporations had contributed to the return of a majority of Tory MPs from the boroughs to James's first parliament. He came to the conclusion that a fresh purge would procure another majority, this time of members who would go along with repealing the Test Act and the penal laws. Consequently in November 1687 James set up a machinery for regulating corporations. The exact workings of this machinery remain obscure, for there are references to commissioners for regulating, lords of the committee for regulating, and other bodies. However, the work seems largely to have been supervised by Sunderland, Jeffreys, Powys, Castlemaine, Father Petre, and Sir Nicholas Butler, and their recommendations to have been carried out by agents, the chief of whom was Robert Brent. The relatively obscure figures Butler and Brent were Catholics, the first a privy councillor, the second, a lawyer. These regulators presided over the purging of over a thousand men from borough corporations. In many cases this involved replacing men who had been installed during the Tory reaction of 1681 and 1686 with their local rivals, sometimes exclusionist Whigs. Some boroughs were purged again and again. Three successive purges at Devizes produced a net turnover of a mayor,

---

[22] J. Carswell, *The Descent on England* (1969), 240.
[23] J. R. Jones, *The Revolution of 1688 in England* (1972), 137.

ten aldermen, fifteen capital burgesses, and twenty-nine free burgesses.[24]

Those responsible for the regulation were highly optimistic as to the prospects of packing a parliament with members who would uphold the policy of repealing legislation which the king found obnoxious. As early as 19 April 1688, after agents had investigated eight counties, they reported that 'for these counties and places which elect a hundred and forty members . . . when Your Majesty shall please to call your parliament you may expect above a hundred will be chosen that will readily concur with Your Majesty in abrogating those Tests and Laws'. Although they could not then account for the rest of the constituencies, they nevertheless believed, following preliminary soundings, 'that the greatest part by far of those that will be chosen for those places will out of inclination readily concur with Your Majesty to abolish those Laws and Tests'.[25]

'It's a question after all', wrote James Welwood in 1700, 'whether the Parliament which K. James was thus labouring to model, would have answered his expectation, had they come to sit.'[26] The question has been debated ever since, and still causes dispute. Professor Jones is convinced that it could have succeeded had it ever been put to the test. This conclusion is endorsed by B. D. Henning, the editor of *The History of Parliament* volumes for the years 1660–89, who regards the success of the campaign as 'at least a possibility'.[27] Others who have investigated particular constituencies, however, are more doubtful. Dr P. E. Murrell's detailed investigation of Bury St Edmunds led her to conclude that a succession of regulations was required to reduce that borough, where only the members of the corporation could vote, to the royal will: 'This raises serious doubts as to whether in the other, more numerous, boroughs where the freemen possessed the vote also, and the king's influence was a stage removed, the progress of the crown's agents can be considered to have been sufficiently

---

[24] L. Glassey, 'Local Government', in C. Jones (ed.), *Britain in the First Age of Party, 1680–1750* (1987), 154.

[25] Bodleian Rawlinson MSS A 139b, fos. 178, 184.

[26] J. Welwood, *Memoirs of the Most Material Transactions in England for the Last Hundred Years Preceding the Revolution of 1688* (1700), 218.

[27] Jones, *Revolution*, p. 165; Henning, i. 42.

advanced to have coped easily with a pending election in the
autumn of 1688.'[28] The duke of Beaufort expressed similar
scepticism at the time about boroughs where 'the election,
having been by prescription, could not be regulated by the new
charters and placed in the magistrates, but continues still in the
freemen, which are very numerous and not subject to be put in
or out at the king's pleasure and generally averse to the taking
away of the Test'.[29] D. H. Hosford also concludes from his
study of the attempts to regulate Derby, Newark, Nottingham,
and East Retford that 'it is by no means clear that the policy . . .
would have produced acceptable parliamentary delegates'.[30]

By 16 September the regulation was regarded as complete,
for writs summoning a general election were issued on that
date. Since they were recalled on the 28th the outcome can only
be surmised. However, the electoral machinery had been
switched on long enough for some estimate of its probable
outcome to be attempted.

The last returns from the agents sent down to regulate
eighteen counties were made on the eve of the abortive polls.
These were rather more cautious than those returned for eight
counties in April. Where the earlier report boasted about having
the result virtually sown up, the latest indicated many constituencies which had still not settled their candidates. It
concluded that 'we have no reason to doubt but there will be an
election of members for the parliament that will readily concur
with Your Majesty in establishing the Libertie proposed by
Your Majesty's most gracious Declaration'.[31] Nevertheless,
there are very good reasons to cast doubts upon that conclusion.
In Queenborough, for instance, there was actually a poll on
25 September. The result was: Robert Crawford, 27; James
Herbert, 16; Captain Wilford, 10; Sir William Booth, 2. The
candidates recommended by the Court, Wilford and Booth,
were thus defeated in this borough despite the fact that it had

---

[28] P. E. Murrell, 'Bury St Edmunds and the Campaign to Pack Parliament,
1687–8', *Bulletin of the Institute of Historical Research*, 54 (1981), 188–9.
[29] Sir George Duckett, *Penal Laws and Test Act* (2 vols.; Oxford, 1882–3), i.
288.
[30] D. Hosford, *Nottingham, Nobles and the North* (Hamden, Connecticut,
1976), 58.
[31] Bodleian Rawlinson MSS A 139b, fo. 186.

been granted a new charter in the spring. The fates awaiting other official candidates had they had to face the voters were probably little better. The earl of Sunderland wrote letters endorsing the candidatures of 105 men. Thirty-seven had represented the constituencies for which they were nominated in 1685, while a few had sat in the Commons during the Exclusion parliaments. Most, however, had very little electoral interest in the boroughs concerned, beyond that created for them by the Court. Only thirteen of them were elected to the Convention parliament. One of these, Charles Bertie, wrote, 'I am obliged to my Lord Sunderland for recommending me to Stamford, which has entirely lost my interest in that corporation, and I cannot blame them for their jealousy.' He was by no means alone in regarding Court backing in 1688 as the kiss of death. At Canterbury, for instance, where the electoral agents were sanguine for the prospects of John Kingsford, the mayor, and Edward Crawford, the recorder, a more objective observer found that 'both the people of the city and country are resolved to oppose the mayor and recorder, who design to stand by his Majesty's commands for Parliament men for this city, and by what I can learn there will be but very few that will give their votes for them'. In Cornwall, a key county with twenty-one boroughs, the leading Court magnate, Lord Bath, was expressing grave doubts about the outcome of the elections there as late as 28 September.[32]

What the regulation failed to take sufficiently into account was the impossibility of completely eliminating the influence of public opinion even in the smallest boroughs. As a contemporary critic of their activities noted early in 1688:

They will have a Parliament per fas et nefas and truly I think they cannot miss to have one, though not this summer, for many of the corporations must be modelled over and over again as they have now

---

[32] Henning, i. 277, 280, 308; *CSPD 1687–9* (1972), 287. Bath was scathing about the inefficiency of the regulation: 'As the case now stands, if they proceed immediately to election of Parliament men, there will of necessity be disputes in most places. Scarce a corporation knows its own magistrates; some of the old ones displaced by mistakes and misnomers, most of the new unduly chosen by reason of their ignorance of the constitutions in the several charters.' See also his dismissive remarks about 'Mr Nosworthy and his fellow regulators' (ibid. 304).

done with some of them. But they take a most effectual way by
reducing the number of electors till they can be sure of a majority. . . .
At Tewkesbury, for instance, the power of electing is put into the
hands of thirteen. . . . But if there could be any end of their modelling
all that would not do their business for even these 13 will fail them. But
they declare they will make the number of electors but three and that
two shall choose the third.[33]

Though this hostile observation was exaggerated, the point
that, no matter how often corporations were purged and the
numbers of electors reduced, the Court would still have
problems finding tools for its business, was valid. They were
not insulated from the opinion of their neighbours, which were
increasingly hostile to James. The regulators conceded this
when they accepted that they had to fight a propaganda war
with the opponents of the king's policies. Besides discussing the
mechanics of electoral manipulation, the agents' reports also
discussed the need to refute the arguments of their critics. In
April they found

that Mons[r] Fagell's Letter and other pamphlets are industriously spread
through all parts with discourses and endeavours to prejudice the
minds of those who are faithful or inclined to your Majesty's interest
and that there's no way yet settled to spread a sufficient number of such
other books as may reform and furnish the country with arguments
to discover and detect the fallacious subtleties of those pernicious
pamphlets.

By September they were able to report

That the books that have been dispersed have had very good effect to
the satisfying and establishing very many, though great endeavours
have been used by the Church party to dissuade people from reading
of them. That a great inconvenience attending this affair is the
suggestions that are propagated by church men and some others
disaffected residing about London.[34]

James does not seem to have appreciated the fact that the Tory
majority in the parliament of 1685 was by no means solely due
to the Court's management of the boroughs. It also owed much
to the swing of opinion against the Whigs after the Oxford

---

[33] Nottingham University Library Portland MSS PWA 2145: 21 Feb. 1688.
[34] Bodleian Rawlinson MSS A 139b, fos. 178, 186.

parliament of 1681 and the Rye House Plot of 1683. The Tory reaction of Charles II's last years was genuinely popular. This was obvious from the election results in the counties and large boroughs in 1685. But the smaller boroughs also went along with the recalling of old charters and issuing new ones, which helped procure a majority of Tories from them. When James flew in the face of public opinion, he revealed that there were severe limitations to the Crown's electoral influence. Sir John Bramston thought the Revolution was unnecessary, since 'people would not be so mad as to send to Parliament such representatives as would cut theire owne throats'.[35]

James, however, was careless of public opinion during these months. He became more than ever convinced that God was on his side, and that he was therefore bound to prevail, when his wife became pregnant in October 1687. That Providence blessed his cause seemed to be confirmed by the birth of a son the following June. 'It has pleased the Almighty,' he solemnly informed the States General, 'who is the sole ruler of Princes and who is uniquely capable of perpetuating their families, to bestow his divine bounty on us and our kingdoms by sending us a son.' More spontaneously he wrote ecstatically to the pope, 'the mercy of God has indulged us with a son. This so much wish'd for pledge of a succession to our kingdoms has been granted to us by the Benevolent Being.'[36]

The king got a rude awakening in September with the shock that a Dutch invasion was in deadly earnest. Realizing that it would probably occur before an election could take place, he promptly panicked and called it off on 26 September. When doing so he reprimanded the regulators, accusing them of betraying his interest by 'making him disoblige the Church of England but were able to do nothing so his Majesty said he

---

[35] Bramston, p. 356. The earl of Clarendon observed in Dec. 1687: 'by some of the changes which are already made it is probable those who are put into those (corporations) will be as averse to what the king would have as those who are put out' (*CSPD 1687–9* (1972), 118).

[36] Algemeen Rijksarchief, The Hague, States General 5915(2): James II to the States General, 11 June 1688; BL Add. MSS 9341, fo. 53: James II to the Pope, 11 June 1688. The Queen also referred to her son as a gift from Heaven: Marquise Campana de Cavelli, *Les Derniers Stuarts à Saint-Germain en Laye* (2 vols.; 1871), ii. 250: Mary of Modena to the Venetian Republic, 27 Aug. 1688.

would have Church of England men every where employed'.
He was as good as his word, reinstating Tories as deputy-
lieutenants of the county militias and justices of the peace. The
whole electoral machine was thrown into reverse. Roger
Morrice noted these moves as an attempt by James to 'rectifie
the fundamental mistake in laying aside the Tories'.[37]

Amongst the 'old friends' to whom James instinctively turned
at this time were the bishops. On 24 September he invited
Sancroft and eight of his episcopal colleagues to meet him. No
fewer than four of those invited to what turned out to be a series
of meetings had been among the seven prosecuted for seditious
libel the previous June. On 3 October the archbishop put to the
king ten recommendations which the bishops had agreed. These
included the dismissal of Catholic officials, the abolition of the
commission for ecclesiastical causes, the restoration of borough
charters, and the speedy summoning of a free parliament.
Although James cannot have liked any of these stipulations, he
responded to them, making some concessions. London's charter
was restored on 4 October. The commission for ecclesiastical
causes was suspended and the bishop of London was reinstated
along with the Fellows of Magdalen College. As one newsletter
observed, 'nothing seems wanting but a free parliament . . . and
then I can't see what the Prince will do'.[38]

Unfortunately for James few were prepared to trust his
sincerity in making these concessions. Since he had previously
projected himself as a monarch whose resolve was adamant,
they were put down to panic. Once the danger was averted it was
assumed they would be withdrawn. Even he himself admitted
that, were he to win, he would be 'absolute master to doe what
he pleased'.[39]

Yet James probably did not intend to resume his tactic of
allying with the Whigs and Dissenters once the storm had

[37] Cumbria RO Carlisle D/Ry/3263a: newsletter, 27 Sept. 1688; Morrice
MS Q, p. 296.
[38] The articles were published in *An Account of the Proposals of the Archbishop
of Canterbury with some other Bishops to his Majesty in a Letter to M. B. Esq* (1688).
The draft articles included several that were dropped before they were
presented to the king: e.g. that he dismiss Petre from the Privy Council and
expel the Jesuits from England (Bodleian Tanner MSS 28, fo. 189; BL Add.
MSS 34487, fo. 30: newsletter, 4 Oct. 1688).
[39] Clarke, *The Life of James the Second*, ii. 211.

passed. After all, it had been the earl of Sunderland who had persuaded him against his better judgement to try it. The dismissal of Sunderland on 27 October was a sign that the king repented of the folly of his ways. But it was too late. Indeed he was now despised for weakness where before his resolute approach had made him respected as 'James the Just'.[40] People turned to the Prince of Orange to obtain cast-iron guarantees for the future conduct of the untrustworthy monarch.

It seems clear that James had no intention of giving such guarantees. His whole autocratic temperament was inimical to the role of a limited monarch. In September he had told the French ambassador that there was not room in the country for both William and himself, and that, if the prince came over, then he would leave the country rather than be subjected to him.[41] At the same time he made contingent plans to get his wife and infant son safely to France.

That fate could only be avoided, in James's view, if God was on his side. Divine assistance was invoked in the special prayers he ordered to be used in all churches 'during this time of publick danger'. Those 'for the king' implored God to 'save and protect him' and to 'give thy holy Angels charge over him'.[42] Initially these seemed to work. James took heart when the first Dutch invasion attempt had to be abandoned after ferocious storms sent the task force back to port in disarray. He was also comforted by the fact that the wind blew continually from the west, pinning William's fleet in those ports for weeks. As he put it to Lord Dartmouth on 20 October, 'I see God Almighty continues his Protection to me by bringing the wind westerly again.' This gave him precious time to make military

[40] Bodleian Tanner MSS 31, fo. 250: Bishop of Norwich to Sancroft, 29 Jan. 1686: 'a prince who is famous (over all Europe) for being firm and steady to his word and thereby hath . . . acquired and deserved the title of James the Just.'

[41] CP(A) 166: Barrillon to Louis XIV, 20/30 Sept. 1688.

[42] J. Gutch, *Collectanea Curiosa* (2 vols.; Oxford, 1781), i. 417. Gutch noted that Edmund Bohun in *The History of the Desertion* was 'fully persuaded these prayers contributed very considerably to the late Revolution . . . the very supplicating God "to preserve our holy religion, together with our laws and ancient Government" necessarily put men in mind they had been endangered, and by whom was well known. And it seemed nonesense and hypocrisy to pray God to preserve these and in the meantime to aid and assist the enemies of both to destroy and ruin them' (p. xvii).

preparations to meet the invader. It was ominous for him when the wind changed, but he still put his faith in Providence. He even thought his nosebleed at Salisbury was providential since had he been well he would have advanced with Churchill towards the prince's lines and, in his own view, been delivered up by the deserter as a captive.[43]

The desertion of key officers, however, caused his nerve to crack. It became all too clear to him that he would not be able to inflict a military defeat upon the Prince of Orange. He therefore resolved to flee rather than to fight. He managed to get the queen and their son to France early in December. Initially he thought of going to Ireland or to Scotland, but then decided to join them instead. His first attempt ended in the fiasco at Faversham. While he was there he showed that providential intervention was very much on his mind by saying that 'he might fall a sacrifice, as Abel did by the hand of Cain, yet he doubted not he and his cause would be accepted by God'.[44]

The reference to the biblical brothers is significant. James was genuinely horrified that the chief conspirator was his own son-in-law. As a dynast who held the royal family dear to his heart, it mortified him when William and his own daughter Mary gave some credence to the rumours that the Prince of Wales was supposititious when they stopped prayers for him in their royal chapel. He was wounded to the quick when his younger daughter Anne left him to join the rebels at Nottingham. The betrayal of his own kith and kin clearly loomed large in his mind when the whole world seemed to have deserted him.

But the greatest betrayal was of his own high command. This broke his nerve and caused him to flee. The sudden end to his reign was astonishing. As Burnet put it, 'a great king with strong armies and mighty fleets, a vast treasure and powerful allies, fell all at once: and his whole strength, like a spider's web, was so irrecoverably broken with a touch, that he was never able to retrieve what for want both of judgement and heart he threw up in a day'.[45]

[43] HMC *Dartmouth*, i. 169; Clarendon, ii. 211.
[44] *Notes and Queries*, 3rd series, 5 (1864), 393.
[45] Burnet, iii. 1.

7

The Constitutional Issues

Thus were we fallen under the greatest misfortune that
could possibly happen to a nation, to have our Laws and
Constitution trampled upon under colour of law.

(*James Welwood, Memoirs of the Most Material Transactions
in England for the Last Hundred Years Preceding the Revolution
of 1688*)

THE nature of the English constitution was at the heart of the
political struggles of the seventeenth century. That it was
a monarchy most men were agreed: the Republic of the
Interregnum was a short-lived expedient which few wanted to
repeat. The basic constitutional question for most of the Stuart
era was, what kind of monarchy did that royal house preside
over?

There were those who urged that it was absolute, and that
kings of England ruled by divine, indefeasible, hereditary right.
The monarch was accountable to God alone for his actions. If he
injured his subjects, there was nothing they could do to remedy
the injury. Since resistance was sinful, they could merely
practise passive obedience.

So far from being subdued by the events of the years 1642 to
1660, such views were revived literally with a vengeance on the
Restoration of Charles II. Swelling chords were played in a
major key on the theme in sermons and pamphlets. Several
statutes enjoined oaths on subjects swearing the inadmissability
of resistance to the Crown on any pretext whatsoever. Above
all such views were enshrined in Robert Filmer's *Patriarcha*,
posthumously published in 1680. This provided a direct link
with the generation which fought the civil wars, for Filmer
wrote the treatise around 1648.

Against these views others argued that the monarchy was limited or mixed. The Crown ruled in conjunction with parliament, the Lords and Commons providing a constitutional check on the royal prerogative. Thus kings were accountable to their subjects' representatives. If they exceeded their limitations, then resistance was legitimate. Among those espousing these arguments the best known today is John Locke, whose *Two Treatises of Government* were written largely in response to the publication of Filmer's *Patriarcha*, even if they were not themselves published until 1689. At the time, however, Locke's views were regarded as radical even by most Whigs, with his stress on the sovereignty of the people based on natural rights. They preferred to assert that kings were ultimately accountable to parliament.

At bottom the debate was about the location of sovereignty. Did it reside in the king alone, or in the king in parliament? It might have seemed that the civil wars had settled the matter once and for all in the latter. But the Restoration Settlement still left the question open. 'The very root of the controversy betwixt the king and subjects of England', observed Dean Granville in 1689, was 'whether the supremacy should be in the king or the people.'[1]

After the legislation of the Long Parliament in 1641, it was reasonably clear that the Crown could not raise taxes without parliamentary consent. James II did so between his brother's death in February and the meeting of parliament in May 1685, when he continued to collect the customs and excise granted for Charles II's life. He justified the collection of the customs on the grounds that to cease doing so would disrupt trade, while the continued levying of the excise was based on the fact that it had been farmed for three years just before Charles died. The loyal parliament of 1685 accepted these excuses, but in 1689 the Declaration of Rights accused James of 'levying money for and to the use of the Crown by pretence of prerogative for other

---

[1] R. Ashcraft, *Revolutionary Politics and Locke's Two Treatises of Government* (Princeton, 1986); *Publications of the Surtees Society*, 37 (1860), 73; for the debate, see M. Goldie, 'John Locke and Anglican Royalism', *Political Studies*, 31 (1983), 61–85; C. C. Weston and J. R. Greenberg, *Subjects and Sovereigns: The Grand Controversy over Legal Sovereignty in Stuart England* (Cambridge, 1981).

time and in other manner than the same was granted by parliament'.[2]

The Declaration made out the case behind the Commons' resolution of 28 January that James had 'endeavoured to subvert the constitution of the kingdom' and had 'violated the fundamental laws'. It declared that the king 'did endeavour to subvert and extirpate . . . the laws and liberties of this kingdom'. To substantiate this accusation, the Declaration made some thirteen particular charges against James. An examination of these in detail demonstrates that the debate on the nature of the monarchy did end decisively in 1689 with the victory of those who argued that it was limited and mixed. For before the Revolution, as we shall see, the case made by the Convention against the prerogative could be answered in favour of the Crown.

The very first charge was that the king had assumed and exercised a power of dispensing with and suspending of laws and the execution of laws without consent of parliament. James's use of the dispensing power to grant immunity from the Test Act had been upheld by the judgment in Godden versus Hales, which had ruled that it was an indispensable prerogative in the kings of England to dispense with penal laws in particular cases. Lord Chief Justice Herbert in his summing up claimed that 'it appeared as clear a case as ever came before this court'.[3]

The Declaration of Rights was equally clear 'that the pretended power of dispensing with laws or the execution of laws by regal authority as it has been assumed and exercised of late is illegal'. To the Whig historian Lord Macaulay, the judgment was perverse and even corrupt. In his view,

the single dissentient, Baron Street, was not removed from his place. He was a man of morals so bad that his own relations shrank from him and that the Prince of Orange at the time of the Revolution was advised not to see him. The character of Street makes it impossible to believe that he would have been more scrupulous than his brethren. The character of James makes it impossible to believe that a refractory Baron of the Exchequer would have been permitted to retain his post.

[2] The most recent edition of the Declaration, which has been published many times, is in L. G. Schwoerer, *The Declaration of Rights* (1981), pp. 295–8.
[3] W. C. Costin and J. S. Watson (eds.), *The Law and Working of the Constitution: Documents, 1660–1914* (2 vols; 1952), i. 257.

There can, therefore, be no reasonable doubt that the dissenting Judge was, like the plaintiff and the plaintiff's counsel, acting collusively.[4]

The dispensing power, however, could only alleviate the lot of individual Catholics, whereas the suspending power could grant them all immunity from prosecution. James simply issued an Edict of Toleration, which proclaimed that all penal laws against nonconformists were suspended. Elizabethan legislation barred them from the Universities and the professions, fined them £20 a month for absenting themselves from the established church, and made it treason to attempt to convert anybody to Roman Catholicism. All prosecutions under these laws were brought to an immediate halt. People sentenced to prison for infringing them were released. Similar edicts, or Declarations of Indulgence as they were called, promulgated by Charles II in 1662 and 1672, had been censured in resolutions of the House of Commons, and Charles had withdrawn them. Yet James also gave out two such proclamations, one in 1687, the second in 1688. The Declaration of Rights condemned both, stating that 'the pretended power of suspending of laws or the execution of laws by regal authority without consent of parliament is illegal'. Macaulay endorsed this verdict. In his words, 'that the Declaration of Indulgence was unconstitutional is a point on which both the great English parties have always been entirely agreed. Every person capable of reasoning on a political question must perceive that a monarch who is competent to voice such a declaration is nothing less than an absolute monarch.' Indeed it was 'the most audacious of all the attacks made by the Stuarts on public freedom'.[5]

The second Declaration of Indulgence gave rise to another of the charges levied against James by the Declaration of Rights. This claimed that his endeavours to extirpate the Protestant religion and the laws and liberties of England included the 'committing and prosecuting diverse worthy Prelates for humbly petitioning to be excused from concurring to the said assumed power'. The trial of the seven bishops was held before the four judges of the King's Bench and a London jury. They pleaded not guilty to the charge that they had published a false, malicious, and seditious libel. Their defence argued that it was

---

[4] Macaulay, ii. 738.   [5] Ibid. 862.

not false, because the matter of the petition was true, that it was not malicious or seditious, because the manner of delivering it was peaceful and legal; and that it was not a libel because the intent was innocent. The prosecution argued that the matter of the petition was false, because the Crown did in fact enjoy a suspending power in causes ecclesiastical; and that it was malicious and seditious, because the proper machinery of petitioning was through parliament; when it was asserted that the bishops should have waited for parliament to meet, people in the court hissed. Finally the counsel for the Crown insisted that it was a libellous petition because it criticized the government.

Only one of the four judges dealt with the question of the legality of the suspending power, and he denied it. Justice Powell claimed:

I do not remember any case in all our law . . . that there is any such power in the King and the case must turn upon that. In short, if there be no such dispensing power in the King, then that can be no libel which they presented to the King, which says that the declaration, being founded upon such a pretended power is illegal. . . . I can see no difference, nor know of one in law, between the King's power to dispense with laws ecclesiastical and his power to dispense with any other laws whatsoever. If this be once allowed of, there will need no Parliament; all the legislative will be in the King, which is a thing worth considering.[6]

It seemed that nobody was prepared to stand by the suspending power in defence of the Crown against the seven bishops.

Indeed the judges were divided. Two directed the jury to find for the Crown, while their two colleagues indicated that they should acquit the bishops. In the event they were acquitted. The verdict was echoed in the statement made in the Declaration of Rights that 'it is the right of the subjects to petition the King and all commitments and prosecutions for such petitioning are illegal'.

The Declaration also accused James of 'issuing and causing to be executed a commission under the Great Seal for erecting a Court called the Court of Commissioners for Ecclesiastical

---

[6] J. P. Kenyon (ed.), *The Stuart Constitution* (2nd edn.; Cambridge, 1986), 410.

Causes' and declared that it 'and all other commissions and courts of like nature are illegal and pernicious'. This tribunal had been established in 1686 after the bishop of London had defied the king's orders to suspend a clergyman who had preached an anti-Catholic sermon. The commission had proceeded to hear the bishop and to suspend him from his spiritual duties for his defiance. To many this was a revival of the Court of High Commission, and therefore patently illegal since the Act of 1641 abolishing that Court had forbidden the creation of any similar judicial body. According to Macaulay, 'lest any person should doubt that it was intended to revive that terrible court from which the Long Parliament had freed the nation, the new visitors were directed to use a seal bearing exactly the same device and the same superscription with the seal of the old High Commission'.[7] It also employed the same notorious procedure of examining *ore tenus*, whereby those arraigned before it had to agree to answer questions put to them orally.[8] Even Lord Burghley had criticized this method of interrogation, claiming that it smacked of the Inquisition. Armed with these powers, the commission had proceeded to attack the privileges of the Universities of Oxford and Cambridge. The vice-chancellor of Cambridge and the Fellows of Magdalen College, Oxford, were deprived of their college livings for refusing to accept the king's instructions to suspend their statutes in favour of Catholics.

This stripping of University dons of their posts was not just an attack on tenure; it was then also an attack on property, since college fellowships were a form of freehold. The fact that the king was prepared to deprive subjects of their properties in pursuit of his Catholic policy led to widespread alarm. There was even fear abroad that he intended to restore to the Catholic Church former monastic lands which had been acquired by laymen after the Reformation. So strong was this rumour that James felt obliged to refute it in the Declaration of Indulgence. Nevertheless the market price of such property actually fell below the level of similar estates which had not formerly been abbey lands. Perhaps more than any other measure the king's

---

[7] Macaulay, ii. 246.
[8] Lowther, pp. 20, 23; Ellis, i. 161.

challenge to the Universities led to the adoption of the slogan 'Liberty and Property' in the Revolution.[9]

Another slogan of the late-seventeenth century was 'no standing army'. James II was the first king to maintain a conspicuously large regular professional force in peacetime. The last occasion when soldiers had been so conspicuous was under Cromwell, for, although Charles II kept on foot rather more men than he is often given credit for, these were largely confined to garrisons at home and abroad, and did not usually give rise to suspicion. Indeed the Disbanding Act of 1660, which demobilized the New Model Army, contained a clause allowing Charles to keep on foot such of them as he thought fit to 'provide for at his own charge'.[10] Parliament did become suspicious, however, in the 1670s when Charles enlarged his forces ostensibly for foreign service. In April 1679 the Commons resolved 'that the continuing of any standing forces in this nation, other than the militia, is illegal, and a great grievance and vexation to the people'.[11] Notwithstanding this resolution, James took advantage of the poor showing of the militia in the duke of Monmouth's rebellion at the outset of his reign to justify retaining an army of some twenty thousand troops. So far from discreetly stationing these in garrison towns, he scattered them throughout the kingdom in winter quarters, making communities aware of a strong military presence for the first time since Cromwell's days; and in summer he concentrated them in camps at Hounslow Heath, just outside London. In the last year of his reign he increased the armed forces to about forty thousand men.[12] After the Revolution the Declaration of Rights accused him of 'raising and keeping a standing army within this kingdom in time of peace without consent of parliament', and declared that 'the raising or keeping a standing army within the Kingdom in time

[9] H. J. Habakkuk, 'Daniel Finch, 2nd Earl of Nottingham: His House and Estate', in J. H. Plumb (ed.), *Studies in Social History* (1955). James was so concerned to counter rumours that he intended to repossess abbey lands that he commissioned Nathaniel Johnstone to write a book against them. Leeds RO Mexborough MSS 48/25 & 35: Johnstone to Reresby, 9 Apr. and 23 June 1687.

[10] J. Childs, *The Army of Charles II* (1976).

[11] L. G. Schwoerer, *No Standing Armies!* (1974), 131.

[12] J. Childs, *The Army, James II and the Glorious Revolution* (Manchester, 1980), 2–4.

of peace unless it be with the consent of parliament is against law'.

Closely linked with these anti-army declarations was the clause charging James with disarming Protestants at the same time as papists were being armed contrary to law. This was a reference to the militia. To James the county levies had proved useless during the rebellions of the earl of Argyll in Scotland and the duke of Monmouth in England, which occurred shortly after his accession. Indeed they were worse than useless, for some had defected to the rebels. He therefore preferred to put his trust in regular forces, and to allow the militias to rust. The Irish militia he regarded as so untrustworthy that he ordered it to surrender its weapons.

The distrust of the militia struck James's critics as being just as sinister as his use of regulars. A citizen militia was regarded as a safeguard of the liberties of the subject, whereas a standing army was held to be an instrument of despotism. When James proceeded to disarm the Protestant militia of Ireland at a time when he was promoting Catholics in the standing army, fears that he was aiming at absolutism seemed to be confirmed. The Declaration of Rights affirmed 'that the subjects which are Protestants may have arms for their defence'.

The final onslaught upon the obstacles in the way of absolutism in the view of James's opponents was his attempt to pack parliament. Having failed to persuade the parliament elected in 1685 to repeal the penal laws and Test Acts, James dissolved it in order to get a more compliant body to implement his religious policy. 'The sanction of a free and lawful Parliament it was evidently impossible to obtain,' observed Macaulay, 'but it might not be altogether impossible to bring together by corruption, by intimidation, by violent exertions of prerogative, by fraudulent distortions of law, an assembly which might call itself a Parliament and might be willing to register any edict of the Sovereign'.[13] Accordingly James set out to subdue parliament to his will. The Revolution, however, overtook all his efforts to get a parliament to accept his proposals. After it the next parliament to meet, the Convention of 1689, passed the Declaration of Rights which condemned him

[13] Macaulay, ii. 966. For the campaign to pack parliament, see above, ch. 3.

for 'violating the freedom of members to serve in Parliament' and declared 'that elections of members of parliament ought to be free'.

In comparison with the clauses concerned with the suspending and dispensing powers, the trial of the seven bishops, the commission for ecclesiatical causes, the standing army, and the campaign to pack parliament, the remaining charges against James made in the Declaration of Rights are relatively trivial.

One accused James of 'bringing prosecutions in the Court of King's Bench for matters and causes cognizable only in Parliament', adding somewhat lamely 'and by divers other arbitrary and illegal causes'. During a debate on the clause it was confessed that it was included 'for the sake of . . . Sir William Williams, who was punished out of Parliament for what he had done in Parliament'.[14] Williams had been Speaker of the House of Commons in 1680, in which capacity he had licensed a pamphlet which the Court of King's Bench judged to have been a seditious libel when he was brought to trial in 1686. There can be little doubt, despite the Declaration of Rights, that the judgment was lawful. More to the point, it was disingenuous of the Declaration to accuse James of bringing Williams to trial, since the proceedings were initiated in 1684, the year before the king's accession.

Indeed two other charges against James avowedly went back before his accession, since they claimed that the alleged offences had occurred 'of late years'. The first charge was that 'partial corrupt and unqualified persons have been returned and served on juries in trials and particularly divers jurors in trials for high treason which were not freeholders'. The treason trials referred to were those of the Rye House plotters in 1683. One of them, Lord Russell, had at the time excepted to a juror on the grounds that he was not a freeholder. The other charge claimed that excessive fines had been imposed. Again all the examples they seem to have had in mind stem from the last years of Charles II's reign. In 1682 Sir Thomas Pilkington, sheriff of London, had been fined the enormous sum of £100,000 for denigrating the duke of York. In 1684 Sir Samuel Barnadiston had been fined £10,000 for writing seditous letters. Although this was reduced to £8,000, it was still a crippling fine.

[14] Grey, ix. 81.

The charge that illegal and cruel punishments had been inflicted, on the other hand, almost certainly refers to James's reign. The exact references, however, are unclear. It is often asserted that the clause condemned the punishment inflicted on the rebels in the aftermath of the duke of Monmouth's rebellion, but there is no overt mention of the so-called Bloody Assizes. Instead the framers of the clause might have been thinking of the sentence imposed on Titus Oates in 1686 after his conviction for perjury. Oates was fined 2,000 marks, severely whipped, given life imprisonment, obliged to appear in the pillory four times a year for the rest of his life, and, as if as an afterthought, defrocked. Or they might have had in mind the Reverend Samuel Johnson, who, upon being found guilty of publishing seditious libels, was fined 500 marks, pilloried, whipped, and also defrocked. In 1689 the House of Commons resolved that the judgment against Johnson was 'illegal and cruel'.

Only one clause referred directly to what many later came to regard as the blackest of all James's crimes, the so-called Bloody Assizes. About 850 people implicated in Monmouth's rebellion were sentenced to ten years' transportation, to be spent toiling on the sugar plantations of the West Indies, where few can have survived to earn their freedom again. They had a market value of between £10 and £15 to the planters. Consequently a lively traffic developed in this gruesome trade. For example, James himself gave 100 of the transported convicts to the Queen's secretary, who sold them for gain. The transportation of over 1,000 rebels also involved the forfeiture of their properties, which likewise gave rise to a sordid auction, as human cormorants joined the carrion that fattened on the fate of the unfortunate rebels in the west. That such pickings were to be had caused bids to be made before some of the accused were convicted. Hence the charge against James in the Declaration of Rights that he had authorized 'several grants and promises of fines and forfeitures before any conviction or judgment against the persons upon whom the same were to be levied'.

These charges stating categorically that James II had acted illegally in fact endorsed a particular view of the law. They assumed that there was a rule of law, that kings were subject to it, and that the legal position was crystal clear in all the cases cited. All three assumptions were open to challenge by defenders of the king's allegedly arbitrary exercise of power.

The claim that the dispensing power was illegal could indeed be questioned. It had been subject to judicial scrutiny on two occasions before the judges reached their verdicts in the case of Godden versus Hales. On the first of these occasions no less an authority than Sir Edward Coke had given an opinion on the matter. Coke distinguished between crimes against the laws of God and crimes against the laws of man. To break God's laws was naturally evil in itself, *malum in se*, and therefore eternally wrong. No king could indemnify a subject from the conse-quences of committing such crimes by royal dispensation. Man-made laws, on the other hand, are relative in time and space. They can be repealed, and therefore violation of them is only wrong while it is prohibited, *malum prohibitum*. Kings could therefore dispense individuals from the penalties incurred by a breach of such legislation.

A case later in the seventeenth century, however, qualified Coke's opinion. This involved a member of the Vintners Company who sold wine by retail without a licence. An informer took him to court in 1674. The vintner claimed that James I had granted a dispensation to members of the company to sell wine without having to hold licences for that purpose. The Lord Chief Justice, however, found against him. He referred to Coke's distinction between crimes which were inherently evil and those which were simply infringements of statute law. He agreed that the king could dispense with the latter in most cases. But when a dispensation damaged the interests of a third party it was invalid. The vintners' dispensation gave them an unfair advantage over other wine retailers who had to pay for a licence. Consequently 'penal laws, the breach of which are to men's particular damage, cannot be dispensed with'. On the other hand, the judgment accepted that 'when the suit . . . is not to the particular advantage of any third person, the King may dispense'.[15]

This was the latest exposition of the law before the Hales case. Neither Coke nor the precedent of 1674 clearly invalidated the dispensation granted to Sir Edward by James. It was not against the law of God, even in seventeenth-century England, for

---

[15] Costin and Watson (eds.), i. *The Law and Working of the Constitution*, 250: the case of Thomas versus Sorrel.

Catholics to hold office under the Crown. Nor could any third party sue Hales for damages arising from his obtaining a commission in the army. There is therefore no need to argue, as Macaulay did, that the verdict was perverse, let alone corrupt. Nor is it necessary to assume that one of the twelve judges dissented from the majority purely for show. The opinion of the remaining eleven that James had the right to dispense with the Test Act to allow individual Catholics to hold office was a reasonably sound one at law. Moreover the resistance of the Universities to James's instructions that they dispense with their statutes to allow Catholics to graduate or hold college fellowships, however admirable it was politically, could scarcely stand up legally. Indeed they were constantly requesting the king to permit unqualified men to become dons notwithstanding their statutes, and had previously been grateful when he obliged by issuing dispensations for that purpose.

The suspending power was another matter. There were resolutions of the House of Commons against Charles II's attempts to issue Declarations of Indulgence, that of 1673 resolving 'that penal statutes in matters ecclesiastical cannot be suspended but by Act of Parliament'. Although none of the judges in the case of the seven bishops seems to have defended the legality of James's Declarations of Indulgence, there was a case for the king's right to suspend the penal laws and Test Act. After all resolutions of the Lower House do not make law. Had they done so, those of the Exclusion parliaments would have prevented James' accession. Moreover James was not claiming to suspend laws in general, but particular ones penalizing Dissenters from the Church of England. He did not even go so far as to suspend the Test Act, but simply declared that the oaths and declarations which it enjoined need not be taken by those employed in his service. And, as if to make doubly sure, he also arranged to grant individual dispensations to those given offices under him who took advantage of this concession. Technically, therefore, James was suspending the penal laws. He could have claimed the power to do this under the terms of the Elizabethan Act of Supremacy. As a contemporary pamphleteer clearly put it, 'if the King be supream head of the Church . . . the King must have a power to dispense with penal laws: for all our lawyers agree the King to have the same power as the Pope had in ecclesiastical dispensations; and that the Pope had a power to dispense with the penal laws in matters of religion, especially in malis prohibitis, was never questioned'.[16] Certainly Charles I had employed the royal supremacy when he suspended the penal laws against Roman Catholic recusants in accordance with his French marriage treaty.

Ironically the Act of Supremacy which recognized the monarch as Supreme Governor of the Church of England, and repudiated the jurisdiction of the pope, gave to a Catholic king almost unlimited powers in matters ecclesiastical. It certainly gave him the right to appoint commissioners for ecclesiastical causes. This was not in fact a revival of the Court of High Commission. It was not even a court. It did not deal with laymen, nor did it fine or imprison. It merely exercised jurisdiction over clergymen, which was undoubtedly allowed by the visitatorial powers vested in the Supreme Governor of the Church of England by the Act of Supremacy.

James could have used the commission to discipline the seven bishops, but unwisely chose instead to have them prosecuted in the Court of King's Bench on a charge of seditious libel. This seems a curious procedure, since the humble petition of seven grave divines scarcely smacks of sedition or of libel. Yet at the same time the law of libel was such that the Crown did not have to prove that the contents of an allegedly libellous work were so in fact. The Solicitor-General cited Coke to support the prosecution's view that, 'if any person have slandered the government in writing, you are [not?] to examine the truth of that fact in such writing, but the slander which it imports to the king or government; and be it never so true, yet if slanderous to the king or government it is a libel, and to be punished'.[17] This sounds like a Humpty Dumpty argument: a thing is what the government says it is. But in point of fact it was a correct exposition of the libel laws. As recently as 1680 Chief Justice Scroggs had maintained that nobody had a right to publish anything relating to government without its permission. The very act of publishing was an offence, regardless of the content

---

[16] *An Answer to a Letter to a Dissenter* (1687), 3.
[17] Costin and Watson (eds.), *The Law and Working of the Constitution*, i. 263-4.

of the publication. As the Lord Chief Justice put it in the trial of the seven bishops,

The only question before me is . . . whether here be a certain proof of a publication? And then the next question is a question of law indeed, whether if there be a publication proved it be a libel? . . . Now gentlemen anything that shall disturb the government or make mischief and a stir among the people, is certainly within the case of *libellis famosis,* and I must give you my opinion, I do take it to be a libel . . . this being a point of law.[18]

Another judge agreed

that no man can take upon him to write against the actual exercise of the government, unless he have leave from the government, but he makes a libel, be what he writes true or false . . . no private man can take upon him to write concerning the government at all, for what has any private man to do with the government if his interest be not stirred or shaken? It is the business of the government to manage matters relating to the government; it is the business of subjects to mind only their own properties and interests.[19]

Draconian though this sounds, it was a perfectly valid summary of the law as it stood. All that the Crown had to prove in court was that the bishops had in fact published their petition. This presented some difficulties, but seems to have been established in fact. If so, the jury had no right to consider whether the petition was or was not libellous. Proving that they had published it was sufficient to have found them guilty of seditious libel. Acquitting them was undoubtedly the popular verdict; but it was not necessarily the right one. Indeed it was not until 1792 that a Libel Act was passed permitting juries to consider whether the content of a publication was indeed libellous as well as whether the prosecution had successfully identified those responsible for publishing it.

While there might have been some legitimate doubts as to the legality of the suspending and dispensing powers, the commission for ecclesiastical causes, and the prosecution of the seven bishops on a charge of seditious libel, there should have been none at all about the king's right to maintain a standing army in peacetime. Again the only qualification was a Commons resolution, which no more made law than the resolutions

[18] Costin and Watson, op. cit. 266–7.   [19] Ibid. 268–9.

against the suspending power. On the contrary, the law clearly recognized the monarch's right to command the armed forces. An Act of 1661 had specifically declared the king to have 'the sole supreme government, command and disposition of . . . all forces by sea and land'. There was not the slightest hint that he required parliament's approval to raise them in time of peace. There can be no question that the Declaration of Rights was not merely clarifying but was changing the law when it declared the maintenance of a standing army in peacetime without parliamentary approval was illegal.

Nor did James go beyond his constitutional rights in his campaign to pack parliament. Indeed he did no more than extend the methods which his brother had used to break the hold of the Whig party on the constituencies after the Exclusion crisis had revealed that they could return majorities to the Commons at general elections despite the influence of the Crown. The purging of the lieutenancies of the county militias and the commissions of the peace, and the calling in of borough charters to remodel the corporations, began in the so-called Tory reaction of the last four years of Charles II's reign. What is more, there is no evidence to suggest that Charles himself was ever going to summon parliament again. All his efforts were devoted to ensuring that James would have a co-operative Commons when he eventually succeeded. If either of them acted unconstitutionally, it was Charles, not James. Charles allowed over three years to elapse after the dissolution of parliament in 1681 without calling another. This was in flagrant defiance of the Triennial Act of 1664, which stipulated that parliament should assemble at least once every three years. By neglecting to summon one Charles unequivocally broke the law.

James might have strained his prerogative to the limit, but he never went beyond it. That he acted impolitically, even rashly, cannot be denied; that he acted unconstitutionally can.

The Crown in fact still possessed great powers under the later Stuarts. Despite the restrictions on the royal prerogative which the Long Parliament had placed, especially on raising money without parliamentary consent, there was plenty of scope for exploiting it to enable the king to rule unchecked either by the law or the legislature. Whether or not this implied absolute monarchy depends on the definition of that term. As Professor Western conceded, James II 'never became an absolute monarch if by that is implied the power to change the laws and social structure of England'.[20] Instead of defining absolutism in the abstract, however, it makes more sense to compare the position of Charles II and James II with that of the archetypal absolute king, their contemporary Louis XIV of France.[21]

'Viewed as a system of government and not just as personal rule the essential features of French absolutism are easily located,' writes David Parker.

These were a standing army, a developed fiscal apparatus, a 'bureaucracy' of venal officeholders foremost amongst whom were members of the judiciary, specialised departments of state and a corps of salaried intendants who were responsible directly to the royal council for the exercise of their comprehensive administrative, financial and judicial powers . . . the exceptionally inflated state apparatus drastically curtailed the role of representative institutions . . . as well as destroying the autonomy of the municipalities.[22]

Not all these elements are discernible in the Stuart state. Certainly there was no real equivalent of the salaried intendants, nor can the state apparatus be described as 'exceptionally inflated'. On the contrary, in comparison with the French model it was modest. If these are 'essential features', then clearly Charles and James were not absolute. Nevertheless enough of the other features can be discerned to suggest that they were moving towards absolutism. Thus they built up a standing army, endeavoured to make the judiciary an instrument of the royal will, began to reform the central organs of government in the interests of greater efficiency, dispensed with parliament, and set about destroying the autonomy of the municipalities.

The army was clearly not intended for foreign fields. Even when it reached its maximum size of 40,000 it was too small to be considered seriously for overseas service. That would have required additional troops beyond James II's stretched resources, and therefore necessitated parliamentary supplies which in the

[20] J. R. Western, *Monarchy and Revolution* (1972), 47.
[21] Cf. J. Miller, 'The Potential for "Absolutism" in later Stuart England', *History*, 69 (1984), 187–207.
[22] D. Parker, *The Making of French Absolutism* (1983), 146.

circumstances he could not contemplate. Indeed the last thing he wanted was a European war.

Instead the army was used to enforce the Crown's will. One of the first occasions when it was clearly employed for that purpose was when an infantry regiment was billeted in Bristol between the autumn of 1685 and May 1686. Bristol was regarded as the most disaffected town in England, and suspected of sympathizing with the rebels in Monmouth's rebellion. To teach its citizens loyalty the regiment 'terrorised the town with its insolence, rapacity and debauchery'. Troops were used in Oxford to protect Catholic converts from attacks by town and gown alike. In Gloucester cavalrymen quartered there were enfranchised in an election which returned a Catholic mayor. Hull was virtually an occupied port. Soldiers were used to put pressure on many towns to fall in with royal policy, which was 'looked upon by some as the commencement of dragooning'.[23]

This highly professional force became increasingly isolated from the rest of English society. The soldiers were an unwelcome intrusion into communities which had not seen them since Cromwell's time. There were insufficient barracks to accommodate them, so they were foisted on innkeepers, whose licences were revoked if they refused to billet them. In Hull, for instance, the garrison had only 195 beds, but by 1688 1,700 men were billeted on the town.

Inevitably disputes arose between soldiers and citizens. In January 1686, for example, there was a virtual battle in York. According to an army officer,

never was men so notoriously abused by the mobbily [*sic*], for there was at least 500 apprentices and lusty young fellows gathered together and begun at Stonegate corner toward the Minster and knock down the sergeants and soldiers . . . there is not a man in the company but that is wounded or bruised in a most terrible manner . . . Several of the mobbily cried out 'let's knock their brains out' and threw great stones and brickbatts at them . . . undoubtedly it is the strangest rebellious place ever I quartered in in my life . . . the soldiers cannot go up and down but they are called redcoat rogue and blackguard dog . . . tis perfect rebellion and they would do as much to his sacred Majesty.[24]

[23] Childs, *Army, James II and Glorious Revolution*, pp. 88, 99, 110, 111.
[24] Leeds RO Mexborough MSS 43/29: George Butler to Reresby, 15 Jan. 1686.

After another clash between the military and civilians in February 1688, the soldiers rounded up the ringleaders and made them ride a wooden horse with their heels tied together until blood came out of their mouths. On learning of this brutal punishment two aldermen intervened to stop it. As an observer reported, 'all the citizens in general are disturbed in an extraordinary manner that townsmen should be punished by marshall law'.[25] Not even municipal office afforded protection, for in Scarborough the mayor was tossed in a blanket by the soliders.[26] Such disputes were at first tried in the ordinary courts. Increasingly, however, they were referred to courts martial, until in March 1688 a standing court martial was set up. This had the effect of freeing the army from common and statute law, thus making it an instrument of the royal will.

Both Charles and James endeavoured to make a similar tool of the judiciary. The key judicial appointments were those of the twelve judges of the Courts of Common Pleas, King's Bench, and Exchequer. Each of these central courts had four judges: a Lord Chief Justice and three Justices in Common Pleas and King's Bench, and a Lord chief Baron and three Barons of the Exchequer. They could be appointed either on good behaviour or at the pleasure of the Crown. The first kind of appointment gave them virtual tenure for life; the second made them vulnerable to immediate dismissal if they displeased the king. By and large Charles II appointed judges on good behaviour during the first decade of his reign, but resorted more and more to appointing them at pleasure in the second. This enabled him to rig the bench to procure judges who would interpret the law in his favour. By the time James succeeded him a bare majority of the twelve was even prepared to approve the new king's policy of granting commissions to Roman Catholic officers in defiance of the Test Act. He proceeded to purge the judiciary further to obtain the favourable verdict from eleven judges in the case of Godden versus Hales. After the trial of the seven bishops in 1688 the two judges who had expressed sympathy with them were dismissed. The very fact that, despite

[25] Leeds RO Mexborough MSS 53/6: anon. to Reresby, 29 Feb. 1688. Thomas Comber deprecated the 'frequent duells and murders in and about York by K. James souldiers' (*Autobiographies and Letters of Thomas Comber* (Surtees Society, 1906), clvi, 18).　　　[26] Ellis ii. 169, 196, 225.

all the dismissals and replacements, two judges could still defy the Crown as late as that shows the limitations of the power of appointment at pleasure in procuring a compliant judiciary. Nevertheless the policy was a deliberate attempt to procure one, and brought both the law and the bench into disrepute. 'The laws', as Lord Halifax expressed it in 1684, had become 'mangled, disguised, made [to] speak quite another language than their own . . . thrown from the dignity of protecting mankind to the disgraceful office of destroying them; and . . . made the worst instruments that the most refined villainy can make use of.'[27] By 1688 the situation was even worse. The judges in the trial of the seven bishops were patently inferior to the defendants' counsel, which included two purged judges, and three future judges, as well as a former Attorney-General and Solicitor-General. It revealed the extent to which the legal machinery had become dependent upon pleasing the king.

Both monarchs also tried to make the administrative machinery more efficient. The Treasury and other departments of state were overhauled in the interests of making them serve the Crown more effectively. Howard Tomlinson has summarized these developments thus: 'the permanent establishment of the Treasury and the creation of a new revenue and credit system; the slow decline of the Privy Council; the consequent extension of the role of the Secretaries of State and the growth of independent departmental administration and the emergence of new conditions of service and more rational administrators.'[28]

The establishment of a more professional Treasury can be dated from the commission of 1667 and the appointment of Sir Thomas Clifford, Sir William Coventry, and Sir John Duncomb to it. These 'rougher hands' asserted the independence of the Treasury from other agencies of government. The Secretary to the Treasury, Sir George Downing, regularized its methods of book-keeping. Another vital development in the administration of the revenue was the abandonment of tax farming. Thus the customs were taken into direct collection in 1671, the excise in 1683, and the hearth tax in 1684.

In other departments of state a secretariat was emerging. The

[27] Halifax, *Complete Works*, ed. J. P. Kenyon (1969), 53.
[28] H. Tomlinson, 'Financial and Administrative Developments in England, 1660–88', in J. R. Jones (ed.), *The Restored Monarchy, 1660–1688* (1979), 95.

two Secretaries of State played an increasingly important part in the business of the Privy Council, while 'their office was gradually acquiring a more public character—in terms of the establishment of salaries, continuity of tenure and business organisation'.[29] The Secretaryship at War changed from being a post of assistant to the commander in chief to a civil office answerable to the king and responsible for recruitment and supply to the army. The post of Secretary to the Admiralty was first given that title in Charles II's reign, and was transformed by Samuel Pepys into an important civil office. In that office, and in that of the Treasurer of the Ordnance, salaries replaced fees. As with judges, so the tenure of office holders was in many cases changed to appointments at pleasure. As J. R. Western observed, 'behind this administrative enterprise there is undoubtedly to be found an admiration for the France of Louis XIV'.[30]

The parallel with French practice can be extended to the curtailment of any check on the monarch by parliamentary representatives. Between the dissolution of the third Exclusion parliament in March 1681 and the summoning of the Convention in January 1689 the two Houses only met for two sessions in 1685. Charles and James achieved independence from them because they succeeded in surviving financially from the revenues which they had voted.

Professor C. D. Chandaman has demonstrated that the 1680s finally realized the revenues which had been voted to Charles II at the Restoration in 1660.[31] The Convention's establishment of a normal supply of £1,200,000 was not niggardly nor designed to keep Charles dependent upon parliament. That the Merry Monarch spent the first twenty years of his reign in a state of constant financial embarrassment was due to his own extravagance and to the fact that the yield on indirect taxes fell short of the amounts estimated in 1660. By 1680 the king's more extravagant youthful excesses, when royal mistresses and their illegitimate offspring were a constant drain on his resources, were largely a thing of the past. More important, a commercial

[29] H. Tomlinson, op. cit. 111.   [30] Western, *Monarchy and Revolution*, 92.
[31] C. D. Chandaman, 'The Financial Settlement in the Parliament of 1685', in H. Hearder and H. R. Loyn (eds.), *British Government and Administration: Studies Presented to S. B. Chrimes* (Cardiff, 1974), 144–54.

expansion had set in, which boosted revenues from the customs up to, and even beyond, the levels voted in 1660. In the last year of Charles II's reign the revenue produced £1,300,000, a little more than was projected at the Restoration. During James II's reign it rose to around £1,600,000 a year. This enabled him to manage without extraordinary revenue and therefore without parliament.

James did not intend to suppress parliament altogether. Instead he strove to rig the electoral system in order to procure a compliant House of Commons, one which would repeal the Test Acts and penal laws. This policy involved a major assault on the autonomy of the localities. In the counties the commissions of the peace were purged, while parliamentary boroughs were regulated.

Purging the commissions of the peace for political purposes was not a policy originated by James himself. Ironically it was first mooted by the Whigs at the time of their ascendancy in the Exclusion crisis, when Charles II had felt obliged to enlarge the Privy Council to make room for some of their leaders. The king had stood firm against their demands that Tory justices should be replaced by Whigs. Instead he began to weed out Whig justices and replace them with Tories, using for the purpose a specially commissioned committee of the Privy Council established in December 1679. By the following April every county in England and Wales had received a new commission. A further purge of the benches followed after the dissolution of the last Exclusion parliament in 1681. The intention was to make the commissions of the peace loyal to the Crown. By 1685 this had been realized. James II was apparently so satisfied with the composition of the commissions that, although he had to get the Lord Chancellor to issue new ones after his accession, he made very few changes for political purposes.

Unfortunately he could not rely on the Tory justices he had inherited from his brother to co-operate with his intention to relax the penal laws against Catholics. On the contrary, they were the most adamant that the laws should be strictly enforced. Consequently, when he came to review the commissions in order to procure benches which would go along with his wishes, he had to reverse his brother's policy and replace Tories with their political and religious opponents. In October 1686 another committee of the Privy Council was commissioned to review the magistracy.[32] As Lionel Glassey concludes from his analysis of its proceedings, 'it is apparent that the primary purpose of the council's regulation was to add Roman Catholic gentlemen to the commissions of the peace'.[33] Nearly two-thirds of those added were Catholics. At the same time a number of prominent Anglican justices were removed, including John Sharp, dean of Norwich, who had offended the king by preaching against popery.

After the dissolution of parliament on 16 July 1687, however, an even more drastic rigging of the commissions began in preparation for a general election. In December the king announced that he would review them in order to sustain the Declaration of Indulgence. This meant eliminating justices who opposed the Edict of Toleration and replacing them with men who supported it. Apparently some three-quarters of the Anglicans appointed in 1685 were no longer on the commissions of the peace by the middle of 1688, mostly through refusing to co-operate with the king's religious policy. They were replaced not only by Catholics but also by Dissenters and former Whigs. These activities attained their peak in the summer of 1688 as preparations for a new parliament reached an advanced stage. By then the boroughs too had been well and truly regulated for electoral purposes.

The campaign against corporations launched in 1687 was also the final phase of a policy of interfering in their independence which can be traced back to the Restoration, and even beyond. Charles II, however, had rather presided over than initiated such interference. At the Restoration the initiative was taken by disgruntled Cavaliers eager to prise power in the localities out of the hands of their former enemies. After the Exclusion crisis vengeful Tories co-operated in the recall of borough charters to get the corporations out of Whig control. The motives for the onslaught on the boroughs during the Tory reaction of the early

[32] Roger Morrice provides a glimpse of it at work, with the Catholic peers Arundel, Dover, and Powys recommending co-religionists as justices from a list which James used as he personally altered names in a book of all the JPs in England (Morrice MS P, 488).

[33] L. Glassey, *Politics and the Appointment of Justices of the Peace, 1675–1720* (Oxford, 1979), 89.

1680s, when 105 new charters were issued, were mixed. Paving the way for another general election was only one of them. Indeed it is far from certain that Charles II intended calling parliament again, and only his unexpected death in 1685 led to an election earlier than had been anticipated. James II certainly benefited from the purging of Whigs from the corporations when the results were announced. Besides preparing the ground for a loyal parliament, however, Charles was also anxious to put the boroughs into the possession of loyalists who would enforce the Corporation Act and the Clarendon Code. In this respect it is significant that not all the boroughs subjected to *quo warranto* proceedings were parliamentary.[34]

By contrast James II's resort to the procedure was undoubtedly to procure a packed parliament. A commission to regulate the corporations was established in November 1687. During 1688 thirty-two boroughs, all returning members of parliament, received fresh charters. In addition sixty-five corporations were regulated under the powers given to the Crown in charters issued during the Tory reaction. Whereas before these powers had been used to purge Whigs and replace them with Tories, now the policy was reversed. Anglican Tories were ousted, and Roman Catholics, Dissenters, and Whigs were put in their place. At the height of the campaign there were Roman Catholic mayors in Cambridge, Carlisle, Gloucester, Newcastle upon Tyne, and Worcester. These moves were less sensational than the Magdalen College case or the trial of the seven bishops, but they probably alienated more people. As J. R. Jones concludes, 'of all domestic policies the campaign to pack parliament was easily the most important in provoking the Revolution, more resented and feared than even the attack on the church and its leaders'.[35]

Certainly if it had succeeded James would have reduced the English parliament to the level of a French provincial estate.

---

[34] J. Miller, 'The Crown and the Borough Charters in the Reign of Charles II', *English Historical Review*, 100 (1985), 53–84; R. G. Pickavance, 'The English Boroughs and the King's Government: A Study of the Tory Reaction, 1681–1685', unpublished D.Phil. thesis (Oxford, 1976); R. J. Skinner, 'Charles II and Local Government: The Quo Warranto proceedings, 1681–1685', unpublished Ph.D. thesis (Rutgers, 1976).

[35] J. R. Jones, *The Revolution of 1688 in England* (1972), 129–30.

There, as John Locke noted when he visited Languedoc, there was all the appearance of a genuine legislative body, but in fact it was completely subservient to the king.[36] One of the attributes of absolutism was to reduce representative assemblies to the status of a rubber stamp. It is interesting to note that Ailesbury claimed the regulators had 'a power not unlike that of the Intendants of provinces in France'.[37]

James II, therefore, did attempt to make royal authority in England absolute. Moreover, as we have seen, there was still plenty of scope for exploiting the power of the Crown under the later Stuarts. Both Charles II and James sought to take advantage of these. From this point of view the 1680s are all of a piece throughout. The growth of the army, the rigging of the judiciary, the professionalization of the major institutions of state, and the attack on local autonomy all began in Charles II's reign. James merely continued a move towards absolutism which his brother had begun. Indeed there is some evidence that he instituted it before his brother died, and that the driving force behind the throne in the early 1680s was the duke of York.[38]

By condemning James II's exercise of the prerogative and asserting parliamentary limits on the power of the Crown, therefore, the Declaration of Rights stated a preference for limited over absolute monarchy. In this respect the Whig view of the significance of the Revolution was correct. The Whig interpretation of the events of 1688 to 1689 was wrong, however, in its claim that limited monarchy was the traditional constitution of the realm and that absolutism was a Stuart aberration. As we have seen, in moving towards absolutism the later Stuarts acted almost entirely within their rights. In claiming that some of their actions, for instance the retention of a standing army in peacetime without consent of parliament, was illegal, the Declaration of Rights made new law in the guise of declaring the old. So far from the Revolution Settlement leaving all the flowers of the Crown untouched, as Macaulay claimed, it uprooted some significant blooms.

---

[36] J. Locke, *Travels in France, 1675–1679*, ed. J. Lough (Cambridge, 1975), 30.   [37] Ailesbury, p. 174.

[38] See above, pp. 40–1. This is not the conclusion reached by the most recent investigation of the politics of the reign, however: J. R. Jones, *Charles II: Royal Politician* (1987), 162–86.

At the time the framers of the Declaration believed that they were simply stating the true state of the law. They distinguished sharply between those assertions of rights which simply needed to be declared, and those which required fresh legislation. Long after the Revolution the historical myth that it had merely restored the ancient constitution retained its cogency. During Walpole's ministry, however, some apologists for his regime began to concede that the settlement of 1689 had established rather than restored limited monarchy. They thus acknowledged that the Glorious Revolution was a turning-point in English constitutional history.

Whether it was a major turning-point, however, is another question. How limited was the monarchy after 1689? When William of Orange read the final version of the Declaration of Rights, he might well have breathed a sigh of relief. He would be irked, undoubtedly, by some of the restrictions upon the prerogative, particularly the requirement that parliament must approve the upkeep of a peacetime army. But the major prerogatives of declaring war and making peace, summoning and dissolving parliament at pleasure, and appointing and dismissing his own ministers without parliamentary restraint, survived the Convention's deliberations. By the end of his reign all had been significantly eroded, most especially by the Triennial Act of 1694, which required him to dissolve parliament at least every three years.

The erosion of the royal prerogatives during the 1690s has been sharply distinguished from the limitations placed on the power of the Crown by the Revolution Settlement itself. Thus it has been claimed that the constitutional developments of William's reign owed more to his foreign policy than to the events of 1688.[39] For example, there was nothing enacted by the Convention which required annual sessions of parliament. The Mutiny Act of 1689 is sometimes cited as one such enactment, since it was passed only for a limited period and had to be frequently renewed. However, this originated as an emergency measure to allow courts martial to deal with mutiny and desertion more speedily than the common law courts at a time when the army was riddled with Jacobitism. Initially it was only

[39] J. Carter, 'The Revolution and the Constitution', in G. S. Holmes (ed.), *Britain after the Glorious Revolution, 1688–1714* (1969), 39–58.

enacted for six months, and it was by no means automatically renewed. On the contrary there was no such statute for several days in 1689 and 1690, nearly three months in 1692, and almost three years from 1698 to 1701.[40] Nevertheless parliament met every year, despite these lapses. The reason was that by then it was absolutely essential to convene the Houses annually to have them vote the supplies necessary to service the debts which had accrued in financing the war against France. Thus the so-called Financial Revolution, involving the creation of a machinery of public credit including the foundation of the Bank of England in 1694, was more responsible for ensuring limited monarchy than was the Glorious Revolution.

There is something in this distinction. Certainly accounts of the Revolution Settlement which include the Act of Settlement of 1701 and even the Regency Act of 1706 beg questions as to how far the upheaval of 1688 and how far the wars against Louis XIV were responsible for these constitutional developments. At the same time, too sharp a separation of the two can be misleading. Members of the Convention were all too aware that they were taking on Louis XIV as well as James II, since backed by the French king James landed in Ireland in March 1689. One of the reasons William urged upon them for dispatch was 'the dangerous condition of the Protestant Interest in Ireland requiring a large and speedy succour'.[41] The ensuing conflict was a war of the English succession as much as of the League of Augsburg.

It is also misleading to seek the nature of the constitutional changes brought about by the Revolution of 1688 in enactments of the Convention. The spirit of a constitution is not confined to documents. While the letter of the law might not have changed greatly, the whole attitude of and towards government altered drastically. There was nothing to stop William, for instance, from appointing judges at the royal pleasure rather than upon good behaviour. When such a change in judicial appointments was suggested as one of the Heads of Grievances, it was dropped from the Declaration of Rights along with those clauses which were deemed to require fresh legislation. It did not become law until it was incorporated into the Act of

---

[40] J. Childs, *The British Army of William III, 1689–1702* (1987), ch. 3.
[41] Grey, ix. 3.

Settlement in 1701, which did not come into force until the accession of George I in 1714. Yet, although they had the right to appoint judges at pleasure, neither William nor Anne did so. Not only had they no personal inclination to make such appointments, but had they done so they would undoubtedly have offended 'revolution principles'.

The men of 1689 believed in the rule of law, that James II had transgressed it, and that they had restored it. They did not believe that they were making a radical break with the past. As one of the Whig architects of the Settlement said of it at the time, 'I hope it will be done as near the ancient Government as can be.'[42] There was a consensus in the Convention for this proposition, which ensured that the necessary technical changes in the machinery of government were kept to a minimum. But their belief in what constituted the rule of law was a very partial one. It clashed with an equally legitimate view that the king had not in fact violated his legal rights. What triumphed in the Revolution Settlement was a version of the rule of law which saw the king as beneath and not above it. This concept found concrete expression in the significant changes made to the Coronation Oath in 1689. Where James II had sworn to 'grant and keep' the Laws 'granted by ye Kings of England' William and Mary undertook 'to govern the people of this kingdom of England . . . according to the statutes in parliament agreed on, and the laws and customs of the same'.[43]

---

[42] Ibid. 29, Wharton's speech.

[43] *The Eighteenth Century Constitution*, ed. E. N. Williams (Cambridge, 1960), 37.

8

The Religious Issues

❦

It is a Church of England loyalty I would persuade you . . .
to keep us true to our Prince, we must be true to our
Church and to our Religion.

(William Sherlock, *A Sermon Preached at St Margarets
Westminster May 29 1685 before the Honourable
House of Commons*)

THE later Stuarts might well have succeeded in their bid for
absolute power if it had not become associated with Catholicism.
For contemporaries did not fear absolutism so much as 'Popery
and Arbitrary Power'. It was the potent mixture of royal
authority and Roman Catholicism under James II which was to
destroy the absolutist state which Charles II had begun to
construct. Without the religious element it is possible that James
could have completed what his brother had started. As he
himself told the Papal nuncio, he would have been the most
powerful ruler England ever had but for his religion.[1]

In many ways the questions raised by religion in the
seventeenth century cannot really be divorced from constitutional considerations. Crucial to them was the role of the
Church of England *as by law established*, and the legal status
of Dissenters from it. As we saw in the last chapter, a
constitutional crisis arose when James II tried to remove the
penal laws against Roman Catholics. However, in the Revolution
Settlement the problem of the king's allegedly arbitrary use of
power and that of the relationship between Anglicans and
nonconformists were dealt with separately, the first by the
Declaration of Rights, the second by the Toleration Act. This
chapter deals with the issues which eventually led parliament to
put a measure of religious toleration on to the statute book.

---

[1] BL Add. MSS 15397, fo. 366: Adda's dispatch, 8/18 Feb. 1686.

Tolerance of dissent could only come about through political rather than through religious conviction. It was not enough to be converted to the view that other denominations might reasonably be treated as fellow Christians and be allowed to worship in peace. Indeed in practice most Anglicans seem to have been prepared to accept this proposition, even of Catholics. Except at moments of acute political tension, Dissenters were normally left undisturbed in local communities. It is not often remarked upon, but it is none the less remarkable, that there was near unanimity amongst the respondents to James II's canvass of opinion in the winter of 1687–8 on the question of whether or not they would live peaceably with their neighbours of all religious persuasions. All but an insigificant minority were prepared to answer 'yes' to this, even though as worded it allowed for the toleration of non-Christians, as well as of Catholics and Protestant Dissenters.

The negative replies to the other questions, however, involving the repeal of the penal laws and Test Acts, reveals that the discrimination was not religious but political. Roman Catholics and Protestant nonconformists were regarded as threats to the constitution in Church and state. This crucial qualification lay behind offers of toleration throughout the seventeenth century. When Charles II offered an indulgence to tender consciences in the Declaration of Breda, he did so with the proviso that it was not on offer to those who disturbed the peace of the kingdom. He probably had in mind Fifth Monarchists, Ranters, Seekers, and other militant sects thrown up during the civil wars. Others might include Baptists, Independents, and Quakers. Certainly these sects remained much more suspect, and prone to persecution, than either papists or Presbyterians for most of his reign. The very fact that they had been spawned during the Interregnum, and largely recruited from the middle or lower orders of society, was enough to identify them with incipient social revolution by the Anglican élite.

It was to take a lot to persuade that élite to accept that such sects were peaceably enough disposed to be granted a measure of toleration. Above all it took the perceived threat from the Catholics, which came to be seen as far greater than any from Protestant nonconformists, to convert the Church of England to tolerate them.

Roman Catholics were regarded as a subversive force because they owed allegiance to a foreign power, the pope. His Holiness was held to be intent on bringing back the whole of Christendom within the fold of Rome by any means. It was widely believed that the Catholics condoned regicide if this would promote the reconversion of the country. Such beliefs lay behind the panic and paranoia of the Popish Plot of 1678, when the wildest untruths perpetrated by the psychopathic Titus Oates were credited. Thus his assertion that there was a plot to kill the king in order to advance the Catholic cause was perfectly compatible with popular perception of the papists.

Indeed the plots against Elizabeth I, the Gunpowder Plot, the Irish rebellion of 1641, and even the fire of London in 1666, were all pressed into service as 'evidence' that the Catholics were constantly planning to overthrow the regime. A stone inscription on 25 Pudding Lane, set up in 1681, claimed that, 'Here by ye permission of Heaven, Hell broke loose upon this Protestant city from the malicious hearts of barbarous Papists, by ye hand of their agent Hubert, who confessed, and on ye ruines of this place declared the fact, for which he was hanged (vizt) that here began that dredful fire, which is described and perpetuated on and by the neighbouring pillar.'[2] The inscription on the monument was even more lurid, blaming the fire on 'the treachery and malice of the Popish Faction . . . in order to the carrying on their horrid plot for extirpating the Protestant religion and old English liberty and introducing Popery and slavery'. James II had this claim erased from the pedestal when he became king, but it was incised afresh after the Revolution and remained there until the nineteenth century, prompting the Roman Catholic poet Alexander Pope to refer to the monument as:

> London's column, pointing at the skies
> Like a tall bully, lifts the head, and lies.[3]

This was nothing to the lies told at the height of the Popish Plot in 1678. One Protestant pamphleteer curdled the blood by asking his readers to imagine themselves looking out over

---

[2] The stone is preserved in the London Museum.
[3] Alexander Pope, *Epistle to Bathurst*, ll. 339–40.

London from the top of the monument should the Popish plot have succeeded:

First, imagine you see the whole town in a flame, occasioned this time by the same Popish malice which set it on fire before. At the same instant, fancy that amongst the distracted crowd you behold troops of Papists ravishing your wives and daughters, dashing your little children's brains out against the walls, plundering your houses and cutting your own throats by the name of heretic dogs . . . casting your eye towards Smithfield imagine you see your own father or your mother or some of your nearest and dearest relations, tied to a stake in the midst of flames, when with hands and eyes lifted up to heaven they scream and cry out to that God for whose cause they die, which was a frequent spectacle the last time Popery reigned amongst us.[4]

Another blood-chilling prophecy envisaged

Your wives prostituted to the lust of every savage bog-trotter, your daughters ravished by goatish monks, your smaller children tossed upon pikes, or torn limb from limb, whilst you have your own bowels ripped up . . . and holy candles made of your grease (which was done within our memory in Ireland) your dearest friends flaming in Smithfield, foreigners rendering your poor babes that can escape everlasting slaves, never more to see a Bible, nor hear the joyful sounds of Liberty and Property. This, this gentlemen is Popery.[5]

The fact that these fantasies were unrealized when a Catholic came to the throne again gave Protestants pause. Catholics pointed out the contrast between the prophecies and the reality, ''Tis evident now, to those that look upon Popery, as it appears here amongst us at this day, with an unprejudiced eye, that it has quite another face, other colours, other features, than those they have seen her painted with for so many years,' observed one Catholic writer in 1687.

All that they have heard of . . . has been full of dread and horror; cruelty in her looks; malice and wickeness in her heart; blood-thirsting in her desires; tyranny and usurpation in her government; oppression

---

    [4] C. Blount, 'An Appeal from the Country to the City' (1679), in J. Miller (ed.), *The Glorious Revolution* (1983), 97.
    [5] Henry Care, 'The Weekly Pacquet of Advice from Rome, or the History of Popery', 19 Nov. 1680, quoted in J. Miller, *Popery and Politics in England, 1660–1688* (Cambridge, 1973), 75. Care later became one of James II's most effective whig collaborators, see below, p. 175.

and slavery for her attendants; danger in her conversation; infection and poyson in her neighbourhood; ignorance in her education; idolatry and sottishness in her religion; follies in their preaching etc. And now she has been in the middle of us for some years, where are all those abominations, those marks of the Beast? Shew . . . where is her cruelty her bloodiness her tyranny her arbitrary power . . . shew us the slaves she has made all this while; where are they whom she has oppressed? How many throats has she cut? where has she wronged her neighbours? Where is the ignorance of her professions, the idolatry of her religion, the follies of her preaching, the absurdities of her doctrine?[6]

At the very least some Protestants must have felt ashamed that they had been led to believe that Catholicism would suppress Protestantism by fire and faggots should it ever achieve power in England again. This feeling probably accounts much for the initial honeymoon period of James's reign, when he was given the benefit of the doubt.

In terms of their numbers the Catholics could scarcely be regarded as a serious threat. By any account they represented at most a mere two per cent of the population.[7] Yet the kind of credulity which cast them in the role of a fifth column ready to seize power is not susceptible to statistical argument. Besides, the statistics need to be qualified. For one thing, religious allegiance was not particularly constant in seventeenth-century England. During the Interregnum episcopalian worship had been proscribed, the country had been officially Presbyterian, while an Independent minority had wielded power. Since then both Presbyterians and Independents had been ousted and persecuted and Anglicanism was established. But it could be argued that the establishment could only sustain its ascendancy if it had official backing. Nonconformity was especially liable to fluctuate according to the relaxation or tightening of the machinery for enforcing the penal laws. Occasional conformity among Dissenters who attended Anglican services as well as their own conventicles was widespread in Charles II's reign, so

---

    [6] *Catholic Representer* (1687), p. xiii.
    [7] *The Compton Census of 1676: A Critical Edition*, ed. A. Whiteman (1986), 2–3. The results of the 'census' were well known to contemporaries. See ibid. pp. lxxx–lxxxii; *Publick Occurrences Truly Stated*, no. 4, 13 Mar. 1688; Bodleian Tanner MSS 28, fo. 7.

much so that it was not easy to establish exactly what constituted a conformist.[8] James II himself even thought that not only was the Church of England sustained by the state, but that without the proscription of popery the kingdom could become Catholic within two years.[9] While this reveals the extent to which he deluded himself, nevertheless when state compulsion was relaxed the numbers of Anglicans did dwindle. Following the first Declaration of Indulgence in 1687, attendance at communion dropped sharply. Referring to earlier resorts to compulsion, a Catholic tract published in that year asserted that 'had not the Church of England taken the lash in hand . . . the Churches had continu'd as empty as they are at this day'.[10]

Another qualification to be made to the statistics is that the Catholics were not evenly distributed throughout the population. Before the influx of Irish immigrants in the nineteenth century the English Catholic community was largely confined to the households of noblemen and gentry. This gave them a much higher profile among the élite than in the rest of the population. When the second Test Act of 1678 debarred them from sitting in either House of Parliament, perhaps as many as 20 per cent of the peerage was kept out of the Lords as a result. Between 7 and 10 per cent of the gentry were probably Catholics too. English Catholicism in the seventeenth century, as Dr Miller has observed, was marked by 'social top-heaviness'.[11]

Above all the association of popery with the highest in the land, the king, made its subversive potential seem formidable. A Catholic monarch could use his authority to give power to his co-religionists out of all proportion to their numbers. It was also feared that even a Catholic queen could influence her husband to extend his favour to them. The fact that all four Stuarts had catholic wives was surely behind the Bill of Rights's insistence not only that future monarchs could not be Catholics but that

[8] In 1676 the curate of Maidstone reported over 300 Presbyterians in the parish, about 10 per cent of the total number of parishioners, 'who doe usually come to Church and to divine service, one part of the day, and goe to a Conventicle the other' (*Compton Census*, ed. Whiteman, pp. xxxviii–ix).

[9] BL Add. MSS 15397, fo. 493: Adda's dispatch, 28 May/7 June 1686.

[10] *The Papist Misrepresented and Represented with a Preface Containing Reflections upon Two Treatises, the One the State the Other the View of the Controversie between the Representer and the Answerer* (1687), p. iii.

[11] Miller, *Popery and Politics*, p. 12.

they could not marry them either, since it had been found by experience to be incompatible with English liberty.

Catholicism in high places reinforced the Crown's inclination towards absolutism according to Protestant critics. Thus Andrew Marvell, in his significantly titled *Account of the Growth of Popery and Arbitrary Government* (1677) claimed that 'there has now for divers years a design been carried on to change the lawful government of England into an absolute tyranny'. It was only when it was seen to be hand in glove with the monarchy that Catholicism appeared to be a more serious threat than Protestant dissent. Catholics were left relatively undisturbed in Charles II's reign until his brother's conversion to that religion became apparent in the 1670s, and again when he came to the throne in 1685. Before 1673, and after the Exclusion crisis, the nonconformists were more feared and hated than the Catholics.

A survey of the enforcement of the Conventicle Acts in eight widely spread counties during the years 1664 to 1680 shows that it was uneven. Much depended on the zeal of local justices of the peace. Sir Daniel Fleming, convinced of the Dissenters' 'great dissatisfaction to the present government both in church and state' kept up a one-man campaign against them in Westmorland. He even prosecuted some in 1670 after the lapsing of the first Act and before the passing of the second! Sir Roger Bradshaigh in Lancashire and Robert Thoroton in Nottinghamshire mounted similar campaigns in their own localities. But their colleagues on the bench were less enthusiastic. By and large prosecutions under both Acts lapsed after initial bouts of enthusiasm. Charles II's Declaration of Indulgence put a stop to prosecutions in 1672, and, although under pressure from parliament he revoked it, the persecution of Dissenters was not revived with the same vigour. By the mid-1670s, after all, fear of popery was much more marked than hatred of dissent.[12]

In the Tory reaction after the Exclusion crisis, however, the second Conventicle Act was enforced most rigorously. The years 1682 to 1686 marked the height of severity against Protestant Dissenters. They were associated with Whiggery and

[12] A. Fletcher, 'The Enforcement of the Conventicle Acts, 1664–1679', in W. Shields (ed.), *Persecution and Toleration* (Studies in Church History, 21; 1984), 235–46.

with the 'good old cause'. Once more, therefore, they became linked with political subversion. As Edmund Bohun expressed it, their 'ultimate object was the destruction of the monarchy and the bringing in a republic'. In Cheshire the number of prosecutions for absence from church services rose dramatically: 310 in 1681; 506 in 1682; 622 in 1683; and 718 in 1684. The number of indictments of conventicles also rose from 8 in 1681 to 144 in 1683. The Quakers fared relatively well in that county, for only nine Friends were recorded as being in prison there on 2 March 1685 out of a total of 1,460 in the whole country. There were over 3,800 arrests in London for breaches of the penal laws, while some four hundred meeting houses were harassed.[13]

James II's general pardon of 1686 temporarily, and his Declaration of Indulgence the following year permanently, ended this period of repression. He expected the Dissenters to be grateful to him for bringing it to an end. His strategy was to win them over to his side and ally them with Catholics against the narrow, persecuting Anglicans. The sincerity of this policy was questioned at the time and has been doubted since. After all, James had identified himself with the Anglican establishment during the period of the Tory reaction. As Lord Halifax warned the nonconformists in his *Letter to a Dissenter*: 'The other day you were sons of Belial, now you are angels of light.' Whig historians were convinced that James was cynically exploiting the Dissenters for his own purposes. Yet he himself announced in his Declaration of Indulgence that 'we humbly thank Almighty God it is and hath of long time been our constant sense and opinion . . . that conscience ought not to be constrained nor people forced in matters of mere religion'.[14]

The key to the apparent contradiction is in the adjective 'mere'. Liberty to tender consciences was permissible if they did not offer any political threat. Before 1686 James could claim that he could not grant an indulgence, despite his religious beliefs, because of his conviction that the Dissenters were politically

[13] Ibid. 242; G. V. Bennett, 'The Seven Bishops: A Reconsideration', in D. Baker (ed.), *Religious Motivation* (Studies in Church History 15; 1978), 268; J. Besse, *A Collection of the Sufferings of the People called Quakers* (2 vols.; 1753), i, p. xxxix.

[14] Halifax, *Complete Works*, ed. J. P. Kenyon (1969), 107; J. P. Kenyon (ed.), *The Stuart Constitution* (2nd edn.; Cambridge, 1986), 389.

subversive. William Penn felt 'obliged in conscience to say that he has ever declared to me it was his opinion that conscience should be free' and even Bishop Burnet conceded that 'when I knew him he seemed very positive in his opinion against all persecution for conscience sake'.[15] Yet the Quakers suffered more than other Dissenters, while all endured persecution in the years 1681 to 1686. James was converted, not to religious toleration, but to the view that, so far from being his political enemies, the Protestant Dissenters could become valuable allies.

The nature of James's conversion to toleration is made clear by the sudden change in his attitude towards those Huguenot refugees who fled to England after Louis XIV's revocation of the Edict of Nantes in 1685. Although it cannot be maintained that he approved of the means employed by the French king, the end, the elimination of the Protestant minority in France, seemed laudable to James. His attitude stemmed more from his perception of their politics than from their religious views. Thus he informed Sir William Trumbull that 'he did not like the Huguenots (for he thought they were of anti-monarchical principles)', while he told the French ambassador that 'he regarded all Protestants as republicans, especially those who fled from France'. At first he suppressed news of their persecution. No mention of it was made in the *London Gazette*, while *The Account of the Persecutions and Oppressions of the Protestants in France* was burned by the common hangman. Beneficiaries of the public subscription organized for their relief had to conform to the Church of England. Only when James parted company with the Anglicans and issued his Declaration of Indulgence did they enjoy full toleration. By then the king was prepared to include them among his political allies.[16]

The Anglicans also experienced a change of heart at the same time for precisely the same reasons. The twin nightmares which they had dreaded, either a papist or a puritan government, had become horrifically real, and were not alternatives but joined together in an unholy alliance against Anglicanism. The prospect of rule by both papists and puritans was too frightful to

[15] M. V. Hay, *The Enigma of James II* (1938), 76.
[16] R. D. Gwynn, 'James II in the Light of his Treatment of Huguenot Refugees in England, 1685–6', *English Historical Review*, 92 (1977), 820–33.

contemplate.[17] Yet the only alternative was to accept the Dissenters as allies against the Catholics, which meant offering them at very least toleration. Political expediency thus dictated the relaxation of the penal laws against nonconformists by James, and the promise to relax them by Anglicans.

There ensued a battle for the hearts and minds of the Dissenters fought between James and his Anglican opponents. Supporters of the king claimed that he alone was genuinely committed to toleration, and that the Anglicans were the worst enemies of the Dissenters. Anglican apologists refuted the king's sincerity and insisted that only a Toleration Act could guarantee liberty of conscience and freedom of worship. A statute passed by both Houses of parliament and the Crown would be unequivocally legal, whereas the legality of the suspending power, on which the Declaration of Indulgence was based, was very much in doubt. Moreover toleration based on the king's will could be reversed if he changed his mind, as Charles II had shown in 1673.

Catholic writers tried to raise scepticism about Anglican claims to be committed to toleration by dwelling on the persecuting zeal of the Church of England, publishing details of the most flagrant cases of insensitivity and downright cruelty. This technique was used most skilfully by Henry Care, one of James II's Whig collaborators, in his newspaper *Publick Occurrences Truly Stated*, which began to appear weekly in 1688. On 20 March in that year he published an account of James Stanton, a bricklayer who got his family together to pray for him when on his death bed. This was reported as a conventicle, and the family suffered a distraint of £20 on the house, for which their goods were seized. 'And as they ransacked the goods of the

---

[17] Humphrey Prideaux, the High-Church Dean of Norwich, expressed these fears vividly to his sister, Mrs Richard Coffin, who sympathized with dissent, e.g. in a letter of 23 Feb. 1688: 'to answer the calumnies of the dissenters who for many years last past made it their constant cry against us that we were all papists in masquerade and would immediately all go over to that religion as soon as it should find any countenance from the Government . . . the present behaviour of our clergy hath sufficiently made it appear how falsely they charged us in this particular and therein how guilty of this they themselves are who are now joined with the papists in the promoting of all methods whereby they hope to bring in that religion amongst us' (Devon RO Pine Coffin MSS, letterbook E).

house for the £20,' alleged Care, 'they would have pulled the bed from under him had it not been for one that had a little more humanity than the rest.'

Care dated this incident 22 February 1685, claiming 'we love not to tell old ungrateful stories, but . . . there are people abroad that instead of acknowledging their crimes have the impudence of the whore in the proverbs, to wipe their mouths after the more egregious villainies and say they have done nothing but according to law'. On 3 April 1688 he retailed an account of an incident in Mildenhall where an Anglican minister broke the windows of a conventicle, 'the fanatical glass being orthodoxly shattered whilst the poor people were peaceably attending a sermon'. On 1 May he reported that a conventicle in Reigate had been vandalized in April by Anglicans who 'broke open the lock, tore to pieces the pulpit and sounding board, cut the pulpit-cloth, cushion and cloth of the communion table all to shreds, broke and sawed asunder the seats and forms; in a word did all the outrage and spoil that the devil could suggest'. As he asked rhetorically apropos of the Mildenhall incident, 'are not these proceedings mighty evidences of their so oft-boasted loyalty? And irresistible arguments to induce dissenters to waive their endeavours for repealing the penal laws, and trust to such churchmen's future good nature and moderation?'[18] *Remarks upon a Pamphlet Stiled A Letter to a Dissenter* remarked upon Halifax's comment 'the other day you were sons of Belial, now you are angels of light': 'And he asserts, that to come so quick from one extreme to another, is such unnatural a motion that you are to look to yourself. Pray do so, and in doing it, remember, that in the word of a King there is power; and that the Church of England, which now hath none to hurt or save . . . styled you a child of Darkness.'[19]

The *Letter to a Dissenter* was the most famous pamphlet to appeal to Dissenters to resist an alliance with the Catholics. Halifax warned the Dissenters of two things. 'The first, is the

---

[18] *Publick Occurrences Truly Stated* nos. 5, 7, 11. That Care's stories were not apocryphal is clear from more objective evidence of provocation by Anglicans against Dissenters. One William Cleeve was particularly zealous in the suppression of conventicles in Middlesex, introducing spies in them as agents provocateurs (Bucks. RO D135/B1/2 and 3).

[19] *Remarks upon a Pamphlet Stiled A Letter to a Dissenter* (1687), 5.

cause you have to suspect your new friends. The second, the duty incumbent upon you, in Christianity and prudence, not to hazard the public safety, neither by desire of ease, nor of revenge.'

His suspicions as to the sincerity of the Catholics in offering an alliance to the Dissenters arose from the fact that it was purely an expedient. There could be nothing of principle in it, since 'wine is no more expressly forbid to the Mahometans, than giving heretics liberty to the papists'. Consequently he concluded, in a celebrated phrase, 'you are therefore to be hugged now, only that you may be the better squeezed at another time'. He admitted that Anglican motives for seeking their alliance were also suspect, in the light of the previous severity of the Church of England towards them. Nevertheless, he insisted, 'the common danger hath so laid open that mistake that all the former haughtiness towards you is for ever extinguished, and that it hath tamed the spirit of persecution into a spirit of peace, charity and condescension'.

Dissenters would endanger the public by acquiescing in a toleration obtained by the royal prerogative. 'The desire of enjoying a liberty from which men have been so long restrained may be a temptation that their reason is not at all times able to resist,' he admitted.

But where, to rescue yourselves from the severity of one law, you give a blow to all the laws by which your religion and liberty are to be protected, and instead of silently receiving the benefit of this indulgence, you set up for advocates to support it, you become voluntary aggressors, and look like counsel retained by the Prerogative against your old friend Magna Carta, who hath done nothing to deserve her falling thus under your displeasure.[20]

Even the Catholics were uneasy about the validity of the Declaration of Indulgence, as their efforts to procure a parliament to make it statutory indicated. It would be much better for the Dissenters to obtain toleration by Act of Parliament.

Some Anglicans were prepared to offer Dissenters more than mere toleration. The issues dividing the Church of England from moderate Presbyterians were not regarded as irreconcilable in some circles on both sides. At various times in the

[20] Halifax, *Complete Works*, pp. 106, 111, 113.

seventeenth century, from the Hampton Court Conference of 1604 to the Savoy Conference of 1661, divines had tried to reach a compromise. During the Exclusion crisis the Whigs had introduced bills into parliament aimed at reconciling the established church and the Presbyterians. Had these attempts been successful the Presbyterians might never had seceded from the established church in the first place, or might have been absorbed back into it in the second. Comprehension, as such absorption was termed, was more attractive in many ways than mere toleration. It retained the ideal of a single national church which comprehended the majority of Englishmen. A measure of religious toleration need only be required for the minority who could not be integrated into such a church: Baptists; Congregationalists; Quakers. Protestant reconciliation against the Catholics during James's reign therefore involved the policy of comprehension as well as converting Anglicans to the idea of tolerating the dissenting sects.

Such a policy was plainly not on for the king. The divisions between Catholics and Protestants ran far too deep for an ecumenical approach to work. What James hoped to achieve was the conversion of most Englishmen to Catholicism. This was not to be done by force. On the contrary, James's sincerity need not be doubted when he deplored the consequences of the revocation of the Edict of Nantes by Louis XIV, and insisted that coercion 'has ever been directly contrary to our inclination, as we think it is to the interest of government, which it destroys by spoiling trade, depopulating countries and discouraging strangers; and finally, that it never obtained the end for which it was employed'. Instead James hoped to convert his fellow countrymen by persuasion. He himself had been converted by the same means, and he was convinced that, if only people would give heed with unprejudiced minds to the tenets of Catholicism, they would like him be persuaded as to their essential truth. As he explained to Lord Dartmouth, 'did others enquire into the religion as I have done without prejudice, prepossession or partial affection they would be of the same mind in point of religion as I am'.[21]

Consequently he encouraged a publicity campaign to dis-

---

[21] Kenyon (ed.), *Stuart Constitution*, 389; HMC *Dartmouth*, i. 36.

abuse Englishmen of their prejudiced misconceptions of the Catholic faith, and to propagate its true doctrines. In turn Anglicans sprang to the defence of the Church of England against what they saw as the errors of Rome.

The King participated personally in the paper debate, publishing 'by his Majesties command' *Copies of Two Papers Written by the Late King Charles II: Together with a Copy of a Paper Written by the Late Dutchess of York*. These explained how his brother and his first wife had been converted to Catholicism. The first, which he claimed to have 'found in the late king my brother's strong box, written in his own hand', asserted that 'Christ can have but one church here upon Earth, and I believe that it is as visible as that the Scripture is in print, that none can be that church but that which is called the Roman Catholick Church'. This pamphlet was published by Henry Hills, the king's printer. So many 'Popish pamphlets' obtained his *imprimatur* that one Protestant writer asserted 'the dreaded names of Henry Hills and Henry Cruttenden in the title page have been a fair warning to the reader not to venture any further'.[22]

Amongst these pro-Catholic publications the most effective was John Gother's *A Papist Misrepresented and Represented*, which appeared in August 1685. Gother argued that Protestant Englishmen had developed a grotesque stereotype of a Roman Catholic, a monster so distorted as to be quite unlike the true believer. He contrasted the two in a double-columned book. On the left was 'the papist misrepresented', as Gother expressed it, 'in those very colours as he is painted in the imagination of the vulgar, foul, black and Antichristian; with the chief articles of his imagined belief, and reputed principles of his profession'. On the right was 'the papist represented', one 'whose faith and exercise of his religion is according to the direction and command of his church'.

He proceeded to contrast the views of these 'papists' on thirty-seven aspects of religious belief and practice, including all the major items of faith wherein Protestants differed from Catholics, such as transubstantiation, praying to the Virgin Mary and to saints, confession, indulgences, and papal

[22] *A Vindication of a Sheet Concerning the Orders of the Church of England Against some Reasons etc.* (Oxford, 1686), 1.

infallibility. Thus he compared the papist of popular imagination with the genuine Roman Catholic on the subject 'of mental reservations'. 'The papist misrepresented' had the following characteristics: 'He is thought to keep no faith with any that are reputed heretics by his Church; and that whatsoever promises he has made (tho never so positive and firm with this sort of people) he may lawfully break and cheat and cozen them without any scruple.' In reality, Gother insisted, the Roman Catholic

is taught to keep faith with all sorts of people of whatsoever judgment or persuasion they be, whether in communion or no; he is taught to stand to his word, and observe his promise given, or made to any whatsoever and that he cannot cheat or cozen whether by dissembling equivocations or mental reservations, without defiance of his own conscience and the violation of God's laws.

Gother summarized the differences between the two in his conclusion.

The Papists believe 'tis convenient to pray before Holy Images and give them an inferior or relative aspect. These describe the Papists praying to Images and worshipping them as Idols. The Papists believe 'tis good to desire the prayers of the saints, and honour them as the Friends of God. These point out the Papists, as believing saints to be their Redeemers, and adoring them as Gods. . . . The Papists worship Christ really present in the sacrament, true God and Man. These say they fall down to and worship a piece of Bread.

So Gother contrasted the bogyman of Protestant paranoia with the Roman Catholic as he ought to be represented.

The former is a Papist, as he is generally apprehended by those who have a Protestant Education; such as whensoever reflected on, is conceived to be a perverse, malicious sort of creature, superstitious, Idolatrous, Atheistical, cruel, Bloody-minded, Barbarous, Treacherous and so Prophane, and every way inhumane, that 'tis be in some manner doubted, whether he be man or no. The other is a Papist whose faith is according to the proposal of the Catholick Church, which by Christ's command he is obliged to believe and hear, and whose whole design in this world, is for obtaining salvation in the next.[23]

---

[23] *A Papist Misrepresented and Represented* (1685), introduction, pp. 41, 74–5.

Gother's book was taken very seriously by Anglican apologists, and spawned '*Answers* and *Reflections* and *Replies*'.[24] Among the more significant of these was Edward Stillingfleet's *The Doctrines and Practices of the Church of Rome Truly Represented*.

Stillingfleet accused Gother of setting up a straw man with his 'papist misrepresented'. 'Did ever any Protestant', he riposted, 'say that Papists are never permitted to hear sermons which they are able to understand, or that they held it lawful to commit idolatry, or that a Papist believes the Pope to be his great God, and to be far above all Angels etc.?' At the same time he took exception to the 'papist represented', since 'several of his representations depend upon his own private sense and opinions, against the doctrine of many others as zealous for that church as himself. . . . As for instance he saith the Pope's personal infallibility is no matter of faith. But there are others say it is, and grounded on the same promises [*sic* premises?] which makes him Head of the Church.' He then went through the thirty-seven points in Gother's book item by item, pointing out that many which he denied to be truly Catholic were upheld by other Catholics. For example, where Gother had contradicted the notion that Mary was co-redemptrix with Christ, Stillingfleet cited other authors who did maintain this doctrine. In the conclusion he too used double columns, with the claims for the 'papist represented' being paralleled by Protestant counter-claims. Thus, against the exposition of transubstantiation in *A Papist Misrepresented*, Stillingfleet wrote, 'we dare not direct our Adoration to the Consecrated Host, which we believe to be the substance of bread and wine (tho consecrated to a Divine Mystery) and therefore not a fit object for our Adoration'.[25]

Although the controversy involved the most learned divines of the Church of England in defence of Protestant beliefs against Catholics, it is not clear, despite Burnet's assertion to the contrary, that they got the best of the argument.[26] Certainly Gother was a formidable adversary. His notion that the popery perceived by Englishmen was at odds with the reality of Roman

[24] William Sherlock convened a meeting to discuss how to answer it: Bodleian Tanner MSS 31, fo. 190.

[25] *The Doctrines and Practices of the Church of Rome Truly Represented* (1686), 5, 6, 110.

[26] Burnet, iii. 104.

Catholicism rings true despite the efforts to refute him. It was also remarkable that, although *A Papist Misrepresented* provoked many answers, they 'appeared to be all from Church of England hands'.[27] Anglicans ruefully admitted that they had borne the brunt of replying to Catholic propaganda, and that the Dissenters had played no part in the debate. *A Catalogue of all the Discourses Printed against Popery* published in 1689 listed 228 Anglican pamphlets against only two attributed to Dissenters.

The effectiveness of these pamphlets in obtaining conversions to Catholicism or restraining Dissenters from supporting the king's policies can only be surmised, since they were but one of several pressures brought to bear on the subjects of James II to make a commitment. They seem, however, to have been widely dispersed.[28] The king himself, though, must have been disappointed with the outcome of his own efforts.

Despite some spectacular conversions to Catholicism among his courtiers, including the blatantly opportunist earl of Sunderland, only a handful of the aristocracy and gentry was converted. Amongst the Anglican clergy, there might have been thirty, including at least nine Fellows of Oxford and Cambridge colleges. The missionary effort was rather more successful amongst the lower orders. It was reported that 'two of the most noted whores in Oxford are gone over'. In Birmingham and Worcestershire 176 conversions were recorded during James's reign. The low number of conversions and the status of most converts led Burnet to conclude that 'there were but very few proselytes gained to popery: and these were so inconsiderable that they were rather a reproach than an honour to him'.[29]

Nor can James have been better pleased with the reception which his Edict of Toleration received from the Dissenters. There was an initial burst of enthusiasm, during which it was noted that the Declaration 'pleases the Quakers, and independents and anabaptists and some of the Presbytery very well'.

[27] *The Papist Misrepresented and Represented*, (3rd part, 1687), p. xxv.

[28] Sir William Strickland of Sizergh made efforts to convert Protestant gentry in Cumbria to his own Catholic faith by sending them tracts, including the third part of *The Papist Misrepresented and Represented*. Sir Daniel Fleming, however, thought that their logic 'was not so self evident as he would have them' (Cumbria RO Carlisle D/Lons/L1/33; Kendal Fleming MSS 3183, 3188.

[29] Leeds RO Mexborough MSS 49/8; Miller, *Popery and Politics*, p. 240; Burnet, iii. 106.

The Quakers, who had suffered grievously from the Anglicans, had least to gain from co-operating with them and most to benefit from the king's policy. It was largely for this reason, and not from motives of self-aggrandisement, that their leader William Penn worked closely with James, actually helping to draw up the Declaration of Indulgence. But while he kept the Friends in line, the other nonconformists soon got cold feet. A campaign to boost the Declaration by formally addressing James to thank him for it, an expression of gratitude he was anxious to receive, produced a very mixed response. Although the pages of the *London Gazette* reported addresses for over a year, from 14 April 1687 to 27 April 1688, in itself an indication of a desperate attempt to maximize their significance, only 197 were published. Moreover a close analysis of these has shown that, with the exception of Penn, the most influential Dissenters refrained from addressing, and urged their flocks to refrain also. There are signs that they were successful. Both the quality and the quantity of subscriptions to addresses indicates that dissenting enthusiasm was largely confined to insignificant minorities. As D. N. Marshall concludes, 'if the addresses represented the barometer of political support which the king his ministers and his opponents seemed to take them for, then the prospects were bleak'.[30]

Prospects for an alliance between dissent and Anglicanism, on the other hand, were no more encouraging until 1688. Despite the notoriety of Halifax's *Letter to a Dissenter*, it does not appear to have been effective immediately after its appearance in the summer of 1687. His assurances that the established church had undergone a change of heart were not particularly convincing. As the Presbyterian Roger Morrice noted on 19 November, 'I do not find that any of the tories, especially of the clergy, are come one inch further towards the Reformed Protestant interest, but still have as great an enmity and disgust against all the reformed churches as ever they had'.[31]

---

[30] PRO 30/53/8, fo. 45, Bridgewater to Lord Herbert, 11 Apr. 1687; J. R. Jones, 'A Representative of the Alternative Society of Restoration England?', in R. S. Dunn and M. M. Dunn (eds.), *The World of William Penn* (Philadelphia, 1986), 64; D. N. Marshall, 'Protestant Dissent in England in the Reign of James II', unpublished Ph.D. thesis (Hull, 1976), fo. 346.

[31] Morrice MS Q.

A more influential pamphlet in persuading them to budge was *Pensionary Fagel's Letter to James Stewart,* 'giving an account of the Prince and Princess of Orange's thoughts concerning the repeal of the Test and Penal Laws'. This 'open' letter to Stewart, dated Amsterdam, 4 November 1687, was published in Dutch and English shortly afterwards. Fagel assured him 'very positively, that their highnesses have often declared . . . that no Christian ought to be persecuted for his conscience'. They therefore offered 'full liberty of conscience' even to Roman Catholics. But they were not prepared to agree to the repeal of the Test Acts. This clarification of their position made it clear to the Anglicans that toleration at least was here to stay, since the next successor was as committed to it as was James.[32]

But what finally converted the majority of Anglicans to the view that some accommodation with the Dissenters had become vital was the second Declaration of Indulgence and the order in Council which bade the clergy read it from their pulpits. The petition of the seven bishops against the order denied that their aversion to distributing the Declaration arose 'from any want of tenderness to Dissenters, in relation to whom they are willing to come to such a temper as shall be thought fit, when that matter shall be considered in parliament and Convocation'. Thus the Church of England, which started the reign still persecuting the Dissenters, came round by the spring

---

[32] *Een Brief geschreven door den Heer Pensionaris Fagel aen Mr James Steward Advocaat*; English translation by Burnet in W. Scott (ed.), *A Collection of Scarce and Valuable Tracts . . . of the Late Lord Somers* (10 vols.; 1813), pp. ix. 183–8. This public letter was the culmination of a curious correspondence between James Stewart in Britain and William Carstares in Holland. Stewart, a Scottish Presbyterian lawyer, returned to England from exile in Holland after the proclamation of the Declaration of Indulgence. He became a Whig collaborator, and in July 1687 began to write, apparently at the king's instigation, to his fellow Scot in exile, Carstares, extolling the policy of toleration. Carstares communicated the contents of the correspondence to Fagel, who showed it to the Prince of Orange. Thus the two Scots acted as go-betweens for James and William. The prince finally made his own position on the question of toleration clear in Fagel's letter. See J. Carswell, *The Descent on England* (1969), 83–4, 96–8, 103–4, 107–10. Extracts from Stewart's letters were published, with Dutch translations, in *Hollandse Mercurius van het Jaer 1688* (1689), 158–66. Mr Carswell believed that Carstares's replies had not survived, but one is preserved in *CSPD 1687–9* (1972), 40–1. See also Carstares to Bentinck, ibid. 44–5.

of 1688 to the view that toleration, if not comprehension, was now essential. The Dissenters, too, for the most part seem to have accepted the olive branch offered in the petition. Certainly there was strong dissenting sympathy for the plight of the seven bishops. When an eminent London nonconformist clergyman expatiated on the Declaration, one of his congregation reportedly 'stood up and desired him to desist, for they payd him for preaching the word of God to them, and if he had a mind to be a politician he might go to Court'. After the acquittal of the bishops, relations between them and 'the chief of the Dissenting ministers' were so cordial that they held several conferences in July together with 'the clergy of London'.[33]

During the Revolution, however, Anglican commitment to accommodating dissent diminished. Two attempts at comprehension, the first in the Convention, the second in Convocation, were abortive. In the event only a limited measure of toleration was placed on the statute book.

The expectations of the summer of 1688 withered largely because they were overtaken by unforeseen, and to many Anglicans unacceptable, events. Archbishop Sancroft and his episcopal colleagues conceived their proposals in the context of a continuation of James II's rule. They put pressure on him to reverse his commitment to Catholics and to restore the status quo which had prevailed at his accession. During the invasion crisis his panic led him to concede many of their demands. This *rapprochement* between Crown and Church persuaded many Dissenters that both had sold them down the river. The archbishop and most bishops were, however, probably sincere in their undertaking to introduce measures of comprehension and toleration into Convocation and parliament, but they assumed that those bodies would be convened by the rightful and lawful king. When he fled, and a Convention assembled summoned by what was to them a usurper, the whole political context on which they had based their scheme was shattered beyond repair. Many of the principal architects of it, including the archbishop himself, refused to recognize the new rulers.

William was particularly suspect to High-Churchmen because he was an avowed Calvinist. His Calvinism, together with his conviction that fellow Protestants were numerous and powerful in England, led him to make some disastrous moves at the outset of his reign. Thus he held out to Dissenters the prospect of a very generous measure of comprehension, 'wherein all the Reformed Churches do agree'. Even more alarming to Anglicans was his announcement to both Houses on 16 March that he was in favour of repealing the Test Act for 'all Protestants that are willing and able to serve'.[34]

These moves rallied the Tories in the Convention. There had been a Tory majority in the Upper House all along, but this was strengthened. More significantly Tories in the Commons, who had been prepared to co-operate with Whigs over the constitutional settlement, now firmly resisted proposals to settle the religious issues on a broad basis. A group of them met at the Devil Tavern and determined to oppose any relaxation of the sacramental test. Moreover their numbers were augmented by many moderate Whigs alarmed at the radical measures being proposed on religion. As Roger Morrice observed, 'the house of commons was stronger by 80 or 100 voices to reform things amiss in the State than in the Church'.[35] The consensus which had marked the debates on the Declaration of Rights evaporated. Two bills for comprehension, one which came down from the Lords, another which originated in the Commons, were dropped, and the question of comprehending Protestant Dissenters within the Church of England was referred to Convocation. When this convened in the autumn it proved to be even more intransigently High Church than were the Tory MPs in the Convention. The mood of the clergy elected to the Lower House was summed up in

[34] G. V. Bennett, 'Conflict in the Church', in G. S. Holmes (ed.), *Britain after the Glorious Revolution, 1688–1714* (1969), 160; H. Horwitz, *Revolution Politicks: The Career of Daniel Finch, Second Earl of Nottingham* (1968), 88. One Tory commented, 'whereas our former fears were of Popery and Arbitrary Government now it is of a Commonwealth and the pressure of the Church by the dissenters' (HMC *Downshire*, i. 304–5).

[35] Morrice MS Q, p. 534. On 9 Apr. 1689 some 160 MPs met at the Devil Tavern 'to draw up an address to the K[ing] to desire him to keep close to the Ch. of England and to hint to him he is in ill hands' (Bodleian Ballard MSS 45, fo. 35). 'Toryism is now in the ascendant,' observed Edward Harley on 26 Mar. (HMC *Portland*, iii. 435).

a speech by its prolocutor: '*Nolumus leges Angliae mutari*.'[36] Thus comprehension was killed by the intransigence of High Church Anglicans alarmed at the accession of a Calvinist king.

All that survived the Anglican alliance with dissent against a Catholic king was the Toleration Act of 1689. But this measure was more restricted than the Declarations of Indulgence, which the churchmen had undertaken to enact in order to give Dissenters the security of statute rather than the uncertainty of a royal proclamation. The Corporation and Test Acts were specifically reinforced. Dissenters had to continue to pay tithes to the established church. Only Protestants who believed in the Trinity were allowed to worship separately from it. The virtual universal toleration introduced by James II was severely curtailed. Such a limited concession after so many reassurances ensured that the friction between Anglicans and Dissenters was long to survive the Revolution, especially since many Tories thought that it went too far. As one put it in a speech objecting to the measure when it was before parliament, 'when James the second published his Declaration for Indulgence (intended for the ruine of the Church of England) these very dissenters joyn with the Papists to ruine the Church of England, and promise to assist the King to gett such a Parliament chosen as would be for his Dispensing Power'.[37] James II's attempt to redraw the religious map of England did not succeed in obliterating the divisions which were deeply entrenched in English society.

[36] 'We do not wish to alter the laws of England' (Bennett, 'Conflict in the Church', p. 162).

[37] Leics. RO Finch MSS P.P.85, fo. 2.

9

The Social Implications

༺♦༻

Things were come to that extremity by the general defection
of the nobility gentry and clergy

(J. S. Clarke, *The Life of James the Second*)

IN the celebrated third chapter of his *History of England from the
Accession of James II* Lord Macaulay painted a vivid picture of
English society in 1685. It was a magnificent *tour de force*, the
more remarkable because he was a pioneering social historian
with scanty materials at his disposal. Often he had to provide
the straw for his own bricks, and sometimes make them
without any. The feat of describing the social structure from
peers to peasants with the rudimentary sources available to him
was truly phenomenal.

Since Macaulay wrote his description, the sources and
resources ready to hand for a similar analysis have increased
enormously. The availability of contemporary records in
private archives and public repositories has transformed the
nature of the evidence at the disposal of the modern historian.
Its exploitation for analysing the social history of later Stuart
England has established features of English society which he
could do little more than delineate or not even touch upon at all.
It is now possible to amend his assertions in the light of recent
research and to provide an updated version of the social context
of the Revolution.

At the same time it should be borne in mind that Macaulay
did not set out merely to describe England in 1685. He also tried
to establish the link between society and politics during the
1680s. While in the event he saw the Revolution as having the
backing of almost all elements in England, he did not regard
them as having equal enthusiasm for the Settlement which
followed. In keeping with his Whig interpretation he sought to
identify the forces of reaction and the forces of progress. The

first were the natural supporters of the Stuarts, and, but for the Catholic aberrations of James II, might well have been expected to defend him against William of Orange and his English allies. The second saw popery and absolute power as barriers to the furtherance of trends which would ultimately transform society. He placed the bulk of the gentry and the rural clergy in the first category, and the business and trading interests, the manufacturing towns and ports, in the second.

'One of the first objects of an inquirer, who wishes to form a correct notion of the state of a community at a given time', he began, 'must be to ascertain of how many persons that community then consisted.' He could only draw upon the intelligent estimates of Gregory King, the religious 'census' of 1676, and Finlaison's nineteenth-century extrapolations. These led him to conclude that 'when James the Second reigned, England contained between five million and five million five hundred thousand inhabitants'.[1]

Thanks to the work of the Cambridge Group for the History of Population and Social Structure we are in a much better position to ascertain how many Englishmen were the subjects of James II. From their computerized analyses of parish records they concluded that the population of England in 1686 was 4,864,762. This is significantly lower than Macaulay's and most modern calculations. In fact they reckon that the population had actually fallen from 5,281,347 in 1656 to its lowest point since 1626, reaching the bottom of a dip from which it was about to rise in the subsequent decade. Even so it did not reach 5,000,000 again until 1701.[2]

The implications of these figures for the Revolution are profound. A falling overall population is not indicative of the kind of demographic stress which might have contributed to social tensions before the civil war, when rising numbers were putting pressure on marginal resources. On the contrary, unless resources too were shrinking, the pressure of population growth on the economy must have eased.

According to Macaulay 'agriculture was in what would now be considered as a very rude and imperfect state'. Improvements

[1] Macaulay, i. 272, 274.
[2] E. A. Wrigley and R. Schofield, *The Population History of England, 1541–1871* (1981), 207–9.

which he attributed to the enclosure movement led him to conclude that 'it seems highly probable that a fourth part of England has been, in the course of little more than a century, turned from a wild into a garden'.[3]

Recent estimates of the expansion of the area of agricultural land in the eighteenth century would place it nearer 5 than 25 per cent.[4] Moreover, while there can be no doubt that the productivity of agriculture improved, partly because of enclosures, the growth in population made England relatively less self-sufficient. In 1685 perhaps as much as 1 per cent of agricultural produce was exported; by 1800 some 10 per cent was imported. This self-sufficiency in foodstuffs was to some extent achieved by the slackening of demand as population levels fell. But it was also accomplished by improvements in food production. Many of the innovations which used previously to be attributed to the eighteenth century, such as the introduction of the turnip and other crops, have recently been pushed back into the seventeenth. Moreover improved productivity did not have to await the enclosure movement of the eighteenth century. Much of England was enclosed by 1700 anyway, while even the traditional open fields saw changes with the adaptation of alternate husbandry, using the same land alternately for arable and pasture. Livestock could be sustained over winter, and not slaughtered at the end of the year as Macaulay believed.

Indeed bounteous yields of farm produce, creating a surplus for export, made the agricultural sector of the economy far more buoyant than Macaulay allowed. It also meant, with a falling population, a fall in prices for foodstuffs, and with them a rise in real wages. Where the decades before the civil war have been seen as among the grimmest facing the mass of the population in English history, in the 1680s Englishmen probably enjoyed a higher standard of living than in any other decade of the Stuart era. This must be borne in mind when we come to assess the motives behind the Revolution.

Inevitably some Englishmen were adversely affected by the fall in the price of farm produce. Farmers of course felt the

---

[3] Macaulay, i. 300, 304.

[4] E. L. Jones, 'Agriculture, 1700–80', in R. Floud and D. McCloskey (eds.), *The Economic History of Britain since 1700*, i. *1700–1860* (1981), 70.

squeeze as their profit margins narrowed. Even if they were amongst those spurred by adversity to improve productivity, they would still find their living standards threatened. Those who were tenants often appealed to their landlords to adjust rents to ease the strain. Such appeals were frequent during the 1680s, which have been described as a decade of 'vicious depression' for the landed interest.

Among the landlords who received cries for help to meet rent arrears were peers and country gentlemen who relied on their tenants for income to sustain their own standards of living. The aristocracy and gentry consequently complained as the depression of agricultural prices hit their rent rolls. Yet the principal landowners, peers and gentry alike, gave overwhelming support to the Crown during Monmouth's rebellion in 1685. In no way can adverse economic trends affecting their interests be cited to account for their alienation from the king during the subsequent three years.

That noblemen tended to take the lead in the localities in the aftermath of William's invasion has been clearly established. The Earl of Danby led a group of Yorkshire gentry to seize the city of York. Other noblemen, accompanied by local gentry and tenants from a number of centres in the Midlands, converged on Nottingham. Lord Delamere marched from Cheshire through Manchester and Derby to reach Nottingham, where he joined the earls of Devonshire and Stamford, who had made their ways there respectively from Chatsworth and Lincolnshire. Nottingham was taken without any serious resistance and was then fortified to resist any loyalist attack. On 29 November four more peers at the head of some five hundred cavalrymen arrived there from Northampton.[6]

Yet to describe these events as a feudal reaction can be misleading. Danby, Delamere, and Devonshire were not typical noblemen. Perhaps only one in ten of the peers took an active part in the Revolution. The typical reaction was not to rush to help William of Orange but to await developments after his arrival in Brixham on 5 November. There were, after all, 160

[5] C. Clay, 'Landlords and Estate Management in England', in J. Thirsk (ed.), *The Agrarian History of England and Wales* (Cambridge, 1985), V. ii. 232.

[6] D. Hosford, *Nottingham, Nobles and the North* (Hamden, Connecticut, 1976).

secular lords in 1688. Thirty-two of these were Roman Catholics, though these did not exactly leap to James's aid either. Lord Molyneux was unusual in raising four hundred men to oppose Delamere in the north-west. Some forty peers were in London in November to answer the king's summons to advise him. The rest were presumably riding out the storm in their country houses.[7]

It could even have been the case that the peers who actively opposed the king were carrying out personal vendettas rather than displaying class solidarity. Certainly many had grudges against James. Danby was chagrined that he had not been reinstated as a chief minister after suffering for his services to Charles II. Devonshire was smarting from the fine of £30,000 imposed on him for a breach of the peace in a royal palace. Two other signatories of the invitation to William of Orange, the earl of Shrewsbury and Lord Lumley, had been stripped of their commissions in the army. Lord Lovelace, who went to the south-west to join William in November 1688, had been haled before the Privy Council the previous February for offering to wipe his backside on a writ served upon him by a Catholic justice of the peace. The earl of Bath nursed a grievance throughout the reign. He had been Groom of the Stole and the recipient of a pension of £5,000 per annum under Charles II. James II gave the post to the earl of Peterborough, and, though he promised to pay the pension, never did. Being Lord-Lieutenant of Devonshire and Cornwall, and Governor of Plymouth, Pendennis's castle, and Falmouth was apparently no compensation, for when William of Orange sent a message to Lord Bath to name his conditions for going over he decided to desert James, clearly hoping the prince would get his former post and pensions back. His defection was crucial, since it removed the vital obstacle of Plymouth from the Dutch line of retreat.[8]

[7] J. P. Kenyon, *The Nobility in the Revolution of 1688* (Hull, 1963). Anthony Wood observed the difference in the behaviour of the nobility in 1685 and 1688. On 6 Nov. 1688 he noted that 'when Monmouth's rebellion broke out there was, every day almost, a duke, earl, or lord, with company, passing through Oxford and making a hurry over all the nation. No man stirs yet' (*The Life and Times of Anthony Wood*, ed. A. Clark (Oxford, 1894), ii. 281).

[8] Bath's grievances against the later Stuarts are fully set out in Northants RO Granville MSS G. 2839. See also BL Add. MSS 32095, fos. 226–9, where

Some of the activists amongst the gentry had also been deprived of lucrative posts. Christopher Tancred was sheriff of Yorkshire from 1685 to 1687. In most counties the office was irksome and expensive, so that local gentry were anxious to avoid holding it at all costs. In Yorkshire, however, it was worth £1,000 per annum to its incumbent. During the general election of 1685 Tancred demonstrated his loyalty by assuring the earl of Sunderland that he would 'send the king a greater number of loyal men to Parliament than ever was known from this county'. After being deprived of the shrievalty, however, he attached himself to Danby, and played a leading role in the seizure of York. It was Tancred who gave the signal for the rising by falsely declaring that 'the Papists were risen'. Afterwards he marched on Leeds and seized £314 of the hearth tax money for the rebel cause. Sir Christopher Musgrave was dismissed from the governorship of Carlisle castle in 1687. At one in the morning on 16 December 1688 he led a party which seized the castle from its unresisting Catholic commander.[9]

Other gentlemen had been ousted from the honorary posts of deputy-lieutenants of the militia or justices of the peace. In Lancashire ten were dismissed from the deputy-lieutenancies in 1687. This was by far the greatest purge of the militia in that county in the period 1660–88, its impact the more decisive because the removals constituted about half of Lancashire's deputy-lieutenancies. The purgings of the commission of the peace in the preparations to pack parliament were also, as we have seen, sweeping. Nor were those who had been removed inclined to forgive and forget when James panicked in the invasion scare of September 1688 and reinstated many. As Sir

---

Bath presents his case to James II on 13 Dec. 1685, assuring him of his 'constancy and unshaken zeal for your Majesty's service which as I have always heretofore so I shall ever continue to my last breath'. James was more surprised by Bath's defection than by anything else which happened since 'his obligations to the Crown were so great, his family always esteem'd so loyall, and himself till then looked upon as uncapable of being shaken or tempted to any ill action' (J. S. Clarke, *The Life of James the Second* (2 vols.; 1816), ii. 230). Bath, however, nursed exaggerated grievances and was also grasping. He later complained that William had offered him a dukedom and the house and park at Theobalds in return for his support in 1688. Northants RO Granville MSS G. 2859.

[9] Henning, iii. 118, 570.

John Bramston put it, 'Some would think one kick of the breech enough for a gentleman.'[10]

They were the more resentful because they felt that they had been replaced by lesser gentry, who had no natural interest in their counties. Sir John Reresby complained that 'the prime of the gentry' had been removed and that 'ordinary persons' had taken their place.[11] This was to do less than justice to the standing of many Catholic and dissenting gentry who were promoted to the local militias and commissions of the peace.[12] Yet there was some truth in it. Eleven obscure names were added to the deputy-lieutenancy in Lancashire in 1687 in place of those dismissed. In Kent, the leading county families were superseded on the bench by nonentities. As Norma Landau has observed of that county

It has been claimed that James II's selection of justices was an affront to the gentry of England. According to the criteria chosen to measure status, it was. Of the total of ninety-seven justices appointed by James, eight-five had not sat upon the bench before—and deservedly so. While 35 percent of the commission in 1679 could proclaim that father or paternal grandfather had graced the bench, only 23 percent of James's new appointees could claim such prestige. Thirty-five percent of the commission in 1679 had attended university, but only 14 percent of the new justices. Forty percent of the justices in 1679 had been registered at the Inns of court, but only 26 percent of the new rulers of the county . . . of the sixty eight justices first placed on the commission by James II who were neither Catholics nor Dissenters, 22 percent cannot be identified. Clearly, James's nominees were marginal

---

[10] D. P. Carter, 'The Lancashire Militia, 1660–1688', in J. J. Kermode and C. B. Phillips (eds.), *Seventeenth-century Lancashire: Essays Presented to J. J. Bagley* (Liverpool, 1983), 180–1, Bramston, p. 326. For the purges, see above, pp. 159–60.

[11] Reresby, p. 494.

[12] A. Fletcher, *Reform in the Provinces* (1986), 35. The Lord Chancellor seems to have been concerned about the effects of the purges on the quality of the bench. When one Fleetwood was proposed as a JP in Staffordshire it was noted against his name '£2000 p. an. a Catholique' (Bucks. RO D135/B1/2). However, the Court virtually admitted that it had not sustained the social status of the commissions of the peace when the purges were reversed in 1688. The Lords-Lieutenants were then asked to name which of the justices were not fit to be in the commissions. The earl of Bath listed 23 in Cornwall and 42 in Devon who were 'of mean quality and small estate and very unacceptable to those worthy gentlemen who are now to be restored' (ibid. 4/1 and 4/12).

members, if members at all, of the community of those who ought to rule Kent.[13]

Moreover, according to Lionel Glassey, 'perhaps Kent suffered less severely than elsewhere'.[14]

Yet, even more than with the nobility, the characteristic response of most country gentlemen to the Dutch invasion was to sit tight to see which way events would move. Macaulay assumed, probably correctly, that they were mostly Tories, and as such would be reluctant to help James II after his treatment of them, but unwilling actively to resist him by joining William.

Macaulay also assumed that they were natural supporters of the Stuarts, because they were reactionary elements in English society, their backwardness characterized by their being 'gross, uneducated and untravelled'.[15] He relied for this impression far too much on literary depictions of booby squires, especially the Sir Jolly Jumbles and Sir Tunbelly Clumsies of Restoration comedy, and the Foxhunter of Addison's *Freeholder* essays. Their own archives, largely opened up since the publication of his *History of England*, reveal a very different set of characteristics. Historians have usually resolved this discrepancy between the stereotype squire of literature, and the literate and even sophisticated gentry who left behind correspondence and other personal papers, by arguing that literary sources illustrate the typical lesser country gentlemen while only the upper ranks of the landowning classes tended to preserve letters and papers. There were something like 16,000 gentry families in England at the time of the Revolution according to Gregory King, and the gap between the wealthiest and the poorest was enormous. Sir Charles Duncombe, a city goldsmith, set himself up as a landowner by purchasing the Helmsley estate from the second duke of Buckingham. He reputedly paid £90,000 for it, which was said to be the biggest single cash transaction between private citizens in the seventeenth century. The sale prompted Pope to pen the sardonic couplet

---

[13] N. Landau, *The Justices of the Peace, 1679–1760* (1984), 302.
[14] L. Glassey, *Politics and the Appointment of Justices of the Peace, 1675–1720* (Oxford, 1979), 89.
[15] Macaulay, i. 312.

> And Helmsley, once proud Buckingham's delight
> Slides to a scrivener or city knight.[16]

Duncombe was exceptional in many ways. The substantial
gentry families of any county, the Lowthers of Cumberland, the
Goodrickes of Yorkshire, the Knatchbulls of Kent, and the
Rolles of Devon, for example, would be in receipt of rent rolls
into four figures per annum. Yet at the other end of the scale
there were gentry who could scarcely boast three-figure annual
incomes. In Restoration Yorkshire, for example, Sir Solomon
Swale inherited property worth only £140 a year, while Sir
Walter Calverley had a net income from his estate of less than
£100.[17]

However, this resolution of the contradiction between the
archives of the country gentlemen and their representation in
creative literature is unsatisfactory for two reasons. First, the
dramatic stereotype was by no means confined to backwoods
squires but took in substantial characters, with fat rentals.[18]
Secondly, the archival evidence is not restricted to the papers of
the upper gentry. Not only have some lesser family archives
survived, but more significantly the correspondence of the most
substantial gentry is by no means confined to their own kind.
Letters from all kinds of correspondents testify to the education
and manners of landed society in late-seventeenth-century
England. Macaulay was very seriously misled by plays and
other literary products into believing that it was marked
by boorish rusticity. Although ignorant boors undoubtedly
existed, most of the landed gentry seem to have been reasonably
civilized if not cultured, and to have been more aware of a wider
world. Take Daniel Fleming of Rydal, for example. A recent
study based on his voluminous papers concluded that they
'show him to be a truly remarkable man. He combined great
intelligence, vast erudition, immense curiosity and great energy,
with a love of documents.'[19]

Fleming lived in a remote corner of the north of England,

---

[16] *Dictionary of National Biography*, article on Duncombe.

[17] P. Roebuck, *Yorkshire Baronets* (1980), 22, 24.

[18] W. A. Speck, *Society and Literature in England, 1700–1760* (Dublin, 1983),
5–12.

[19] A. Macfarlane, *The Justice and the Mare's Ale* (Oxford, 1981), 42.

which Macaulay described as being the most backward region in the kingdom. As he put it,

a large part of the country beyond Trent was, down to the eighteenth century, in a state of barbarism . . . In the reign of Charles the Second, the traces left by ages of slaughter and pillage were distinctly perceptible, many miles south of the Tweed, in the face of the country and in the lawless manners of the people. . . . The irregular vigour with which criminal justice was administered shocked observers whose life had been passed in more tranquil districts. Juries, animated by hatred and by a sense of common danger, convicted housebreakers and cattle stealers with the promptitude of a court martial in a mutiny; and the convicts were hurried by scores to the gallows.[20]

Alan Macfarlane has shown how inaccurate Macaulay's picture was as far as Westmorland was concerned:

We encounter less than half a dozen persons suspected of murder or homicide during the fifty years 1650–99 for the county. Of really serious and brutal assaults involving the loss of limbs or serious injuries, there are very few indeed . . . Nor is there much evidence of . . . rape, arson and large-scale cattle rustling. There are no documented cases of any of these for Kirkby Lonsdale in the hundred years after 1650, and scarcely a case for the whole of Westmorland in the surviving records for 1650–99.[21]

Instead he came across burglary, highway robbery, and counterfeiting, the characteristic crimes of allegedly advanced societies. He therefore concluded that there was little difference between the behaviour of the inhabitants of the Lake District in the reign of James II and those who were subjects of Queen Victoria.

Whilst Macaulay and more recent historians have assumed that 'pre-industrial society' was very different from their own communities, so that it is salutary to be reminded of the continuities of English social history, it is redressing the balance too far to suggest that the subjects of the later Stuarts were no more violent than modern Englishmen. The aristocracy and gentry lived then by a rigid code of honour, breaches of which provoked innumerable duels. The resort to cold steel to avenge insults, real or imagined, was commonplace amongst the upper

[20] Macaulay, i. 274, 276.
[21] Macfarlane, *Justice and the Mare's Ale*, p. 186.

ranks of society. At least eight gentlemen who sat in the House of Commons between 1660 and 1689 killed an opponent in a duel. Sir John Reresby, a noted duellist himself, recorded in his diary in January 1681 that 'two gentlemen of my acquaintance who dined with me a few days afterwards fought a duel . . . The first killed the other.'[22] This casual violence, accepted as an everyday risk by every armigerous gentleman, marked a rather different behaviour from today's upper classes.

Duelling was of course condemned by the clergy as an affront to the law of God. Yet their censures were largely ignored by the laity to whom they were addressed, showing that there were limitations to the influence of clergymen even in that religious age.

In other spheres of life the clergy were still immensely influential. Macaulay drew a distinction between the urban clergyman and his rural colleague. 'The Anglican priesthood', he maintained,

was divided into two sections which, in acquirements, in manners and in social position differed widely from each other. One section, trained for cities and courts, comprised men familiar with all ancient and modern learning . . . The other section was destined to ruder and humbler service. It was dispersed over the country, and consisted chiefly of persons not at all wealthier, and not much more refined, than small farmers or upper servants.[23]

Here again, as with the gentry, he seems to have been misled by the sources available to him. His view of the clergy was based to a large extent on the hostile account of John Eachard's *The Grounds and Occasions of the Contempt of the Clergy and Religion*, first published in 1670. 'Whatever . . . does at present lessen the value of our clergy', it claimed, 'may be easily referred to two very plain things; the ignorance of some and the poverty of others of the clergy.'[24] Eachard, a Cambridge don, had a lofty view of the intellectual pretensions of the rural clergymen. In fact, they were not as ignorant as he implied. The vast majority were graduates of Cambridge or Oxford Universities. Many had

---

[22] Leeds RO Mexborough MSS MX/242, fo. 18.

[23] Macaulay, i. 319–20.

[24] John Eachard, *The Grounds and Occasions of the Contempt of the Clergy and Religion* (9th edn.; 1685), 3.

obtained the degree of MA. Nor did they neglect their learning after they graduated. As a local study concluded, 'probate inventories show that almost all late-Stuart Leicestershire parsons had libraries of some sort, a few of which were valued at over £100; an average clerical library was worth about £10, and Immanuel Bourne's, valued at £5, ran to 120 volumes'. Ten per cent of the ministers in Restoration Leicestershire even published something.[25]

It is true that many of the clergy were, as Eachard claimed, poor. In 1670 just over a quarter of the livings in Leicestershire were worth under £60 a year to their incumbents. Yet even the extent of clerical poverty can be exaggerated. Thus in Leicestershire 'clerical incomes covered a wide range in the late-Stuart period. Middling parsons received incomes which Gregory King thought comparable to those of middling freeholders, and for every parish where an incumbent struggled to feed and clothe his family, there was another where the parson's standard of living was among the highest in the village.'[26]

There was a similar spectrum of incomes for the higher clergy. The poorest bishoprics, Bangor and Llandaff, were worth respectively £131 and £154 a year in 1680. By contrast Ely brought in £2,134 and Canterbury £4,233.

Seven of the twenty-six bishops, by presenting a petition to James II, set off a sequence of events which were to precipitate the Revolution. Moreover, once the momentum had been established, members of the episcopate kept the initiative. That they should have taken the lead, making the Revolution, at least in its initial stages, more clerical than feudal or bourgeois, was

---

[25] J. H. Pruett, *The Parish Clergy under the Later Stuarts: The Leicestershire Experience* (1978), 45. Eachard was ambiguous about the ignorance of the clergy, for he criticized not only those who lacked learning but also those who paraded it before ignorant rustics 'spreading themselves in abundance of Greek and Latin to a company perhaps of farmers and shepherds . . . when such stuff as this (as sometimes it is) is vented in a poor parish, where people can scarce tell what day of the month it is by the Almanack, how seasonable and savoury is it likely to be?' (*Grounds and Occasions*, pp. 49, 52).

[26] Pruett, *Parish Clergy*, p. 100. Pruett's findings for Leicestershire have been confirmed for Wiltshire too. See D. A. Spaeth, 'Parsons and Parishioners: Lay-Clerical Conflict and Popular Piety in Wiltshire Villages, 1660–1740', unpublished Ph.D. thesis (Brown University, 1985), fos. 325–31.

unexpected. The High-Church leaders amongst the nobility, Lords Clarendon, Nottingham, and Rochester, gave a very poor lead in the crisis. Only Clarendon advised not reading the Declaration, while Nottingham and Rochester urged compliance. Characteristically Halifax 'was so very cautious that he would give no advice at all'.[27] It certainly surprised James, who expostulated that the presentation of the petition was 'a standard of rebellion' and, more reasonably, that he did not expect it from some of them.

He had every reason not to have expected some of the seven to challenge him, because he had promoted most of them himself. During the Tory reaction of 1681 to 1685 Charles II had set up a commission for ecclesiastical promotions, over which James, as duke of York, had commanded considerable influence.[28] His brother-in-law, the earl of Rochester, had worked closely with Archbishop Sancroft on the commission to ensure that supporters of the duke and his claim to the succession were promoted. Three of the seven had received their first episcopal appointments from the commissioners: Thomas Ken of Bath and Wells; John Lake of Chichester; and Francis Turner of Ely. In the first year of his own reign James had promoted two more, Jonathan Trelawny to Bristol and Thomas White to Peterborough.

In deciding to appeal against the order in Council requiring the second Declaration of Indulgence to be read out in churches, they worked closely with leading lower clergymen, such as Simon Patrick, Edward Stillingfleet, and John Tillotson, whom James dubbed 'the Deans', because they were respectively deans of Peterborough, St Paul's, and Canterbury. There was also close collaboration at this time with London clergy, notably Thomas Tenison, vicar of St Martin's in the Fields. These men were all singled out by Macaulay amongst the urban ministers who distinguished themselves in comparison with their rural colleagues. It is clear that he was making as much of a political as a social point. The rural clergy, like the gentry, were inclined to be Tories. The leading London divines were more sympathetic towards dissent. Indeed, until the crisis created by the

---

[27] Morrice MS Q, p. 255.
[28] R. A. Beddard, 'The Commission for Ecclesiastical Promotions, 1681–1684: An Instrument of Tory Reaction', *Historical Journal*, 10 (1967), 11–40.

second Declaration of Indulgence, the four mentioned had been at loggerheads with the seven bishops over this issue. Where Sancroft and his episcopal colleagues had been zealous in the prosecution of dissent, Patrick, Stillingfleet, Tenison, and Tillotson had advocated reconciliation.[29]

It is possible that the urban environment created more sympathy for nonconformity since nonconformists were more likely to be encountered in towns than in the countryside. There were, of course, Dissenters in rural areas, perhaps especially in woodland or pasture districts, which were rather less amenable to the social control of squire and parson than the nucleated villages of arable farming districts. Moreover the very concept of urban areas opposed to rural is somewhat anachronist when only London could measure its population in six figures and perhaps half a dozen other towns had over 10,000 inhabitants. Most so-called towns were little more than villages. Urban historians are divided over what constituted a town. Contemporaries used the term to describe tiny communities. Thus Gregory King's idea of a small town was one with about 650 inhabitants. There were about five hundred market towns or ports with between 500 and 2,500 residents around 1700. Above them were some sixty or seventy with populations between 2,500 and 11,000.[30] It was in such centres that dissent retained its most tenacious grip. As Michael Watts has put it, 'The evidence of the Evans list, the episcopal visitation returns, and the Quaker burial registers all suggest that Dissent was more urbanised than the population at large.'[31] The Dissenters who addressed James II to thank him for the first Declaration of Indulgence were mainly townsfolk. For example, addresses from Yorkshire came from Hull, Leeds, Sheffield, and York.

Macaulay drew a distinction between towns such as these.

---

[29] The political significance of this group is clearly indicated in their inclusion among 'the clergy of London that deserve a more particular regard from your Highness', drawn up for the Prince of Orange apparently in 1688. It lists Patrick, Tenison, who 'has done more against Popery than any man whatsoever', Stillingfleet, 'the learnedest man of the age', Sharp, Sherlock, and Wake, 'the most popular divine now in England' BL Add. MSS 32681, fo. 313.

[30] P. Borsay, 'Urban Development in the Age of Defoe', in C. Jones (ed.), *Britain in the First Age of Party, 1680–1750* (1987), 198–9.

[31] M. Watts, *The Dissenters from the Reformation to the French Revolution* (1978), 285.

Thus York he classed amongst the 'ancient capitals of shires', while Leeds and Sheffield he placed amongst the 'younger towns' which were to develop into the great industrial centres of the nineteenth century.[32] His Whig bias is discernible behind this categorization. In his view the county capitals were backward looking, while the rising manufacturing towns belonged to the future. Places like Shrewsbury and Worcester were the resorts of the minor county gentry, the backbone of the Tory party, while Birmingham and Manchester were inhabited by businessmen who were more receptive to Whiggism.

The distinction, economically speaking at least, was anachronistic. Some of the 'ancient capitals of shires' were still major manufacturing centres. In the early reigns of James I and Charles I the manufacture of woollen cloth, England's staple commodity, suffered severely from recession brought about partly through bottlenecks in the finishing process, but mainly through the interruption of the markets caused by the outbreak of the Thirty Years War. Those areas which met the challenge by manufacturing the lighter cloths known as the New Draperies, such as the West Riding of Yorkshire, East Anglia, and the West Country, survived the depression better than others. In Norwich the textile industry revived and prospered in the seventeenth century. The main market for East Anglian cloth seems to have been domestic rather than foreign. By contrast West Country textiles were very much in demand abroad, so much so that the cathedral town of Exeter, by any account an ancient county capital, emerged from the crisis as one of the more prosperous ports, exporting well over a quarter of all English cloth bound abroad by the 1680s.[33]

Meanwhile, however, colonial produce began to make up an increasingly large proportion of English overseas trade as colonies were successfully established in the sugar islands of the West Indies and the tobacco region of the Chesapeake Bay. Other extra-European produce re-exported by English merchants included coffee, tea, spices, and silks. There was also domestic demand for these products created by the fall in the price of

---

[32] Macaulay, i. 326, 328.

[33] C. Wilson, *England's Apprenticeship, 1603–1760* (1965), 189; P. J. Corfield, 'A Provincial Capital in the Late Seventeenth Century: The Case of Norwich', in P. Clark (ed.), *The Early Modern Town* (1976), 246.

foodstuffs and the corresponding availability of cash to spend on other commodities. This expansion boosted particularly the western ports of Bristol, Liverpool, and, for a time, Whitehaven. Liverpool's population expanded rapidly, from 1,000 or 1,500 to over 5,000 between 1660 and 1700, while the new town of Whitehaven was developed in the 1680s.[34]

Historians are disagreed as to whether recession or boom was the salient characteristic of the late-seventeenth-century town. Some larger county towns, such as Northampton, Nottingham, and Norwich, were apparently prospering in the 1680s, but this was at the expense of smaller towns which were in decline. Small market towns, especially in areas hard hit by the depression in the cloth trade, like the Cotswolds, were also struggling to survive. Yet overall buoyancy rather than depression seems to have been more common. One historian has described the decades after 1680 as 'the urban renaissance'.[35]

The most rapidly growing urban centres were the future industrial towns such as Birmingham, Leeds, Manchester, and Sheffield.[36] Above all London continued to expand and to prosper. Despite the national population growth slackening and even, perhaps, going into reverse between 1650 and 1680, the number of inhabitants in the capital increased from 375,000 at mid-century to 490,000 by 1700. In 1650 London contained 7.2 per cent of the population of England; by 1700 this had risen to 9.7 per cent.[37]

London was thus a giant dwarfing the next largest town, Norwich, which had only 30,000 inhabitants. The implications for the national economy of the sheer scale of the capital are only just beginning to be worked out. Certainly the economic health or otherwise of the city was a vital factor in the well-being of the whole country. During the 1680s it profited hugely from the boom in overseas trade which characterized that decade. Yet the

---

[34] A. McInnes, *The English Town, 1660–1760* (1980); R. Millward, 'The Cumbrian Town between 1600 and 1800', in C. W. Chalklin and M. A. Havinden (eds.), *Rural Change and Urban Growth, 1500–1800* (1974), 216–18.

[35] P. Borsay, 'The English Urban Renaissance: The Development of Provincial Urban Culture, *c.*1680–1760', *Social History*, 5 (1977), 581–603.

[36] P. Clark and P. Slack (eds.), *English Towns in Transition 1500–1700* (1976), 38–45.

[37] A. L. Beier and R. Finlay (eds.), *The Making of the Metropolis: London 1500–1700* (1986), 39.

prosperity did not benefit every trade or merchant equally. Monopoly companies with a royal charter, such as the East India Company, prospered in these years. Those kept outside the legitimate Eastern trade when Charles II granted a new charter to the Company in 1683 felt particularly aggrieved. The Company, led by Sir Josiah Child, became largely Tory. Its critics, prominent amongst whom was Thomas Papillon, tended to become Whigs. Papillon, a Dissenter of Huguenot extraction, later fled to Holland. When James II began to woo the Dissenters in 1685, Papillon was pressed to return.[38]

Dissent was a major dimension of London politics. There were perhaps 100,000 nonconformists in the capital. A significant proportion of aldermen and common councilmen were from dissenting congregations. When Charles II revoked the charter and issued a new one, many of these were purged. Later James began to reinstate them in his bid for the support of the Dissenters against the Anglicans. Ailesbury in his *Memoirs* recalled a Lord saying to him that 'all the jolly, genteel citizens are turned out, and all sneaking fanatics put into their places'.[39] James made a direct connection between religious toleration and economic prosperity in this bid. As he put it in his Declarations of Indulgence, religious intolerance was contrary 'to the interest of government, which it destroys by spoiling trade'. Here he was drawing directly on Whig arguments to sustain his appeal. Slingsby Bethel, for example, in *The Interest of Princes and States*, published in 1680, had asserted that 'it is the undoubted Interest of his Majesty, to advance and promote Trade, by removing all obstructions'. Amongst the obstacles he cited was 'imposing upon Conscience in matters of Religion', which, he claimed, was 'a mischief unto Trade, transcending all others whatsoever'. Bethel, however, also advocated measures which would not have pleased James, such as opening up companies to all comers, and establishing banks like those in Amsterdam and Venice, concerning which he confessed 'there are no thriving and flourishing examples, save under Republics'. Such sentiments inspired Dryden to depict Bethel as one who advocated that 'Kings were useless, and a clog to trade'.[40]

---

[38] A. F. W. Papillon, *The Memoirs of Thomas Papillon of London, Merchant* (Reading, 1887), 239.   [39] Ailesbury, pp. 175–6.

[40] J. Dryden, *Absalom and Achitophel*, ed. P. Roberts (1973), ll. 614–15.

Dryden put his finger on a key issue concerning the link between politics and society in the 1680s. The decade was one of commercial expansion on an unprecedented scale. The merchant interest prospered and played a role in English social and economic affairs which made its presence felt more perhaps than ever before. The visible sign of its wealth and clout was the rapid rebuilding of London following the fire of 1666. As the City rose from the ashes, grander and more impressive than it had been before, contemporaries marvelled at this manifestation of its buoyant economy. Here clearly was an interest to be reckoned with politically.

In the reign of James II both the king and the traditional ruling class which he had antagonized made attempts to win that interest to their side. James preached the virtues of religious toleration as a promoter of prosperity. 'Trade he had much at heart', claimed Ailesbury, 'and his topic was liberty of conscience and many hands at work in trade.' The instructions given to judges going on circuit in 1688 emphasized this theme. James designed the happiness of his people so 'that trade may increase'. Toleration 'had already much increased the trade at home' and, if continued, would make England 'the chief seat of trade in Christendom'.[41] The king's opponents argued that liberty in general, and not just religious freedom, was vital for commerce to thrive. Absolutism in their view was detrimental to business, while more liberal regimes boosted it. Both cited the Dutch Republic as a model of a country where trade had flourished as a direct result of its polity. Where the king connected this with the fact that in religious matters the Dutch were the most tolerant people in Europe, his antagonists stressed that its republican constitution was more significant.

London was not just a port in James II's reign, but was also a significant centre for manufacturing. Indeed in the outer parishes to the north, east, and south, including Southwark, which grew much more rapidly than those within the walls, production was more important than distribution. It has been estimated that by 1680 these parishes made up 61 per cent of the capital's population, and that production in them accounted for 70 per cent of their economic activities while trading took up a

---

[41] Ailesbury, p. 103; *Publick Occurrences Truly Stated*, no. 14, 13 Mar. 1688.

mere 8 per cent. Manufacturing developed outside the walls to a large extent because it was not restricted by the gild regulations operating in the old city. Thus apprenticeship was not required in many of the trades in the suburbs. Along the river the maritime trades, not surprisingly, were prominent: anchorsmiths, caulkers, ropemakers, sailmakers, for example. Elsewhere there was a dramatic rise in the numbers of cordwainers, glovers, tailors, and others connected with the clothing industry; also cutlers, leatherworkers, smiths. In fact there was a growing profusion of producers for the huge market which lay at their doorsteps.[42]

These trademen and craftsmen would be aware of the religious and political issues of the age, if not from the press, then from the arrival of some 50,000 or 70,000 Huguenots in England during the 1680s. Many of those fleeing from persecution in France were artisans who made their way to the east end of London, bringing with them tales of their ordeals which doubtless lost nothing in the telling. They would also bring home to Londoners vividly the connections between popery and arbitrary power, however unfair such an equation was when applied to James II rather than to Louis XIV.

This association was made repeatedly in Whig propaganda during the Exclusion crisis. One of several prints executed by Stephen College was called *A Prospect of a Popish Successor: Displayed by Hell-bred Cruelty*, *Popish Villainy*, *Strange Divinity*, *Intended Slavery*, *Old England's Misery etc*. Even if they could not read the captions, they could see the symbolism of martyrs burning at the stake, the city on fire, and the figures of the pope, a cardinal, a devil, and other Catholic stereotypes presiding over the scene. During the Tory reaction there were popular prints against the Dissenters. One depicted a monstrous griffin-like creature, representing 'the Commonwealth ruling with a standing army'. The beast consumes crowns, churches, episcopacy, nobility, laws and statutes, and defecates liberties and taxes.[43]

Politicians of all persuasions, therefore, used the press to promote their views. In 1662 the Crown attempted to control

---

[42] A. L. Beier, 'Engine of Manufacture: The Trades of London', in Beier and Finlay (eds.), *The Making of the Metropolis*, pp. 141–67.

[43] J. Miller, *Religion and the Popular Prints, 1600–1832* (1986), 121, 127.

all publication by the Licensing Act, which set up a machinery of state censors to vet any material before it could be printed. During the Exclusion crisis the Act lapsed, and the Whigs took advantage of the relaxation of the censorship to release a flood of propaganda. The Crown reimposed the controls as soon as possible, first by obtaining a judicial opinion to uphold its right to regulate the press notwithstanding the lapsing of the Licensing Act, and then by renewing it in the parliament of 1685. Although this effectively stifled the English press, much propaganda against James was printed in Holland for dispersal in England. William of Orange had 60,000 copies of his Declaration made by Dutch presses for English consumption.[44]

How far such propaganda had any influence on public opinion, however, is difficult to assess. Election results might appear to offer a gauge of its effectiveness. But the fact that the Whigs won the three general elections held in 1679 and 1681, while there was a massive swing to the court in 1685, cannot be directly attributed to changes in the views of voters. The electoral system was too restrictive for the electorate as a whole to register its support freely for one side or the other.

There were 269 constituencies in England and Wales after the enfranchisement of Durham and Newark in Charles II's reign. The franchise in the fifty-two counties was uniform, having been restricted to the ownership of freehold property worth forty shillings a year. In the 217 boroughs, however, it varied considerably. Apart from the unique cases of Oxford and Cambridge Universities, where the MAs returned MPs to parliament, Yorkshire contained every type of borough, and can therefore be used to illustrate them. Burgage properties conveyed the right to vote to their proprietors in Boroughbridge, Knaresborough, Malton, Northallerton, Pontefract, Richmond, Ripon, and Thirsk. Only the members of the Corporation could vote in Scarborough. The freemen were enfranchised in Beverley and Hedon. Freemen and forty-shilling freeholders voted in Hull and York, for they were counties in their own right as well as cities. Finally in Aldborough the vote ultimately rested on a residential qualification. There could be disputes about the extent of the franchise in every type of parliamentary

[44] BL Add. MSS 41816, fo. 237: D. Petit to Middleton, Amsterdam, 5/15 Oct. 1688.

borough, but those like Aldborough, where inhabitants voted, were the most fruitful of them. In February 1679, for instance, Sir John Reresby claimed that only nine burgage holders could vote there, while his opponents insisted that all inhabitants paying scot and lot, or rates for the church and the maintenance of the poor, could vote. These numbered about seventy. The House of Commons upheld their case and Reresby was declared not duly elected.

Although Reresby recorded that 'there was a great dispute as to elections over all England at this time, as men stood affected to the government and to the then ministers, and as men believed them well intentioned or otherways', there is little evidence that this dispute affected the electors of Aldborough. On the contrary, as Reresby also noted, 'in most of these little boroughs, which consisted of mean and mercinary people, one had noe man sure longer than you was with him, and he that made him drunke or obliged him last was his first friend'. Having spent £20 entertaining the Aldborough burgesses trying unsuccessfully to get back into parliament at the second general election held in 1679, he had good grounds for his complaint. At the next election he spent £43 on entertainment and was not even opposed.[45]

Even in such boroughs, however, there are signs that some of the electors were swayed by national political considerations. Members of parliament for Aldborough, Boroughbridge, and Knaresborough, for example, regularly kept their constituents informed about proceedings in parliament. On one occasion Sir Henry Goodricke's newsletter to the burgage holders of Boroughbridge provoked a heated debate. When he informed them that he and his fellow MP had voted against the first Exclusion Bill, some hissed and accused their representatives of being papists. At this the parson of the parish took umbrage and said angrily 'that though God should in revenge set over us even a Devil incarnate yet ought we of the Church of England to be obedient for conscience sake in what was not directly opposite to God's express will in the Scriptures'. For his pains he was taken to be a crypto-papist himself.[46]

There was, moreover, a difference between 'most of the little

---

[45] Reresby, pp. 169, 186.
[46] Leeds RO Mexborough MSS 14/75: E. Morris to Reresby, 8 June 1679.

boroughs' and the cities and counties. Constituencies with under five hundred voters, and above all those with under a hundred, could be venal or subservient to their local élites. Election results were rarely the outcome of swings in public opinion in such boroughs. Where over five hundred could poll, however, they were in a position to exercise some freedom of choice, and to base that choice on opinion. In 1685 Sir John Reresby found electioneering at York, which had nearly two thousand electors, rather different from his experiences at Aldborough. It is true that he had to entertain and to spend money. Indeed he spent £350, a good deal more than in the smaller borough. Yet he noted that 'it cost them more that lost it'. The contest did not just hinge on the financial outlay.[47]

About three years before he stood as a parliamentary candidate for the city, Reresby had drawn up an account of York for the marquis of Halifax. This made it clear that it was divided from top to bottom into Whigs and Tories.

The loyall party in York is much inferiour in nomber to the factious. The first consists of the gentry, clergie, officers and dependents of the Church, militia officers and souldiers; and about a fourth part (as is computed) of the cittyzens; the secound of the Maior and whole magistracy (two aldermen only excepted) the sheriffs and most of the common council, with the rest of that citty. . . . It is now come to that, that ther is not only a separation of interests, but few doe buy of, or have any commerce but with thos of their own principle.[48]

The regulation of the boroughs for electoral purposes exploited such separations of interests. Exeter became 'miserably divided and distracted' by it, according to the earl of Bath.

You may easily imagine it to be a great mortification to them to see the most substantial, rich, loyal citizens turned out of the government for no offence and never so much as asked any questions by the regulators . . . to be domineered over by a packed chamber of Dissenters, and to see the sword, which was never known in the memory of man in this city, carried every Sunday before the Mayor in state to a conventicle.

In Norwich, too, the substantial citizens who made up the ruling Anglican-Tory group were superseded not even by prominent Whigs but by men with little local status, one of

[47] Reresby, p. 358.   [48] Ibid. 579.

whom, a new alderman, had to borrow horses to appear with suitable dignity at the assizes.[49]

The gentry, clergy, and magistrates were not the only politically aware sections of society. The lower orders, too, could become very involved in politics. It is usual to assume that they were almost entirely in sympathy with the Whigs. Certainly the first earl of Shaftesbury could get the crowds out on the streets, for example by holding massive pope-burning processions on the anniversaries of the Gunpowder Plot and Queen Elizabeth's accession in 1679 and 1680. Similar demonstrations took place in James II's reign, despite the king's attempts to ban them. And mob attacks on Catholic targets reached a crescendo in an orgy of destruction during the crisis of the Revolution in 1688. Chapels were attacked and many gutted in provincial towns such as Newcastle upon Tyne, Norwich, and York, and above all in London. The most spectacular incident was the sacking of the Spanish ambassador's residence on 11 December. On the other hand, Timothy Harris has established that it is erroneous to think of a single homogeneous London crowd under the later Stuarts. There were popular demonstrations showing Tory as well as Whig sympathies. In November 1682 a correspondent in the capital informed Sir John Reresby that on the fifth 'the streets were filled with the rabble and the usual conflicts between whig and tory'. The November celebrations witnessed the burning of Jack Presbyter by Tories as well as effigies of the pope by Whigs. Similar ceremonies took place in Norwich on 29 May 1682, the anniversary of Charles II's Restoration, and in Wells on 9 September 1683, the day of thanksgiving for the suppression of the Rye House Plot.[50]

Wells was, however, a royalist town. Two years later the duke of Monmouth could only recruit thirteen men from amongst its inhabitants, compared with ninety-five from Lyme Regis, and 354 from Taunton. His rebel army took their

---

[49] *CSPD 1687–9* (1972), 305; J. T. Evans, *Seventeenth Century Norwich* (1979), 314.

[50] Leeds RO Mexborough MSS 22/27: T. Harris, 'The Politics of the London Crowd in the Reign of Charles II', unpublished Ph.D. thesis, (Cambridge, 1985); W. L. Sachse, 'The Mob and the Revolution of 1688', *Journal of British Studies*, 4 (1964), 23–40.

revenge on Wells by desecrating the cathedral during their temporary occupation of the town. Three-quarters of Monmouth's three thousand or so followers came from Somerset, and most of those from an area bordered by Bridgewater in the north, Axminster in the south, and Wellington in the west. Indeed half the rebels came from some seventeen places, many of them textile towns experiencing depression. They consisted largely of clothworkers and craftsmen. There were hardly any gentry and, for a predominantly rural area, relatively few farmers or farm labourers. Not that crude economic determinism can be cited in explanation of their motivation. There were personal factors too. Recruitment was relatively easier where populations were concentrated. Communication made it harder for scattered inhabitants to make contact with Monmouth. He landed at the height of the hay-making season, aggravating the problem for farmers and their labourers. Moreover, as we have seen, craftsmen were better off in the 1680s than at any other time in the seventeenth century. Many of them were Dissenters, with strong religious reasons for preferring 'King' Monmouth to King James. They were probably not veterans who could remember the Interregnum and were still supporting the 'good old cause', but young men in their teens and early twenties.[51]

Nevertheless, the fact that the élite of the south-west not only refused to join Monmouth but worked assiduously to crush his rebellion did exacerbate social tensions between them and the rebels. The duke's forces extracted a contribution from Longleat House by the simple expedient of threatening to burn it down. The houses of Sir William Portman and Lord Stawell were plundered. Such excesses revived memories of the civil wars, and a horrified gentry voted the king ample sums to crush the rebellion. In 1685 they feared social upheaval from below, and rallied to the Crown. By 1688 they had come to fear it from the king himself.

For James's determination to find allies to assist him in his campaign to remove disabilities from Catholics led him to seek them amongst social groups which had not enjoyed power since the Interregnum. The refusal of the substantial landed gentry to co-operate with his policy forced him to go below that level in

---

[51] P. Earle, *Monmouth's Rebels* (1977); R. Clifton, *The Last Popular Rebellion* (1984).

an attempt to find collaborators: minor gentry in the counties; business and professional men in towns. In this respect James was as much of a social revolutionary as Cromwell. Indeed the parallels between the two men can be quite striking. Both sought religious toleration; both were military leaders who rode roughshod over parliaments which stood in their way and strove to find more compliant ones; and both terrified the ruling classes, who feared a radical upheaval from below.

The eventual outcome of the social and political changes of the Interregnum was a reassertion of the authority of the landed élite at the Restoration, coupled with a reaction against those inferior bodies which had usurped it. On the surface a similar result can be discerned in the Revolution. Reacting to the subversive activities of a radical monarch, the territorial magnates cashiered him and installed another on terms which assured their own ascendancy. Certainly the aristocratic rather than the bourgeois nature of the post-Revolution regime is clear.

And yet the ruling groups which emerged from the Revolution were significantly different from those which triumphed at the Restoration. Although the landed interest was still predominant, there were bourgeois elements which were much more evident under William and Anne than they had been under Charles II. Among those which were admitted to a greater share of power were the commercial classes, especially of the City of London. Merchants and financiers loomed larger in the political nation after 1689 than they had done before.

The accommodation of commercial and financial interests in the post-Revolution polity was the pay-off for the deal which they had made with the landed interest during the reign of James II. Landowners honoured their debt in hard cash, by accepting direct taxation on their estates. They also accepted the creation of a machinery of public credit. As with the religious settlement, the day of reckoning did not find the political nation united. Many Tories resented the social implications of the alliance which had been forged to forestall James II's attempt to create an alternative structure of politics. Thus the problems of absorbing the different interests into a ruling class were to remain on the agenda for at least another three decades.

10

Reluctant Revolutionaries

֍

I see the Duke of Somerset, the Earl of Burlington, the Earl
of Scarsdale and some other Lords who had all been active
to bring in the Prince speak in another strain. Some said the
thing was gone further than they expected, others that they
never believed the Prince would contend for the Crown.

(Sir John Reresby, *Memoirs*, 3 Feb. 1689)

Lord Abingdon made great protestations to me, that if he
had thought this revolution of government would have
happened he would never have gone in to the Prince of
Orange.

(The earl of Clarendon, *Diary*, 9 Mar. 1689)

JAMES II's actions eventually alienated a majority of his English
subjects. But they did not all react in the same way to his
measures. Many acquiesced in them, not wishing to risk the
consequences of resistance. Memories were still vivid of the
civil wars and the devastation which they had inflicted upon
society. For a few years it seemed as though the world had been
turned upside down. The king had been executed. Bishops and
lords had been abolished. England had become a republic. The
fabric of county communities was also torn as first parliament
and then the army had interfered with the running of local
government. Under the Major-Generals the counties themselves had even been superseded, and England had become in a
contemporary expression 'cantonized'. Although the traditional
administrative areas survived, the leading landowners who
traditionally administered them had been in many instances set
aside and replaced by lesser gentry.

At the Restoration in 1660 the institutions of local government were restored along with king, bishops, and lords at the
centre. The county militias and commissions of the peace were

also put back into the hands of the magnates and squires. These formed the backbone of the Tory party, which emerged during the Exclusion crisis to support the principle of divine, indefeasible hereditary right against the Whigs who sought to dispossess the heir to the Crown. They accused the Whigs and their dissenting allies of reviving the 'good old cause' of the regicides and republicans. The Tory reaction which followed the dissolution of the Oxford parliament owed much to the fear of civil war engendered by Whig militancy.

It also owed much to the alliance of Church and Crown. 'No bishop no king' had become proverbial by the late-seventeenth century. The notion that the Church of England was a bulwark against anarchy, levellers, and republicans was deeply engrained in the Tory mentality. Anglican monopoly of power, whether in boroughs as a result of the Corporation Act of 1661, or under the Crown as guaranteed by the Test Act of 1673, was regarded by Tories as essential to preserve the constitution in Church and State.

The advent of a Catholic ruler was therefore deeply disturbing to them. What would happen when the Supreme Governor of the Church of England was an avowed papist? Whigs had warned that such an anomaly would strain the constitution to breaking point. Tories hoped against hope that they could maintain their traditional principles of allegiance to both Crown and Church. They faced a major dilemma of principle when it dawned on them that they might have to choose between them.

The dilemma was slow to dawn. At first James's assurance that he would 'endeavour to preserve this government in church and state as it is by law established', which he gave to the Privy Council immediately after his accession, and repeated in his speech at the opening of parliament, reassured them. 'This speech was soon printed', observed Burnet, 'and gave great content to those who believed that he would stick to the promises made in it.' Sir John Reresby also recorded that it 'in a great measure did quiet the minds and apprehensions of people'.[1]

Reresby, who was both a staunch Anglican and Governor of York, tried more than most to reconcile his loyalties to Church

---

[1] Grey, viii. 344; Burnet, iii. 7; Reresby, p. 353.

and Crown. By the end of the reign, although he still protested his allegiance to both, it seems that he had compromised his religious conscience to retain his post. In this respect he was not unlike Thomas Bruce, future earl of Ailesbury, whose maxim was 'not to make one step against my conscience, on the other hand to be silent and to keep my place in court as long as I could'.[2] Others decided that they could not serve God and Mammon.

The time taken to reach the decision varied with individuals. Among the first was the archbishop of Canterbury, who refused to serve on the commission for ecclesiastical causes when it was set up in 1686. More dramatic was the resolution of the earl of Rochester to quit as Lord Treasurer early in 1687. Although he had been prepared to serve on the ecclesiastical commission, and even to entertain the notion of a conversion to Catholicism, his removal from office was a major signal that James could no longer work with High Church Anglicans to achieve his ends. The Declaration of Indulgence and the assault upon Magdalen College, Oxford, seemed to most of them to be in breach of the assurances he had given to the Church of England at his accession.

The problem, though, was what to do about it? What could men do when the monarch was behaving in ways which were intolerable to them? There were not many options open to the subjects of James II when he began to pursue aims which they found unacceptable. Resistance was a possibility only for a tiny minority. For most it was out of the question. Even those ousted from the commissions of the peace and replaced by justices they regarded as inferiors continued to co-operate with the new benches on the grounds that the king's business must be carried on.[3]

They could hope that he would hold a session of parliament, and that the peers and MPs would represent their views to him. It is significant that towards the end of the repeated prorogations members of both Houses turned up in some force, either to

---

[2] Ailesbury, p. 153.
[3] On this, see a remarkable letter from Sir Daniel Fleming to 'T.B. Esq', Rydal, 27 July 1688. Anticipating his own removal from the commission, Fleming instructed the recipient how to continue proceedings which were in train (Cumbria RO Kendal Fleming MSS 3235).

prevent the king taking advantage of low attendance to rush his measures through, or in genuine hopes that debate would be allowed. But this potential safety valve was removed when parliament was dissolved in July 1687.

Indeed the whole idea of parliament acting as a constitutional check on the monarch was jeopardized by the king's decision to pack a new one in order to get it to endorse his measures. Until James tried this his subjects could take comfort from the thought that there were legal limitations to his power which would ultimately safeguard the Church of England. As Sir John Kaye had expressed it in a letter to Sir John Reresby at the height of the Exclusion crisis, 'So long as we transgress not the laws of the land, but make them, loyalty to our Sovereign and the Protestant religion as we have it now by Law happily established amongst us, the rule of our actions, we may bid a defiance to all Popish fooleries and fopperies and phanatical and enthusiastical treacheries and perfidiousness.'[4] The fact that the Church of England was 'by law established' seemed to offer it protection from both quarters. But when its Supreme Governor became a Roman Catholic, and used the royal prerogative to undermine its privileges, then Kaye's position became harder to sustain. It could be maintained by the arguments that the dispensing and suspending powers as James employed them were illegal. The king was ultimately subject to the rule of law and therefore in the end would be bound to retract. But when the very legislature was capable of succumbing to his will, this hope faded. James could get the prerogative powers endorsed by a parliament 'shuffled, cut and packed by Mr Brent and his missionaries'.[5] Then Kaye's faith in the law would be confounded. It is significant that he was one of the magistrates of the West Riding who collectively signed answers to the three questions which denied their very legality.

Being there is no commission produced from the King neither any authority appears to us by the Statutes of the Militia whereby answers to the questions may be required, we take leave to make this

---

[4] Leeds RO Mexborough MSS 15/69: Kaye to Reresby, 20 Nov. 1680.

[5] *A Modest vindication of the Petition of the Lords Spiritual and Temporal for the Calling of a Free Parliament* (Exeter, 21 Nov. 1688). The gentry were reported by a newsletter to believe it 'the most fatal of all things that something may be made like laws by the power of the Papist' (*CSPD 1687–9* (1972), 388).

Declaration that we think ourselves under no obligation to reply to them otherwise than to show our willingness to express our obedience whenever and by whomsoever the King's name is made use of.

1. If any of us be chosen members of parliament we judge we ought not to preingage ourselves by consenting to the demands before arguments may be heard and considered in parliament. And we are further sensible that the Protestant church may be deeply concerned herein as to its security which church we are bound to support by all lawful means.

2. Until such penal laws and Test may be made appear to be repugnant to the Protestant interest we cannot contribute to any such election.

3. We shall live peaceably with all men as it's every good christian's duty to do and in what may be required of us we shall endeavour to acquit ourselves with a due regard to the laws and the discharge of good conscience.[6]

The canvassing of opinion by James was the first move in his campaign to pack parliament. It alarmed people about his intentions. At the same time, as replies were concerted and the results became known, they took heart, since it revealed that a majority were strongly opposed to the king's measures. Previously, with no national forum for debate following the prorogation of parliament in November 1685, and with a relatively effective censorship, they had been in the dark about the attitudes of subjects across the kingdom. Now it became clear that public opinion was not in favour of relaxing the laws debarring Catholics from holding office. As a correspondent of Willem Bentinck observed, the canvass 'has not only healed our sores by uniting people, but has been the happiest occasion to show the people that they are united'.[7]

The Prince of Orange indicated that he shared their views in *Pensionary Fagel's Letter to James Stewart* dated 4 November 1687. This gave 'an account of the Prince and Princess of Orange's Thoughts concerning the repeal of the Test and the Penal Laws'. It was almost as if they were giving their own answer to the king's three questions. Thus they asserted 'that it is their opinion that no Christian ought to be persecuted for his

---

[6] Bodleian Rawlinson MSS 139a, fo. 233: 'The answers of the gentlemen justices taken at Pontefract the 20th of August 1688.' There is a copy in Cumbria RO Carlisle D/Lons/L1/1/34/6. Kaye was among the conspirators who seized York for William.

[7] Nottingham University Library Portland MSS Misc. PWA 2103.

conscience', which implicitly answered the third. 'And if his majesty shall think fit farther to desire their concurrence in the repealing of the penal laws,' the tract continued, 'they are ready to give it, provided always that those laws remain still in their full vigour, by which the Roman Catholicks are shut out of both houses of parliament and out of all publick employments, ecclesiastical, civil and military.'[8]

William's intervention in English politics signalled the end of a period in which the king had made most of the running. Until the fall of 1687 most Englishmen seem to have adopted an attitude of wait and see. Some clearly thought that, given enough rope, James would hang himself. His policies were doomed to failure. He could never hope to achieve the permanent relaxation of the penal laws which he sought. But his determination to pack a parliament to repeal them led people to the realization that it was at least a possibility. Moreover the announcement in November that the queen was pregnant also concentrated minds. If she produced a son, then the appalling prospect of another Catholic successor dawned. No longer, therefore, could they afford to wait upon events. Something had to be done to divert their course before it became too late. It is at this stage that the Glorious Revolution entered the cloak-and-dagger phase. A secret correspondence was established between the more discontented of James's subjects and William Bentinck, a confidant of William of Orange. ''Tis certainly believed by all our wise men except Mylord Halifax', Bentinck was informed on 8 December, 'that we shall have a Parliament, and they say more certain, that it will be a packed one, chose only by those that return it, and that the prince should take his measures what he will do in that case, for that we must never expect to see a free parliament here under the present state of affairs.' A week later information was conveyed to the Dutch about a conspiracy in the army.

There is at present in agitation a proposal (which HM likes mightily) to make the army by way of address promise to HM to concur with him in taking off the penal laws and Test. Many will not do it, come what will. Many are poor, and will not do it, if they can have any assurance of bread. Some of the best officers of the army have been with

---

[8] *A Collection of Scarce and Valuable Tracts . . . of the late Lord Somers*, ed. W. Scott (2nd edn.; 1813), ix. 183–8.

Mr Sidney about this. He told them much could be done, but they might be sure all that the Prince and other Protestants could do for them would be done.[9]

According to Burnet, Henry Sidney was 'the man in whose hands the conduct of the whole design was chiefly deposited'. He had been envoy to Holland from 1679 to 1685, during which time his brother Algernon Sidney had been executed for his alleged implication in the Rye House Plot. Undeterred by this he co-ordinated the Orangist conspiracy of 1688, which culminated in the invitation to William of 30 June to which was appended his cipher and that of six other conspirators. Sidney's contacts with 'some of the best officers of the army' enabled the Immortal Seven to assure William that 'we do upon very good grounds believe that their army then would be very much divided among themselves, many of the officers being so discontented that they continue in their service only for a subsistence (besides that some of their minds are known already)'. Among those whose minds were known were John Churchill, Percy Kirke, and Charles Trelawny. Churchill wrote to William personally on 4 August, informing him that

Mr Sidney will let you know how I intend to behave myself: I think it is what I owe to God and my country. My honour I take leave to put into Your Royal Highness' hands, in which I think it is safe. If you think there is any thing else that I ought to do, you have but to command me, and I shall pay an entire obedience to it, being resolved to die in that religion that it hath pleased God to give you both the will and power to protect.

Such assurances that the high command of James's army would desert probably persuaded William of Orange to risk an invasion more than any other calculation.[10]

Certainly he would have been foolhardly to have trusted much to the more general claims made by the invitation that 'nineteen parts of twenty of the people throughout the kingdom . . . are desirous of a change and . . . it is no less certain that much the greater part of the nobility and gentry are as much

---

[9] Nottingham University Library Portland MSS Misc. PWA 2087–178. See W. A. Speck, 'The Orangist Conspiracy against James II', *Historical Journal*, 30 (1987), 455–6.

[10] Burnet, iii. 277; Dalrymple, II, ii. 299, 239.

dissatisfied'. The answers to the three questions, while they revealed that a majority of those canvassed did not approve of James's religious proposals, nevertheless indicated a substantial degree of support for them. And it would have been rash to conclude that those who opposed them were ready to rise when William landed.

Indeed he might have questioned how far the Seven were 'the most prudent and most knowing persons that we have in this nation', as Sidney claimed in the letter which accompanied the invitation. Although revered as the Immortal Seven, they were hardly household names, and even Macaulay's omniscient schoolboys might well have had difficulty in identifying them all. Danby would no doubt spring instantly to mind. He had dominated the political scene as Lord Treasurer for most of the 1670s. The earl of Devonshire had achieved notoriety in James's reign for incurring a swingeing fine after being convicted of brawling at court. The bishop of London had also attracted considerable attention after being deprived of his episcopal functions by the commission for ecclesiastical causes. Lord Lumley, Edward Russell, and the earl of Shrewsbury, however, although they became prominent figures after the Revolution, could scarcely be numbered amongst front-rank politicians at the time. Lumley was a landowner in County Durham, who ironically became a convert to Protestantism from Roman Catholicism during James's reign. Russell, like Sidney, had a more celebrated brother who had been executed for involvement in the Rye House Plot. Charles Talbot, earl of Shrewsbury, was a wealthy local magnate in Oxfordshire, who reputedly loaned William £30,000 during the Revolution. In April William had indicated that he would respond to an invitation from 'some men of the best interest, and the most valued in the nation'.[11] He must have been disappointed that the Seven were the best Sidney could come up with.

The really substantial politicians whom James had offended declined to become involved. Halifax, prudent and cautious as ever, would not commit himself. The earl of Nottingham at first joined in, then got cold feet and backed down. 'He saith 'tis scruples of conscience', observed Sidney, 'but we all conclude

[11] Burnet, iii. 240–1.

'tis another passion.' They were only partly right. Nottingham admitted that he 'did not dare to proceed in an affair of which the next step would be high treason'. At the same time he consulted two clergymen, Stillingfleet and the bishop of St Asaph, as to whether one could 'in conscience endeavour to oppose by force a manifest design of destroying our religious and civil rights and liberties?' They both advised him that it could not be done.[12]

It is highly significant that the High–Church Tory sought the advice of Anglican clergy at this juncture. For the bishops and leading London divines took a very different line from that of the Orangist conspirators. In this respect the bishop of London was most untypical. The circumstances surrounding the petition of the seven bishops showed that there was another alternative to merely acquiescing in the king's measures than playing the Orange card.

About the time that the earl of Nottingham was consulting clerical friends with his case of conscience, some London clergymen sought his advice as to whether or not to read the Declaration of Indulgence to their congregations. 'He was utterly against their refusal', according to Roger Morrice, 'unless they were unanimous therein.'[13]

In fact there was near unanimity amongst the Anglican clergy not to obey the order in Council requiring them to read the Declaration during divine service. Their refusal gave a moral lead to Englishmen reluctant to resist the king, and a signal to him that he could no longer rely on the passive obedience of his subjects. The clergy felt themselves to be in the front line of the battle against popery, and had suffered casualties from the suspension of the bishop of London to the ejection of the Fellows of Magdalen College, Oxford. They were sceptical of the king's commitment to toleration, since it seemed a strange kind of tolerance which would not tolerate the expression of views held by the majority of his subjects. Now a stand had to be made.

Their refusal to obey the king required considerable courage given the Church's special relationship with the Crown.

[12] H. Horwitz, *Revolution Politicks: The Career of Daniel Finch, Second Earl of Nottingham* (1968), 52–3.
[13] Morrice MS Q, p. 255.

Tremendous pressure was put on those in the dioceses of Chester, Durham, and St Davids by their time-serving bishops. Cartwright of Chester sent orders to his clergy to read the Declaration, together with a 'menace of suspending such of the ministers as should fayle to reade it'. Notwithstanding his threats it was read in only one church in Chester, and then after most of the congregation had gone out, while very few churches in the county heard it.[14] Lord Crewe, bishop of Durham, likewise urged the clergy in his diocese to obey the order, yet even in his own cathedral he could prevail with 'not one major or minor canon resident'. It was read in only sixty-five churches within the bishopric.[15] From Wales it was reported that 'the Bishop of St Davids plays the fury amongst our Welsh clergy . . . and is about suspending . . . several of the best clergy for not reading the king's declaration and has ordained 20 silly ignorant people who will comply'.[16]

Elsewhere the disobedience was even more universal. One informed estimate was that 'of 9000 churches in England but 400 ministers read it'. Above all the London clergy took the lead in defying the king's instructions. After several consultations between bishops and leading London divines, it was agreed to present a petition to James requesting him not to insist upon their reading the Declaration.[17]

What they expected the king to do when the bishops petitioned him is not quite clear. They could scarcely have

[14] PRO 30/53/8, fos. 60, 63: A. Newport to Lord Herbert, 19 May, 9 June 1688.

[15] *Publications of the Surtees Society* (1865), xlvii, 147. Crewe was alleged to have suspended 133 clergymen for refusing to read the Declaration (Algemeen Rijksarchief, The Hague, Fagel Archive 1:10:19:2017, newsletter, 10 Aug. 1688). He was also accused of having put three questions to his clergy, to the effect that it was a matter of conscience and expediency to obey the order, but he emphatically denied it, blaming his Dean for the rumour (BL Egerton MSS 3335, fo. 4; Cumbria RO Kendal, Fleming MSS 3198: bishop of Carlisle to Sir Daniel Fleming, 14 May 1688).

[16] Bodleian Carte MSS 130, fo. 317: R. Price to the duke of Beaufort, 30 June 1688.

[17] *The Life and Times of Anthony Wood*, ed. A. Clark (Oxford, 1894), ii. 267; R. Thomas, 'The Seven Bishops and their Petition', *Journal of Ecclesiastical History*, 12 (1961), 24–5; G. V. Bennett, 'The Seven Bishops: A Reconsideration', in D. Baker (ed.), *Religious Motivation* (Studies in Church History, 15; 1978), 280–3.

thought that he would actually rescind the order. He had shown his inflexible determination to pursue his aim of religious toleration too single-mindedly to back down now. Moreover, they did not object to that goal. On the contrary, they indicated their readiness to consider measures of comprehension and toleration in Convocation and parliament, though ominously for James only for Protestant Dissenters and not for his co-religionists. It even seems that he was prepared to accept objections to his aims. What took him aback was the petitioners' attack upon his suspending power. By declaring it to be illegal, they challenged the very foundation of his attempt to get by his prerogative what he had failed to obtain through parliament. He was bound to retaliate vigorously to this challenge.

Perhaps that was the intention of the petitioners. By petitioning against the suspending power, they brought the question of its legality to a head. The dispensing power had been tried before the judges in the case of Godden versus Hales. Then all but one of them had declared in its favour. Although many thought the judgment perverse, it had nevertheless settled the matter for the time being. There had been no similar trial of the suspending power. All that the petition could cite in support of the claim that it was illegal were resolutions of the House of Commons declaring it to be so. By challenging it head on they virtually forced James either to bring the issue to a proper trial or by refusing to do so implicitly to acknowledge the illegality of his actions.

The king accepted the challenge by prosecuting the bishops. Although technically the prosecution was for seditious libel, which need not have involved the suspending power at all, everybody at the time accepted that the prerogative was on trial as well as the bishops. During the proceedings 'the dispensing power was banded on both hands'.[18] The verdict, therefore, was a shattering blow to the power of the Crown. By acquitting the seven bishops, the jury in effect found James guilty. The implication was that all who held office under the Crown and who had not taken communion in the Church of England according to the Test Act, unless they had received individual dispensations, were unlawfully appointed. While many of the

[18] PRO 30/53/8, fo. 65. Anon. to Lord Herbert, 30 June 1688.

Crown's servants at the centre had been granted dispensations, the great majority of local officials in the commissions of the peace and the corporations depended upon the Declarations of Indulgence for their legitimacy. James's government was coming apart at the seams before William of Orange invaded. There was a widespread refusal to serve under Catholics whom James had appointed to offices with dispensations from taking the religious tests. Thus on 7 October Roger Kenyon noted 'that the Protestant gentry will not, can not, joyne in Lancashire in the execution of any office with such as will not qualify themselves to act according to law'.[19] Only a packed parliament prepared to put the Declaration on the statute book could have undone the damage. When the king decided not to go ahead with the planned general election, therefore, the reversal of many of his measures became inevitable.

This is what the bishops and many of their supporters were waiting for. They were not revolutionaries, and certainly not Orangists. What they wanted was for the king to come to his senses and realize the error of his ways. In their eyes, since the removal from office of the Hyde brothers, Lords Clarendon and Rochester, James had been hijacked by a small clique of Catholics and careerists led by the earl of Sunderland.

They took heart when James consulted them, agreed to reverse many of his schemes, and dismissed Sunderland. It seemed as though they had obtained their objective, and that things were being restored to the situation which had obtained when the reign began. However, as Robert Beddard has observed,

The fruits of this attempted reconciliation were disappointingly small. The straitness of time, royal ineptitude, a divided episcopate, a peerage that had fallen victim to faction and the persistent and well-nigh universal feeling of distrust throughout the kingdom—all these contributed to frustrate the renewed efforts of James's 'old friends' to resettle 'things upon the foot they were at his coming to the crown'. James's first escape undoubtedly complicated their task, while his

[19] HMC Kenyon, p. 198. Compare the refusal of the deputy-lieutenants of Derbyshire to serve under a Catholic Lord-Lieutenant and that of the gentry in Yorkshire to accept commissions in the militia if any Catholics held them. HMC Seventh Report Appendix: *Graham*, p. 412; Cumbria RO Carlisle D/Lons/L1/1/34/8.

second removal fearfully perplexed his supporters, who were left in the unenviable situation of having to fight, as best they could, a rearguard action in a desparate bid to salvage both their master's kingship and their own claims to political consideration.[20]

The fact was that 'the counter revolution of the loyalists', as Dr Beddard calls it, was rendered abortive by the Revolution itself. Between William's landing in Torbay on 5 November and the flight of the king to France on 22 December, events took on a momentum which swept aside all attempts to stop them in their course. Support for the intervention of the Prince of Orange, above all for the summoning of a 'free' parliament, was so overwhelming that nothing short of the military defeat of the Dutch invaders could have prevented their realization.

William's Declaration appealed for mass support. 'We do', he proclaimed,

invite and require all persons whatsoever, all the peers of the realm, both spiritual and temporal, all Lords Lieutenants, deputy lieutenants, and all gentlemen, citizens and other commons of all ranks, to come and assist us, in order to the executing of this our Design, against all such as shall endeavour to oppose us, that so we may prevent all those miseries which must needs follow upon the nation's being kept under arbitrary government and slavery, and that all the violences and disorders, which may have overturned the whole Constitution of the English government, may be fully redressed, in a free and legal Parliament.[21]

The response to the invitation was disappointing in terms of those who actually joined him. Even the immediate neighbour-hood where he landed in Devonshire did not rush to his standard, though it bore the legend 'For the Protestant Religion and Liberty'. It was not until 16 November, eleven days after the landing, that significant numbers of gentry joined him in Exeter. Then, according to a pamphlet intended to impress Londoners, and therefore doubtless exaggerating for propaganda purposes, 'every day the gentry from all parts of Devon and Somerset etc. flocked to him in great numbers'. In welcoming them William could not forbear to say 'we expected you that

---

[20] R. A. Beddard, 'The Loyalist Opposition in the Interregnum', *Bulletin of the Institute of Historical Research*, 90 (1967), 102.

[21] Cobbett, v. 11.

dwelt so near the place of our landing would have joined us sooner'.[22] Certainly he had not been joined by the 'great numbers' promised by the Immortal Seven in their invitation.

They had also promised 'to attend Your Highness upon your landing'. Three actually accompanied the prince in the invasion fleet. The other four, however, Danby, Devonshire, Lumley and the bishop of London, were not in a position to join him in Exeter, being many days' march away in Yorkshire and the Midlands, and cut off from Devon by the royal forces. When William planned a western invasion, Danby plotted a northern uprising in support of it. The headquarters were at Ribston Hall, near Knaresborough, home of Sir Henry Goodricke. Danby was joined there by the earl of Devonshire on 1 October. They resolved 'that on November 1st they will seize York'.[23] The plan had to be postponed when it was learned that William's first attempt to launch the expedition in October had been beaten back by storms. On 7 November, however, they received the news that he had landed in Torbay.

This was the signal they had awaited. Sir Henry Goodricke proposed holding a meeting of the gentry and freeholders of the county at York on the 22nd, ostensibly to draw up a declaration of loyalty to the king in that time of danger. The Governor of York, Sir John Reresby, unsuspectingly agreed that it was an excellent suggestion. 'Accordingly a paper of summons was written and dispersed to give notice throughout the county.' Sir John himself signed it, along with other deputy-lieutenants of the three Ridings.[24]

With singularly inept timing James II chose that week to announce the dismissal of nearly thirty of the principal gentlemen of the West Riding from the commission of the peace, including Goodricke. As Reresby, who despaired on

[22] *A Letter from a Gentleman in Exeter to his Friend in London* (1688); J. Whittle, *An Exact Diary of the Late Expedition of his Illustrious Highness the Prince of Orange into England* (1689), 51; BL Egerton MSS 2621, fo. 45. Bentinck attributed the reluctance of the Devon gentry to their being intimidated by the savage suppression of Monmouth's rebellion in the West (Japikse, II, ii. 626).

[23] A. M. Evans, 'Yorkshire and the Revolution of 1688', *Yorkshire Archaeological Journal*, 29 (1929), 271.

[24] Reresby, p. 526; HMC Seventh Report Appendix; *Graham*, 415–16. The original letter to the deputy-lieutenants of Yorkshire summarized on p. 416, now in the British Library, contains Reresby's signature.

hearing the news, observed, 'I fear this matter being unseason-
ably notified at such a time may change the good measures we
were upon and divide the country.' Though the gentlemen at
York did not seem unduly concerned at it, the news doubtless
stiffened the resolve of those who had plotted to use the meeting
as a pretext to seize the city for William of Orange. Instead of
drawing up a declaration of loyalty, they drew up a petition for
a free parliament. When the draft was being circulated for
signatures, Christopher Tancred ran into the hall and cried out
'that the papists were risen and had fired at the militia troops'.
This was the pre-arranged pretext for Danby and about one
hundred mounted gentlemen to rush up to the militia calling out
'a free parliament and the Protestant religion and no Popery'. Sir
John Reresby was completely taken aback, 'not believing
it possible that men of such quality and estates (however
dissatisfied) would engage in a design so desperate, and so
contrary to the laws of the land and the religion which they
professed'. The militia refused to obey his orders. Sir Henry
Bellasis, who according to Reresby 'had commanded a regiment
in Holland under the Prince, and lurked long here in Yorkshire
for his services', put the Governor of York under house arrest.[25]

After seizing York, the rebels sent a detachment led by
Thomas Fairfax to Leeds to collect contributions for the Prince
of Orange. Amongst those raised was £314 which they
appropriated from the receiver of the hearth tax.

The most important strategic centres in the county besides
York were Scarborough and Hull. Danby had contacted the
garrison in Scarborough castle at the time when plans were
being made to capture York. When news came that the county
town had fallen, the garrison entered and took Scarborough,
declaring for a free parliament. On learning of the success at
Scarborough, Danby wrote to William of Orange to inform
him that the castle was taken, along with 'a very good magazine
both of cannon and ammunition' and that he had 'put a garrison
in the place to secure it'.[26]

He also told the prince that he was 'in some hopes of making
myself master of Hull, but dare not assure myself of it'. Hull

[25] Reresby, pp. 526–9.
[26] A. Browning, *Thomas Osborne, Earl of Danby* (3 vols.; Glasgow, 1944–
51), ii. 144.

was a major garrison town, with nearly two thousand troops under the command of the Catholic Governor, Lord Langdale. Langdale, who had conscripted civilians to strengthen the town's fortifications, assured James that he could withstand a siege—Danby's doubts about the feasibility of seizing a town so heavily fortified seemed to be eminently justified.

However, the earl had a fifth column in the Hull garrison led by Sir John Hanmer, a lieutenant-colonel in the regiment commanded by the Catholic Lord Montgomery. Hanmer was encouraged by the promise of the enormous bribe of £5,000, to be paid within a month of the town's being taken for the Prince of Orange. He was also promised the help of one thousand men from York. In the event Hull fell without this assistance. Hanmer was able to prevail upon the Lieutenant-Governor, Lionel Copley, to surprise Langdale, Montgomery, and other Catholic officers in a night operation with the support of Protestant soldiers. Copley took over as Governor, and declared 'for the King and the Protestant religion'. This was not the declaration for a free parliament which had been made at York and Scarborough, and Danby confessed to William of Orange that the Protestant officers of Hull were 'not so free in their declaration as I could wish'. Nevertheless the securing of Hull for the Protestant cause was a major blow to the king, notwithstanding the loyalty which the rebels declared for him. Years later an eyewitness claimed that 'King James was never startled until he was informed that [Danby] had secured Hull and York'.[27]

Meanwhile the conspirators had raised the prince's standard in the Midlands. On 15 November Lord Delamere issued an appeal to his tenants to join him the following day, providing either a horse or money. 'I impose on no man', he insisted, 'but let him lay his hand on his heart and consider what he is willing to give to recover his religion and liberty.' When his tenantry mustered, he led them to Nottingham. The earl of Devonshire also raised his tenants and marched into Derby on 17 November, where he issued a declaration for a free parliament, before adjourning to Nottingham, which he entered unopposed on the 20th. There he was joined by Lord Delamere, and they issued a

---

[27] A. Browning, op. cit. 142–3; Bodleian Ballard MSS 45, fo. 20, Jones to Charlett, 4 Dec. 1688; Evans, 'Yorkshire and the Revolution', p. 274.

joint declaration calling for a free parliament and appealing for support against the king.[28]

Active support for these activities was not, however, very encouraging for the rebels until 2 December, when the bishop of London brought Princess Anne into Nottingham. Her arrival was a crucial turning-point in the revolutionary upheaval in the Midlands. Now gentlemen flocked into Nottingham, since, though they might have scruples about declaring for the Prince of Orange, they could with a clear conscience protect the princess.

Anne had fled from her father following the desertion of her closest friend, Lord Churchill, and her husband, Prince George of Denmark, to William. She anticipated that James would confine her and her confidante, Lady Churchill, on account of the treason of their husbands. They put themselves under the protection of the bishop, who took them from London to Nottingham, moving from country house to country house.

As they progressed, they picked up a host of supporters. Sixty-two gentlemen joined them in Northampton alone. On 30 November the cavalcade entered Leicester, where many local gentlemen attached themselves to it. Once Anne was safely in Nottingham castle it became almost a public duty to safeguard her. Thus the earl of Chesterfield, who had turned down a plea from Danby to participate in the northern uprising, took a hundred men on horseback to Nottingham.[29] Orders were sent from there to Warwick to raise the militia, informing the recipient that 'the Princess of Denmark is now here of whose safety all imaginable care must be taken'.[30]

Although the seizures of Nottingham and York were the most spectacular events in the provinces remote from the Prince of Orange's headquarters, they were not the only

[28] *CSPD 1687–9* (1972), p. 354; D. Hosford, *Nottingham, Nobles and the North* (Hamden, Connecticut, 1976), 78–119.
[29] Northants. RO IL 3982: 'The names of those gentlemen who listed themselves under the command of the Right Hon[ble] and Right Rev[d] Father in God Henry Lord Bishop of London to guard her Royal Highness Princess Anne of Denmark at Nottingham Anno Dom 1688 being the year of the happy Revolution'; BL Althorp Papers, H1: Chesterfield to Halifax, 16 Dec. 1688.
[30] Compton Papers, 1108: draft endorsed 'probably from George 4th earl of Northampton to "Sir"'; it ends 'I suppose this will not seem strange to you since you have so many precedents of the same nature'!

demonstrations of force on his behalf. As we have seen, Hull and Scarborough were also wrested by insurgents from James's supporters. Other garrisons were taken too, including Berwick, Carlisle, and Tynemouth, putting all the north into the hands of William's adherents. The duke of Norfolk ordered troops into King's Lynn and Norwich with instructions to disarm Roman Catholics, welcoming the arrival of the Prince of Orange, which 'has given us an opportunity to declare for the defence of . . . the laws, liberties and Protestant religion'. Lord Herbert of Cherbury and Sir Edward Harley 'and most of the gentry of Worcestershire and Herefordshire' entered Worcester and then seized Ludlow castle, where they imprisoned the Catholic sheriff of Worcestershire.[31]

Although there was more potentially violent activity in the provinces during the Revolution than is often acknowledged, there can be no denying that those who took part in it were an unrepresentative minority. The majority hesitated to commit themselves to treasonable activities. There were, however, two ways of showing support for the Dutch invasion short of actual treason. One was to join in the Association to protect William of Orange. The other was to pick up the cry for a free parliament.

Burnet, who accompanied William to England and was present in Exeter when the Association was mooted, described how it came about at the instigation of Sir Edward Seymour.

As soon as he had been with the prince, he sent to seek for me. When I came to him, he asked me, why we had not an association signed by all that came to us, since, till we had that done, we were as a rope of sand: men might leave us when they pleased, and we had them under no tie; whereas, if they signed an association, they would reckon themselves bound to stick to us. I answered, it was because we had not a man of his authority and credit to offer and support such an advice. I went from him to the prince, who approved of the motion as did also the earl of Shrewsbury, and all that were with us. So I was ordered to draw it. It was, in few words, an engagement to stick together in pursuing the ends of the prince's declaration; and that, if any attempt should be made on his person, it should be revenged on all by whom or from

[31] J. M. Rosenheim, 'An Examination of Oligarchy: The Gentry of Restoration Norfolk', unpublished Ph.D. thesis (Princeton, 1981), fo. 287; *Great News from Salisbury*, 6 Dec. 1688.

whom any such attempt should be made. This was agreed to by all about the prince. So it was engrossed in parchment, and signed by all those that came in to him.[32]

The Association was printed for general distribution. Those associated in defence of the Protestant religion and the ancient government, laws, and liberties of England, Scotland, and Ireland solemnly engaged to protect the prince against 'desperate and cursed attempts of Papists and other bloody men'. Although originally confined to 'the gentlemen of Devon', it was distributed about the country. Sir John Bramston noted that 'in very many counties the nobilitie and gentrie rise and associate. Some say it is for defence of themselves against the Papists, who are armed and imbodied; others declare for defence of the Protestant religion, the laws and liberties which have been invaded, and are yet in dainger of beinge utterly subverted by Priests and Papists.' The earl of Bath communicated it to Cornwall. In the Midlands several peers signed it, including the bishop of London, and the earls of Devonshire, Manchester, and Northampton.[33] Before James II's flight from London some of the nobility and gentry hesitated to become involved in the movement. Their hesitation might have been prompted by the knowledge that the king regarded it as rebellious.[34] Thus the earl of Chesterfield led resistance to it in the Midlands. Despite the fact that it had originated at the suggestion of the Tory Seymour, it seems to have been more enthusiastically taken up by Whigs, while Tories were apparently more hesitant. In Kent Sir John Knatchbull urged caution, on the grounds that 'itt was very hazardous to us and the Prince's cause to declare for him

[32] Burnet, iii. 337.

[33] Bramston, p. 338; *CSPD 1687–9* (1972), 369, 371. The roll of parchment on which the Assocation was recorded accompanied the Prince of Orange on his progress and was offered to his supporters for their signatures (Clarendon, ii. 216).

[34] Among the reasons which James gave for his flight was that he 'could no longer resolve to expose myself to no purpose to what I might expect from the ambitious Prince of Orange and the *associated rebellious Lords*' (HMC *Dartmouth*, i. 226: James II to Dartmouth, 10 Dec. 1688 (my italics)). James also told Feversham that he 'expected that he and all other loyall both officers and soldiers would keep themselves from Associations' (BL Add. MSS 34487; fo. 50: newsletter, 16 Dec. 1688).

out of season'.[35] After James fled, however, this reluctance disappeared. Even the dons of Oxford University signed when William of Orange invited them to do so.[36]

While signing the Association became to some extent a partisan demonstration of support for the prince, the slogan 'a free parliament' was universally taken up. It had the virtue of uniting the aspirations of all those anxious to change the course of events which the king had precipitated without specifying the precise nature of the changes. Thus those who merely wanted to persuade James to reverse his policies and those who aimed ultimately at ousting him from the throne could subscribe to the demand for the summoning of a parliament. On 17 November, just before the king went to Salisbury, he was presented with a petition signed by twelve peers and seven bishops requesting such a summons. James's immediate reaction was to refuse, claiming that it was impossible to hold a general election while an invading army was occupying the West Country. During the following days demands for a free parliament were raised all over the country. The insurgents at Nottingham and York made it the main plank in their platform. Elsewhere petitions were drawn up demanding an election. Thus 'the gentlemen of Westmorland and Cumberland' assembled at Penrith on 1 December and signed the following address:

Whereas it is the concurrent opinion of the Lords spiritual and temporal and all ranks and degrees of men within this Kingdom that there is no expedient so proper to remove the miseries and secure the religion and properties of this nation as a free parliament we . . . do hereby declare our full consent and concurrente in that opinion.

On the same day 'a great concourse of gentry' attended by friends and servants met the mayor and aldermen of Norwich and made a similar declaration.[37] Meanwhile James had returned

[35] P. C. Vellacott, 'The Diary of a Country Gentleman in 1688', *Cambridge Historical Journal*, 2 (1926–8), 57. Knatchbull wrote thus on 8 Dec. On the 29th after James's second flight he received the Association in Kent and arranged for its distribution (*Notes and Queries*), 6 (1984), 121).

[36] BL Althorp Papers, H1: Chesterfield to Halifax, 16 Dec. 1688; Burnet, iii. 350.

[37] Cumbria RO Kendal Fleming MSS 3363; BL Egerton MSS 3336, fos. 18–19; *Norfolk Lieutenancy Journal, 1676–1701*, ed. B. Cozens Hurly (Norfolk Record Society, 1961), xxx. 93–4. The duke of Beaufort 'and several other

to the capital, to be confronted by another request to summon a parliament from all the bishops and peers in town. This time he agreed, and issued a proclamation on 1 December for a parliament to meet on 15 January 1689.

Being obliged to summon a parliament was in fact the last straw for the king. For what was a 'free' parliament going to do? The Cumbrian gentry were convinced it was the most proper expedient 'to remove the miseries and secure the religion and properties of this nation'. As far as James was concerned this could only be bad news. At best it would revive projects for limitations on the prerogative such as his brother had proposed as a compromise during the Exclusion crisis. At worst it could lead to the revival of Exclusion itself, if not of the reigning monarch then of the son and heir born to him in the summer. Certainly there would be a parliamentary inquiry into the circumstances of the birth and the rights of the child, with William of Orange looking on. William had demanded as much in his Declaration prior to the invasion. The least that could be expected was that the Prince of Wales should be educated as a Protestant. Such a prospect was so intolerable to James that within a week of issuing the proclamation he got his wife and child out of the country and safe in France. He had already made up his mind to join them there. Any parliamentary limitations on the prerogative were unacceptable to a monarch who had aspired to become absolute.

It was not his absolutism, however, so much as his Catholicism which alienated his subjects. Their paranoia about popery was vividly shown in the panic which swept the country when a wild rumour arose that Irish troops making their way from London north were pillaging unchecked by any authority.[38] Protestants of all persuasions closed ranks as the reports aroused irrational anxieties. It was reported that Birmingham had been fired by the Irishmen, and that men, women, and children had been murdered. Then Nottingham and Stafford were alleged to have been sacked. The panic spread

persons of quality of the county of Gloucester' also petitioned the king 'for the speedy calling of a parliament', as did the gentry of Devon and Lancashire: HMC Seventh report Appendix: *Graham*, pp. 350, 416; HMC *Kenyon*, p. 212.

[38] G. H. Jones, 'The Irish Fright of 1688', *Bulletin of the Institute of Historical Research*, 55 (1982), 148–53.

into Yorkshire with the news that Doncaster, Penistone, and Huddersfield were on fire. Ralph Thoresby, the dissenting historian of Leeds, who clearly believed the rumours, described how that city took alarm. He claimed that some seven thousand men were assembled in Leeds 'in defence of their lives and liberties, religion and property, against those barbarous and inhuman wretches'. When it was reported that they were in the suburbs,

The drums beat, the bells rang backward, the women shrieked and such dreadful consternation seized upon all persons; some men with their wives and children left all behind them (even monies and plate upon the tables) and ran for shelter to the barns and haystacks in the fields. Their horror was so great and universal that the aged people who remembered the civil wars said, they never knew any thing like it. Thousands of lighted candles were placed in the windows, and persons of any courage and consideration (if such a thing was to be found) ran with their arms to the bridge, and so marched towards Beeston; so that in a very small time some thousands appeared, and I among the rest, with horse and arms; and blessed be God! the terror disappeared, it being a false alarm taken from some drunken people, who cried out horribly, murder! murder![39]

Still the terror swept north, a newspaper recounting its progress to Boroughbridge:

As distempers of the head commonly affect the whole body so the reported Irish massacre which began in London has defused itself into most counties and towns of note throughout England; for on Friday the 28th [December] the frenzy had possessed the country people of Boroughbridge in Yorkshire as also the neighbouring towns who in few hours were assembled to the number of 3000 and so marched towards Ripon expecting the child eating Irish but they were quickly undeceived the massacre vanishing in an instant.[40]

[39] *London Mercury: Or, the Moderate Intelligencer*, 24–7 Dec. 1688; Kendal RO Fleming MSS 3393; *The Diary of Ralph Thoresby*, ed. J. Hunter (2 vols.; 1830), i. 188–91.

[40] *London Mercury: Or, the Orange Intelligencer*, 3–7 Jan. 1689. The furthest north that the rumours reached appears to have been Kendal, where on 19 Dec. the mayor 'fired the beacon upon a sham report of his man that a Proclamation was made in Settle of the Irish having burnt Halifax etc. All false' (Cumbria RO Carlisle D/Ry box 119: Sir Daniel Fleming's account book 1688–1700/1). See also *A Hewitson Diary of Material on 1688 and War in Ireland*, ed. Bellingham D. Thomas (Preston, 1908), 36–7.

The episode is a stark reminder of the paranoid mentality of many English Protestants in the seventeenth century. It helps explain how the doggerel song 'Lilliburlero' set to a jaunty marching tune could become the anthem of the Revolution. Burnet claimed that 'the whole army, and at last all people both in city and country, were singing it perpetually. And perhaps never had so slight a thing so great an effect.'[41] Its author, Thomas Wharton, later boasted that it had whistled a king out of three kingdoms. Fear of popery was the most potent emotion uniting the subjects of the Stuarts, from the suspicions of the influence of Catholics in the counsels of Charles I to the fire of London, the Popish Plot, and the Glorious Revolution.

Anti-popery contributed more than anything else to the consensus which characterized the elections to the Convention and the deliberations of the Commons when it assembled in January 1689. The kind of sentiments informing electors and members alike were summed up in a tract 'addressed to all members of the next Parliament':

The Church of Rome is still the same Church it was a hundred years ago, that is, a mass of treachery, barbarity, perjury, and the highest superstition; a machine without any principle or settled law of motion, not to be mov'd or stopt with the weights of any private or publick obligations; a monster that destroys all that is sacred both in Heaven and Earth, so ravenous that it is never content unless it gets the whole world into its claws and tears all to pieces in order to salvation; a Proteus that turns itself into all shapes, a chameleon that puts on all colours according to its present circumstances, this day an Angel of Light, tomorrow a Beelzebub.[42]

Religion was thus at the heart of the Revolution. This is manifest not only in the crucial issue of Catholicism but also in the way both sides appealed to Providence to justify their cause. Just as James II took refuge in the belief that Providence was on his side, until the success of the Dutch invasion forced him to the contrary view, so the supporters of William of Orange found justification in the notion that the Revolution had divine approval. Burnet even cited the storm which caused the first expedition to return to Dutch ports, and which James saw as

[41] Burnet, iii. 336.
[42] *Popish Treaties not to be Rely'd on: In a Letter from a Gentleman at York to his Friend in the Prince of Orange's Camp* (1688), 3.

evidence of divine disapproval on the invasion, to prove that God had blessed the prince's mission. 'We on our part', he maintained, 'looked on it as a mark of God's great care of us, who . . . had preserved us while we were in such apparent danger, beyond what could have been imagined.' Sir George Treby, Recorder of London, attributed the eventual success of the undertaking to assistance from above when he addressed William on 20 December:

Reviewing our late danger, we remember our Church and State overrun by Popery and Arbitrary Power, and brought to the point of destruction, by the conduct of men (that were our *true* invaders) that broke the sacred fences of our laws, and (which was worst) the very Constitution of our Legislature . . . When we look back to the last month, and contemplate the swiftness and fulness of our present deliverance, astonished, we think it miraculous. Your Highness, led by the hand of Heaven, and called by the voice of the people, has preserved our dearest Interests.[43]

The Declaration of Rights expressed similar sentiments when it said of the Prince of Orange, 'whom it hath pleased Almighty God to make the glorious instrument of preserving this kingdom from popery and arbitrary power'. When enacted as the Bill of Rights it gave the claim that Providence had directly intervened in the Revolution the solemnity of statute.

These twin convictions, that popery was incompatible with liberty, and that God was on their side, persuaded Protestant Englishmen to overcome their reluctance to resist James II's measures, though not the king himself. Most of them probably hoped that the king would come to his senses if he was made to realize the error of his ways. Few can have dared to hope that instead he would flee to France rather than accept parliamentary limitations on his regal authority. In a bizarre sense the least reluctant revolutionary was James himself, whose actions did most to ensure that the year 1688 would be marked by a bloodless if perhaps not altogether glorious revolution.

Certainly the impact of the king's decision to flee rather than to fight was devastating on his most loyal supporters. As Clarendon wrote on hearing the news of his second departure, 'it

---

[43] Burnet, iii. 313; *The Speech of Sir George Treby Knight . . . to the Prince of Orange December the 20th 1688.*

is like an earthquake'.[44] Among the most loyal was Peter Shakerley, Governor of Chester. As late as 7 December he was ready to assure James of his fidelity, 'from which I shall never swerve'. Two days later he was asking the War Office whether he should proceed against some deserters by common or martial law. Then the news of James's first flight reached him. On 13 December he was writing, 'the loyalty and fidelity I paid to my king will not I hope be imputed to me a crime by the victorious Prince of Orange whose commands I now humbly awayt and shall steadfastly obey'. Like many who were reluctant to resist James II, Shakerley withdrew his allegiance and transferred it to William of Orange when the king abandoned his people. Another was Lord Dartmouth, the commander of James's fleet. William of Orange wrote to him on 29 November inviting him 'to joyne the fleete under your command with mine and to declare as I have donne in my Declaration for the Religion and Liberties'. For some reason this letter did not reach Dartmouth at Spithead until 12 December. By then he must have been aware of the king's flight, and wrote accepting the prince's suggestion. Had the letter arrived two or three days earlier, Dartmouth might well have sent a very different reply. His loyalty was shaken by James's decision to go, and his despair rings through a letter he wrote to Feversham, 'Oh God what could make our master desert his kingdoms and his friends?'[45]

Perhaps the most shattered were Archbishop Sancroft and his High-Church colleagues. They had worked closely with James when he was duke of York, supporting him against the exclusionists and sharing in the triumph of the Tory reaction in the last four years of Charles II's reign. When James succeeded his brother, however, so far from continuing the alliance against 'fanatics', he had allied with their opponents. The despair felt by Sancroft in the darkest days of the reign was communicated by him in a letter to Princess Mary. 'It hath seem'd good to the infinite wisdom to exercise this poor Church with trials of all

---

[44] Clarendon, ii. 234.
[45] BL Add. MSS 38695, fos. 92, 100, 103; HMC *Dartmouth*, i. 219, 235, 279. It seems possible that military men were influenced by the Hobbesian notion that the sovereign must be obeyed as long as he could protect you, but that allegiance ended at the point when he could no longer afford protection.

sorts and of all degrees', he wrote. Their very loyalty to the hereditary monarch 'imbitters the very comforts that are left us, it blasts all our present joys and makes us sit down with sorrow in dust and ashes'. Only the thought of her succeeding eventually gave him any grounds for optimism: 'Blessed be God who in so dark and dismal a night hath caused some dawn of light to break forth upon us from the eastern shore in the constancy and good affection of your Royal Highness and your excellent prince towards us; for if this should fail (which the God of Heaven and Earth forbid) our hearts must surely break.'[46] Unfortunately this light at the end of the tunnel was extinguished by the birth of the Prince of Wales at the time when Sancroft was on trial for seditious libel in June 1688.

Then the cloud had seemed to lift. Threatened with invasion, James had panicked, dropped his plans to build up an alternative political system to the alliance of Crown and Church, and turned once more to his 'old friends'. It must have seemed that Good King Charley's golden days were back. But that dream turned to a nightmare when William invaded and the king capitulated. The last thing Sancroft and his colleagues wanted was what happened in the winter of 1688 to 1689. They desired nothing more than to cement the old alliance of king and bishops under James II. They tried their best to retain him as monarch, but his departure made life impossible for them. The archbishop and six of his episcopal colleagues, including three who had signed the petition with him which led to their trial, refused to take the oaths to the new regime. Along with about four hundred clergymen, they were deprived of their livings and survived into the post-Revolution world as nonjurors, a perpetual prick to the consciences of other High Churchmen who recognized William and Mary as king and queen *de facto* if not *de jure*.

Even some of those who conspired to bring about the Dutch invasion did not will its eventual outcome. 'I can take God to witness that I had not a thought when I engaged in it,' wrote the earl of Danby's son '(and I am sure my father neither) that the prince of Orange's landing would end in deposing the King.'[47] Lord Ailesbury later claimed that he had advised James to

---

[46] Bodleian Tanner MSS 29, fo. 111: Sancroft to Mary, 3 Nov. 1687 (draft).
[47] Henning, iii. 185.

'march to York where the Earl of Danby is with his broom-sticks and whishtail militia, and some raw bubbles he has drawn in, who will all run away'. He also recalled meeting Danby in December 1688 and asking him, 'what course would you have taken, had we marched to York?', to which he replied, 'to submit ourselves, and to crave his pardon'.[48] The story is self-serving and was recounted years after the Revolution. But there is no reason to doubt its intrinsic veracity. Danby's nerve might easily have failed if he had been confronted by James at the head of a professional army.

Had James stayed, therefore, there can be little doubt that events would have taken a different turn from the sequence which ensued as a result of his flight. His departure meant that those few real revolutionaries who had all along intended to replace him with William of Orange, including the prince himself, succeeded beyond their wildest dreams. The object of their desire fell into their hands almost without a struggle.

But that is not to say that there would have been no significant political and constitutional changes if James had remained. His actions had alienated enough of his subjects for some curbs to be forced upon him. They might have been reluctant actually to resist him. But they were not prepared to acquiesce any longer in his rule. Even Sancroft and his colleagues had only agreed to co-operate with him on their own terms. Englishmen in 1688 were for the most part reluctant revolutionaries. Yet they were even more reluctant to put up much longer with a king who rode roughshod over what they considered to be the rule of law.

They therefore welcomed the intervention of the Prince of Orange since he promised to restore that rule. The sentiments of

---

[48] Ailesbury, pp. 195–6. Danby told Sir John Reresby that before his second flight James had sent a message to him by Charles Bertie soliciting his protection. According to Reresby, Danby had replied that 'if his Majesty would bring a considerable party with him, and came without the papists, he would sooner lose his life then his Majesty should be injured' (Reresby, pp. 557–8). Danby's biographer, however, expresses scepticism about this story, especially since Charles Bertie never went to York. (A. Browning, *Thomas Osborne, Earl of Danby* (3 vols.; Glasgow, 1944), i. 412). Yet Ailesbury and Reresby both register Danby's wavering immediately after the Revolution. Certainly he was disgruntled at William's allegedly ungrateful acknowledge-ment of his services (Browning, pp. 424–5).

most (Protestant) Englishmen around Christmas time in the year 1688 were admirably summarized in a Declaration drawn up in Lancashire on 23 December by the Lord-Lieutenant, sheriff, deputy-lieutenants, justices of the peace, militia officers, 'and other Protestant Gentlemen'.

> We being hearty and zealously concerned for the Protestant Religion, the Laws of the Land, and the Liberties and Properties of the subject cannot (without being wanting in our duty) be silent under those calamities wherein late prevailing Popish councils have miserably involved these Kingdoms: And we do therefore unanimously resolve to apply ourselves to his Highness the Prince of Orange who with so great kindness to these realms, so vast expence and such hazard to his person, hath undertaken by the endeavouring to procure a free Parliament to rescue us with as little effusion as possible of Christian blood from the eminent [*sic*] dangers of Popery and Slavery.[49]

It was the demand for a free parliament, and not the desire to replace King James with King William, which united Englishmen in the closing months of James II's reign. Advocates of divine right and contractual kingship could all accept the need for parliamentary curbs on the prerogative. Although the events of early 1689 were to divide them again, for a few brief weeks there was a rare consensus. As one contemporary put it, 'I question if in all the histories of empire there is one instance of so bloodless a Revolution as that in England in 1688, wherein Whigs, Tories, princes, prelates, nobles, clergy, common people, and a standing army, were unanimous. To have seen all England of one mind is to have lived at a very particular juncture.'[50]

---

[49] Cumbria RO Kendal Fleming MSS 3406.
[50] *An Apology for the Life of Colley Cibber, Comedian . . ., Written by Himself* (1925), i. 35.

11

Conclusion

❦

1688. Novemb. 5. About the end of this year happen'd here in England the greatest revolution that was ever known.

(The Diary of Abraham de la Pryme)

Whether or not the events of 1688 deserve to be remembered three hundred years later as a revolution depends on what is meant by the term. Like 'feudalism' and 'class', it is one of those words which historians use all the time. Indeed, despite warning each other that it is constantly being employed in an imprecise and even nebulous way, they continue to spawn new usages for it. Thus it has had the adjectives 'agricultural', 'commercial', 'financial', 'industrial', 'moral', 'sexual', and even 'Thatcherite' attached to it. Clearly this is a debasement of the term, so much so that some scholars have recommended its removal from the historical lexicon altogether. Yet we seem to be stuck with it, not least because it is a useful shorthand.

Several attempts have been made to give it a more precise definition. Thus models have been extrapolated from events which everybody recognizes as revolutionary, such as those in France in 1789 or in Russia in 1917, and used to test the claims of other upheavals to the same status. One problem with this approach, however, is that the analyses have come up with different and even conflicting definitions. After reviewing some of the rival models, Theda Skocpol concluded that 'there are enormous differences among the major types of social–scientific theories not only about how to explain revolutions, but even about how to define them'.[1]

Yet to deny that there can be precision about a word which has produced so much confusion is not to disclaim the value of

---

[1] T. Skocpol, *States and Social Revolutions* (Cambridge, 1979), 12–13.

attempting to define it. Clearly it should be possible to distinguish between *coups d'état*, rebellions, and revolutions, if these expressions are to serve any useful purpose. Since historians cannot define them to everybody's satisfaction, they should at least make explicit the criteria which they would require for them to be valid.

As we saw in the Introduction, Marxist historians prefer to describe what occurred in 1688 as a *coup d'état*, reserving the term 'revolution' for the events of the 1640s and 1650s. Yet contemporaries preferred to distinguish the earlier episode as a rebellion, and to dub the later a revolution, or rather as *the* Revolution. They seem to have been drawing a distinction between a political movement which, for all its spectacular initial success, ultimately failed in their eyes with the Restoration of 1660, and one which was successful. They were also, of course, condemning the first and applauding the second, though in History that amounts to very much the same thing. Although they did not use the word revolution in any of the senses in which it is generally employed today, this does not necessarily mean that they are inappropriate.

Most historians nowadays would distinguish political from social revolutions. A political revolution is seen as one which changes the polity of a society but does not alter its social structure, whereas a social revolution transforms the structure of society and its dominant ideology.

The argument of this book has been that England did experience a political revolution in 1688 and 1689. Absolutism gave way to limited monarchy. While this might seem to be nothing more than a reassertion of the classic Whig case, however, there are several major qualifications to be made to that interpretation. There was nothing unconstitutional about the bid for absolutism under the later Stuarts. Nor was it doomed to failure. Above all it is too subjective to load the change with value judgements, deploring absolutism and approving limited monarchy.

Both Charles II and James II worked for the most part within the letter of the law. The notion that there were legal limitations on their authority imposed by an ancient constitution, requiring them to account for their actions to parliament, was a Whig myth. Provided they did not violate statutes or common-law precedents their prerogative powers were still formidable. Moreover, they were backed by powerful sections of the political nation who regarded the Crown as an essential ally of the Church of England. As long as the later Stuarts kept up the alliance of Crown and Church they bade fair to make the monarchy as absolute in the 1680s as it had ever been since the accession of their House to the English throne. It was not as if the civil wars had never happened. On the contrary, it was precisely because they had occurred that the bulk of the political nation rallied to the Crown when it seemed there was the awful possibility that 'forty-one' would happen again.

It was James II's Catholicism which severed the link between Crown and Church. When, in pursuit of his aim of achieving toleration for Catholics, he was prepared to jettison the Anglican Tories and turn for support to Dissenters and former exclusionist Whigs, then the alliance broke down. Those who had formerly been the most devout supporters of the Stuarts became alienated from them. At the same time he failed to convince the majority of the Dissenters and Whigs to rally to him. Although he was sincere in his offer of religious toleration to all who could not conform to the established church, they remained suspicious of his motives and unhappy about his methods of achieving his goal.

Those who were alienated did not for the most part take their opposition as far as outright resistance. In the event relatively few took up arms against James II. But they withdrew their allegiance from him, not being prepared to lift a finger to help him when he was challenged by the Prince of Orange. The contrast with the reaction to the duke of Monmouth's rebellion is remarkable. In 1685 the political nation fell over itself to assist the king against the rebels. Not only did parliament immediately vote an Act of Attainder and extraordinary supplies, but the provinces too responded positively in demonstrations of loyalty to the regime. Addresses of abhorrence poured in to clog the pages of the *London Gazette*. One from remote Kendal echoed the general sentiments:

We cannot but with the greatest horror and detestation reflect upon the late most desperate and damnable attempts of those incorrigible sons of rebellion who after so many repeated miracles of Divine Providence in frustrating all their hellish plots and confounding their most wicked devices, durst again presume to fight against God and lift up their sacriligious and bloody hands against his anointed . . . we do here again unfeignedly renew our former vows of serving with our lives and fortunes your Majesty, your heirs and lawful successors against all rebels and enemies whatsoever.[2]

In 1688, so far from addresses abhorring the invasion filling the nation with noise, there was a deafening silence. 'It is not to be admired that we have so little intelligence', the earl of Middleton informed his fellow Secretary of State from the king's camp on 23 November, 'since none of the gentry of this or the adjacent counties come near the Court and the Commons are spies to the enemy.'[3] This created a situation in which the Prince of Orange could succeed where Monmouth had failed. In any resistance movement to a regime only a minority are actively involved. The attitude of most people can only be to give support to the government or comfort to its enemies. Yet this can be a crucial consideration in the success or failure of the movement. In 1685 the loyalty of his subjects contributed to the king's successful crushing of the rebellion. In 1688 the alienation of his subjects helped the cause of the Revolution.

The silence was eventually broken by petitions for a free parliament. Again these contrast sharply with the addresses of 1685. The petition from Ipswich conveys their gist:

being very sensible of the present troubles and distractions this nation is under [we] do believe no way better to give ease and relief to the nation than by a free parliament, and joining together in the maintenance of the true Protestant Religion do unanimously declare that [we] will readily and heartily join with all those that are for a free Parliament and for the maintenance of the Protestant Religion against all persons whatsoever that shall be opposers thereof.[4]

Demands for a free parliament united all those Englishmen who were anxious for a change in 1688, from those, probably a majority, who hoped it could be achieved under James II, to those who desired that William of Orange should replace him. Anglican Tories desperate to put a brake on the king's use of

---

[2] Cumbria, RO Kendal Fleming MSS 2943.

[3] *CSPD 1687–9* (1972), 360.

[4] Ipswich Great Court Book, 14 Dec. 1688. I owe this reference to Pat Murrell.

the prerogative looked to a parliament elected without his influence to provide it. Whigs and Dissenters who had been persuaded that toleration could only properly be established by statute and not by royal edicts also took up the slogan.

Nor was it just a slogan. The survival of parliament free from royal interference was a central concern of all those whom James had alienated. It is significant that no fewer than four of the original 'public grievances' which formed the basis of the Declaration of Rights dealt with this problem.[5] One asserted that the right and freedom of electing members should be preserved. Another claimed that parliaments ought to sit frequently and that 'their frequent sitting should be secured' or, in another formulation, 'be suffered to sit'. A third insisted on 'no interrupting of any session of parliament till the affairs which are necessary to be dispatched at that time be determined'. Where this harked back implicitly to Charles II's reign as well as to James II's, a fourth explicitly referred only to the Cavalier parliament: 'that long continuance of the same parliament be prevented.' The decision to separate grievances which required new legislation from those which could be immediately incorporated in the Declaration led to the loss of two of these clauses and the dilution of the other two. After all, James II had not broken the law, even if he had stretched his prerogative in his bid to pack parliament. Charles on the other hand had undoubtedly done so when he failed to convene parliament in 1684 despite the Triennial Act of 1664. Yet in the final form of the Declaration of Rights Charles was disregarded. The consensus behind the Declaration could only be sustained as long as it concentrated on James and ignored his brother. There was little which it could declare, therefore, on the subject of parliament except to assert that 'election of members of parliament ought to be free' and that 'parliaments ought to be frequently held'.

These are sometimes dismissed as mere pious exaltations. Yet the concern for free and frequent parliamentary elections and sessions remained of central importance to the Revolution Settlement. The Triennial Act of 1694 stemmed directly from

[5] *The Publick Grievances of the Nation Adjudged Necessary by the House of Commons to be Redressed* (1689); Sir Charles Graham Papers, vol. '1688', fos. 311–12.

the concerns expressed in the Convention. Although no statute required annual sessions to be held, nevertheless had William attempted to rule without parliament he would have flown in the face of what became known as 'Revolution principles'.

The permanence of parliament and its regular meeting after 1689, where before it had been ephemeral and irregular, wrought a major transformation in the English polity. Revisionist historians of early Stuart England have objected to traditional views which treat parliament as a central institution, preferring to regard it as an event. There is much truth in this. After all parliament met in only eleven of the first forty years of the seventeenth century. The Long Parliament, which survived in one form or another from 1640 to 1653, became something of an institution, but under Cromwell parliaments became once more unpredictable events. Even after the Restoration the long survival of the Cavalier parliament could not have been predicted. Nor was it in continuous session, for there were frequent prorogations, one of which lasted for fifteen months. During the decade 1679 to 1689 parliaments met in only four years.

In 1689 parliament was finally transformed from an event into an institution. The consequences were far-reaching. Once men realized that there was a permanent legislative machine available at all times they made use of it. The history of private legislation really dates from the Revolution. So does the history of parliamentary lobbying.[6]

The permanence of parliament is what distinguished the limited monarchy which the Revolution established from the absolutism to which the Stuarts had aspired. This change transformed the dominant ideologies. It is no longer possible to argue that the doctrines of Filmer were replaced overnight by those of Locke. Historians of political thought have shown that divine-right theories obstinately survived, despite the events of

---

[6] J. Styles, 'An Eighteenth-century Ruling Class? Interest Groups, Lobbying and Parliament in Eighteenth-century England'. I am grateful to John Styles for a copy of this unpublished paper. The resort to legislation after the Revolution can to some extent be indicated by the number of statutes placed on the statute book in the twenty-one parliamentary sessions held from 1660 to 1685 compared with the twenty-one held after 1689. In the first period 562 Acts were passed, in the second 1,373.

1688. They have also demonstrated that it is anachronistic to regard Locke as the philosopher of the Revolution. On the contrary, at the time, his stress on contract and the right to resist was regarded as on the extreme radical fringe. Nevertheless a sea-change can be detected in Tory and Whig thought, which placed parliament at the centre after 1689. Tories continued to uphold the doctrines of passive obedience and non-resistance, but came to accept that the sovereign power which it was not lawful to resist was not the monarch alone but the king in parliament. Whigs even more quickly got round to arguing that sovereignty lay not in the people at large but in the legislature, which consisted of King, Lords, and Commons.[7]

The rejection by most Whigs of the concept of popular sovereignty raises the question of how far the Revolution deserves to be commemorated as a milestone in the history of human liberty? The Whig interpretation assumed that it was. Although the people were not sovereign, nevertheless they were represented in the House of Commons. Yet, as a Tory member of the Convention, Sir Robert Sawyer, pointed out, 'the third estate, which is the House of Commons . . . are not the fourth part of the Kingdom . . . Copy-holders, lease-holders, all men under 40s a year are people.'[8] He might have added all women, too, not to mention children. The Revolution did nothing explicitly for them.[9] Sawyer, moreover, was right to assess the electorate at about 25 per cent of adult males. Although this was a higher proportion that some historians have estimated, it nevertheless remained a minority.

The Whig interpretation also regarded the change from absolute to mixed monarchy as one for the better. Such a moral view of 1688 is rather at a discount now. Indeed it has been argued that the lot of most Englishmen actually became worse after 1689 than it had been before. Although 'Liberty and

---

[7] H. T. Dickinson, *Liberty and Property* (1977); J. P. Kenyon, *Revolution Principles* (Cambridge, 1977); M. Goldie, 'The Revolution of 1689 and the Structure of Political Argument', *Bulletin of Research in the Humanities*, 83 (1980), 473–564; R. Ashcraft and M. M. Goldsmith, 'Locke, Revolution Principles and the Formation of Whig Ideology', *Historical Journal*, 26 (1983), 773–800.

[8] Grey, ix. 22.

[9] L. Schwoerer, 'Women and the Glorious Revolution', *Albion* (1986), 195–218.

Property' was the motto for the revolutionaries, the emphasis soon came to settle on the second word. Thus in defence of property the number of offences against it punishable by death rose rapidly, until paradoxically England had the bloodiest penal code in enlightened Europe.[10]

It is a paradox because such leading philosophers of the Enlightenment as Montesquieu and Voltaire held up England as a model precisely because its constitution seemed much more liberal than the authoritarian governments on the Continent. Were they misguided in making this contrast? Certainly it has been asserted that the differences between eighteenth-century England and Europe have been exaggerated, and that under the Hanoverians it was essentially an *ancien régime*. By implication the Revolution had changed hardly anything, and should be ignored as virtually a non-event.[11]

This is to take the case against the revolutionary claims of 1688 to absurd lengths. The conventional wisdom about it in the eighteenth century became that it had ensured the survival of the finest constitution that it was humanly possible to devise. The balance of monarchy, aristocracy, and democracy achieved at the time offset the inevitable tendency towards tyranny, oligarchy, or anarchy which each type of government was prone to on its own. It also made England superior to any other country in the world. So far from being comparable with the regimes of continental Europe, the English polity came to be regarded as unique. Such boasts exaggerated in the opposite direction, sustaining the view that the Revolution was Glorious. There was not much glory in 1688. But there was a revolution.

At least there was a political revolution. Whether or not it also added up to a social revolution again depends upon definitions. If by social revolution is meant the overthrowing of one class by another, then nothing of the kind occurred in 1688. For one thing the very existence of classes in seventeenth-century England is highly debatable. Some contemporaries used the term to describe divisions in society, but even they were not doing so in the sense of a broad horizontal layer. That usage

---

[10] A. McInnes, 'The Revolution and the People', in G. S. Holmes (ed.), *Britain after the Glorious Revolution, 1688–1714* (1969), 80–95.
[11] J. C. D. Clark, *English Society, 1688–1832* (Cambridge, 1985).

only became general during the eighteenth century.[12] Earlier the word 'class' signified type, such as might be employed today to distinguish classes of battleship. Most seventeenth-century Englishmen used categories such as rank, degree, or sort. One which came into increasing use during the century was the concept of interest. Society was seen as being composed of various sectional interests, which together made up a national interest. The landed interest was held to be predominant. Alongside it, however, were newer ones, such as the monied interest. Interests were not classes, since they were vertical rather than horizontal fissures in society. Thus the landed interest held together all those involved in the agricultural sector of the economy, from the greatest landlord to the poorest labourer. Where the notion of rank, degree, or sort implied a fairly static model of society, the concept of interests was more dynamic. Moreover, it was a conflict model. The interests were regarded as rivals engaged in competition. For example, the rise of the monied interest was held to be a threat to the hegemony of the landed interest.

Historians on the whole have disregarded these anxieties. They have been played down as paranoid exaggerations fostered by politicians and propagandists to serve purely political ends. The reality was much more complex, and the alleged division of society into rival interests dissolves upon close inspection. There were too many links between land and money, for example, for them to be taken seriously as distinct, let alone as being irreconcilable. Thus landowners invested in commercial enterprise, while merchants bought land.

Above all it is alleged to be preposterous to suggest that the landed interest was threatened by other interests since it kept control of the commanding heights of power. Indeed, in so far as the word 'class' has been accepted by historians of the period, it has been to describe the major landowners, peers, and substantial country gentlemen, as a ruling class. There can be no doubt that in terms of personnel they dominated the institutions which exercised power. The ministers of the Crown came overwhelmingly from the landed aristocracy after 1689 as before. Both Houses of parliament were dominated by territorial

[12] P. J. Corfield, 'Class by Name and Number in Eighteenth-century Britain', *History*, 122 (1987), 38–61.

magnates in the eighteenth century, as they had been in the seventeenth. In this respect the Revolution made no difference, which appears to lend some credence to the view that in essentials the *ancien régime* survived from the Stuart into the Hanoverian era.

However, as John Styles has pointed out, it can be misleading to analyse the country's political institutions purely in terms of the social status and economic activities of those who ran them. 'We need to ask a question which historians have been remarkably reluctant to address,' he insists; 'to what extent were landowners able to translate their undoubted hold on the institutions of political power into policies that privileged their own interests as a sector of the economy, to the detriment, if necessary, of competing interests?'[13]

In this respect the most significant rival to the landed interest was the state itself. To see the state as being merely the instrument of the ruling class is to accept a very crude model of how power operates. For, as Theda Skocpol has demonstrated, the state has an autonomous power of its own.[14] It can pursue ends different from and even inimical to the aspirations of the so-called ruling class. To some extent of course this was obvious under the later Stuarts. Charles II's foreign and religious policies were frequently at odds with the dominant attitudes of the class which chiefly upheld his regime. James II antagonized it even more. One of the major causes of the Revolution was the determination of the ruling class to call a halt to the erosion of its status and privileges.

After 1689, however, the state positively encouraged the development of other interests literally at the expense of the landed interest. Above all the creation of a machinery of public credit benefited the monied interest and hit landowners where it hurt, in the pocket. This was the price necessary to pay for the wars against Louis XIV, no doubt. But it was also the pay off for the alliance which the landed class had forged with the financial interests, especially of the City of London, to offset the appeal which James II had made to them in his attempt to build up an alternative political structure. The removal of Crown support for privileged monopolies granted to overseas trading

---

[13] Styles, 'An Eighteenth-century Ruling Class'.
[14] Skocpol, *States and Social Revolutions*, pp. 24–33.

companies, and permitting former interlopers access to previously protected markets was another. And the Toleration Act, which mainly benefited an urban bourgeoisie rather than landowners, was yet another.[15]

These were major adjustments to the way the state operated after 1689. They did not amount to a social revolution in the sense of a bourgeoisie overthrowing a landed aristocracy. But they did mark an acceptance that emergent interests which had received a powerful boost from the commercial boom of the 1680s should be granted greater political clout. In this modest respect 1688 deserves to be regarded as marking a shift in the process whereby England became recognized not as an *ancien régime* but as a nation of shopkeepers.

[15] The argument in this paragraph is greatly indebted to the most stimulating study of the relationship between politics and society in the later Stuart period to have appeared this decade: G. S. de Krey, *A Fractured Society: The Politics of London in the First Age of Party, 1688–1715* (Oxford, 1985).

Select Bibliography

꧁꧂

Place of publication for printed works is London unless otherwise stated.

PRIMARY SOURCES

1. Manuscripts

Algemeen Rijksarchief, The Hague
  Fagel Archive 1:10:19: 2017, 2019, 2021
  States General 5915
Bodleian Library
  Ballard MSS 21, 45
  Carte MSS 130
  Rawlinson MSS 139a and b
  Tanner MSS 28–31
British Library
  Additional MSS 9341; 15397; 17677GG–HH; 32095; 32681; 34487;
    38695; 40621; 41816
  Althorp Papers
  Egerton MSS 2621; 3335; 3336; 3344
Buckinghamshire Record Office
  D135/B1–4: Jeffreys Papers
Cambridge University Library
  Additional MSS 4403
Cheshire Record Office
  Cholmondley MSS
  DDX 383/2: Diary of Sir Thomas Mainwaring, Bt.
Cumbria Record Offices:
  Carlisle:
    D/Lons: Lowther MSS
    D/Ry: Fleming MSS
  Kendal:
    Fleming MSS 2838–3474
Devon Record Office
  Pine Coffin MSS
Dr Williams Library
  Morrice MSS P and Q

Leeds Record Office, West Yorkshire Archive Service, Sheepscar
   Library
  Mexborough MSS
Leicestershire Record Office
  Finch MSS
Ministère des Relations Extérieures, Quai d'Orsay, Paris
  Correspondance Politique (Angleterre), 155, 165–6
  Correspondance Politique (Hollande) 149–157
National Library of Scotland
  Yester MSS
National Library of Wales
  Brogyntyn: Clenennau Letters and Papers
  Canon Trevor Owen MSS
  Coedymaen Group I
  Kemeys-Tynte Correspondence
  Ottley MSS
Northamptonshire Record Office
  Finch Hatton MSS
  Granville MSS
  Isham Correspondence
Nottingham University Library
  Portland MSS
Private Papers
  Sir Charles Graham, Bt. (Preston MSS now in BL)
  Compton Papers, Castle Ashby, Northampton
Public Record Office
  PRO 30/53/8: Herbert MSS
  PRO 31/3/155–78: Baschet transcripts of French dispatches, 1683–8
Staffordshire Record Office
  Dartmouth MSS

2. *Printed Works*

a. Pamphlets and Periodical Publications

Animadversions on a Late Paper Entitled a Letter to a Dissenter (1687).
An Answer to a Discourse intitled Papists protesting against Protestant Popery
  (1686).
An Answer from the Country to a Late Letter to a Dissenter (1687).
An Answer to a Letter to a Dissenter (1687).
An Answer to the Letter to a Dissenter (1687).
A Catalogue of all the Discourses Printed against Popery (1689).
Catholic Representer (1687).
The Citizen's Lament for the Lord Chancellor's Loss of the Purse (1688).
The Clergy's Late Carriage to the King Considered (1688).

Considerations Proposed to the Electors of the Ensuing Convention (1688/9).

Copies of Two Papers Written by the Late King Charles II (1686).

Eachard, John, *The Grounds and Occasions of the Contempt of the Clergy and Religion* (9th edn.; 1685).

Een Brief geschreven door den Heer Pensionaris Fagel aen Mr James Stewart Advocaat (1687).

Ellys, E. *A Clergyman of the Church of England his Vindication of himself for Reading his Majesty's Late Declaration* (1688).

    An Epistle to the Truly Religious and Loyal Gentry of the Church of England (1687).

    A Second Epistle to the Truly Religious and Loyal Gentry (1687).

    A Third Epistle to the Truly Religious and Loyal Gentry (1687).

English Currant (Dec. 1688).

Gother, J., *A Papist Misrepresented and Represented* (1685).

Great News from Salisbury (1688).

Halifax, *Complete Works*, ed. J. P. Kenyon (1969).

His Majesty's Reasons for Withdrawing Himself from Rochester (1688).

Hollandse Mercurius van het Jaer 1688 (1689).

L'Estrange, Sir Roger, *An Answer to a Letter to a Dissenter* (1687).

A Letter from a Gentleman in Exeter to his Friend in London (1688).

A Letter in Answer to Two Main Questions of the First Letter to a Dissenter (1687).

A Letter to a Friend Advising in this Extraordinary Juncture how to free the Nation from Slavery for ever (1688/9).

London Courant (Dec. 1688).

London Gazette (1681–9).

London Mercury: or, the Moderate Intelligencer (Dec. 1688).

London Mercury: or, the Orange Intelligencer (1688–9).

A Modest Censure of the Immodest Letter to a Dissenter (1687).

A Modest Vindication of the Petition of the Lords Spiritual and Temporal for the Calling of a Free Parliament (Exeter, 1688).

Orange Gazette (1688/9).

The Papist Misrepresented and Represented with a Preface Containing Reflections upon Two Treatises, the One the State the Other the View of the Controversie between the Representer and the Answerer (1687).

Papists Protesting against Protestant Popery (1686).

Payne, H., *An Answer to a Scandalous Pamphlet Entitled a Letter to a Dissenter* (1687).

Popish Treaties not to be Rely'd on: In a Letter from a Gentleman at York to his Friend in the Prince of Orange's Camp (1688).

Publick Occurrences Truly Stated (Mar.–Oct. 1688).

A Rare a Show: Or England's Betrayers Exposed (1688/9).

Reasons Humbly Offered for Placing his Highness the Prince of Orange Singly on the Throne during Life (1689).

Reflections upon the Answer to the Papist misrepresented (1685).

Remarks upon a Pamphlet Stiled A Letter to a Dissenter (1687).

A Review of the Reflections on the Prince of Orange's Declaration (1688).

A Second Letter to a Dissenter (1687).

Sherlock, William, *A Papist not Misrepresented by Protestants* (1686).

—— *A Sermon Preached at St Margaret's Westminster May 29* (1685).

A Speech of a Commoner of England to his Fellow Commoners of the Convention (1689).

A Speech to his Highness the Prince of Orange by a True Protestant of the Church of England (1689).

Stillingfleet, Edward, *The Doctrines and Practices of the Church of Rome Truly Represented* (1686).

A View of the Whole Controversy (1687).

A Vindication of a Sheet Concerning the Orders of the Church of England Against some Reasons etc. (Oxford, 1686).

b. Personal and Public Records

An Apology for the Life of Colley Cibber, Comedian . . ., Written by Himself (1925).

Autobiographies and Letters of Thomas Comber (Surtees Society, 1906).

The Autobiography of Sir John Bramston, ed. Lord Braybrooke (Camden Society, 1845).

Bruce, Thomas, earl of Ailesbury, *Memoirs*, ed. W. E. Buckley (2 vols., Roxburgh Club, Edinburgh, 1890).

Burnet, Gilbert, *History of his Own Time* (6 vols.; Oxford, 1833).

Calendar of State Papers Domestic, 1685–1689 (3 vols.; 1960–72).

Cavelli, Campana de, *Les Derniers Stuarts à Saint-Germain en Laye* (2 vols.; 1871).

Clarke, J. S., *The Life of James the Second* (2 vols.; 1816).

Cobbett, W., *Parliamentary History of England* (36 vols.; 1806–20), vols. iv and v.

The Compton Census of 1676: A Critical Edition, ed. A. Whiteman (1986).

The Correspondence of Henry Hyde, Earl of Clarendon . . . with the Diary, (ed. S. W. Singer (2 vols.; 1828).

Correspondentie van Willem III en van Hans Willem Bentinck, ed. N. Japiske (vol. i in two parts; vol. ii in three parts; The Hague, 1927–37).

Costin, W. C. and Watson, J. S. (eds.), *The Law and Working of the Constitution: Documents, 1660–1914* (2 vols.; 1952).

Dalrymple, Sir John, *Memoirs of Great Britain and Ireland* (vol. i in one part, vol. ii in two parts; 1771–3).

The Diary of Abraham de la Pryme, ed. C. Jackson (Surtees Society, 1870).

The Diary and Autobiography of Edmund Bohun, ed. S. Wilton Rix (Beccles, 1853).

The Diary of Ralph Thoresby, ed. J. Hunter (2 vols.; 1830).

The Diary of Sir John Knatchbull, Bt.: (i) *Notes and Queries*, 3rd series, 5 (1864), 391–3; 6 (1864), 1–3, 21–3, 41–3, 81–2, 121–2; (ii) P. C. Vellacott, 'The Diary of a Country Gentleman in 1688', *Cambridge Historical Journal*, 2 (1926–8), 48–62.

Duckett, Sir George, *Penal Laws and Test Act* (2 vols.; Oxford, 1882–3).

The Ellis Corespondence, ed. G. A. Ellis (2 vols.; 1829).

Grey, Anchitel, *Debates of the House of Commons from the Year 1667 to the Year 1694* (10 vols.; 1763).

Gutch, J., *Collectanea Curiosa* (2 vols.; Oxford, 1781).

Historical Manuscripts Commission Reports

    Fifth Report Appendix: *Pine Coffin MSS*

    Seventh Report Appendix: *Graham MSS*

    Dartmouth MSS

    Kenyon MSS

    Portland MSS

    Rutland MSS

'A Jornall of the Convention at Westminster Begun the 22 of January 1688/9', ed. L. G. Schwoerer, *Bulletin of the Institute of Historical Research*, 49 (1976).

'Journaal van Constantyn Huygens den zoon van 21 October 1688 tot 2 September 1696', *Werken Uitgegeven door het Historische Genootschaap*, NS 23 (Utrecht, 1876–8).

The Life and Times of Anthony Wood, ed. A. Clark (2 vols., Oxford, 1894).

Lowther, Sir John, *Memoirs of the Reign of James II*, ed. T. Zouch (York, 1808).

Memoirs of Sir John Reresby, ed. A. Browning (Glasgow, 1936).

Miscellaneous State Papers from 1501 to 1726, ed. Philip Yorke, second earl of Harwicke (2 vols.; 1778).

Norfolk Lieutenancy Journal, 1676–1701, ed. B. Cozens Hurly (Norfolk Record Society, 1961).

Négociations de Monsieur le comte d'Avaux en Hollande depuis 1684 jusqu'en 1688, ed. E. Mallet (6 vols.; Paris, 1752–3).

Quadriennium Jacobi: Or, the History of the Reign of King James II from his First Coming to the Crown to his Desertion (1689).

The Rev. Oliver Heywood, 1630–1702: His Autobiography, Diaries, Anecdotes and Event Books, ed. J. Horsfall Turner (4 vols.; 1882).

Simpson, A., 'Notes of a Noble Lord, 22 January to 12 February 1688/9', *English Historical Review*, 53 (1937).

Somers, John, 'Notes of Debate, January 28, January 29, 1689', in

Miscellaneous State papers from 1501 to 1726, ed. Philip Yorke, second earl of Harwicke (2 vols.; 1778).

Welwood, J., *Memoirs of the Most Material Transactions in England for the Last Hundred Years Preceding the Revolution of 1688* (1700).

Whittle, J., *An Exact Diary of the Late Expedition of his Illustrious Highness the Prince of Orange into England* (1689).

SELECT SECONDARY WORKS

1. *Books*

Ashcraft, R., *Revolutionary Politics and Locke's Two Treatises of Government* (Princeton, 1986).

Baxter, S., *William III* (1966).

Browning, A., *Thomas Osborne, Earl of Danby* (3 vols.; Glasgow, 1944–51).

Carswell, J., *The Descent on England* (1969).

Childs, J., *The Army of Charles II* (1976).

—— *The Army, James II and the Glorious Revolution* (Manchester, 1980).

—— *The British Army of William III, 1689–1702* (1987).

Clifton, R., *The Last Popular Rebellion: The Western Rising of 1685* (1984).

Coleby, A. M., *Central Government and the Localities: Hampshire 1649–1689* (Cambridge, 1987).

Dickinson, H. T., *Liberty and Property* (1977).

Earle, P., *Monmouth's Rebels* (1977).

Fletcher, A., *Reform in the Provinces: The Government of Stuart England* (1986).

Glassey, L., *Politics and the Appointment of Justices of the Peace, 1675–1720* (Oxford, 1979).

Henning, B. D. (ed.), *The History of Parliament: The Commons, 1660–1689* (3 vols.; 1983).

Holmes, G. S. (ed.), *Britain after the Glorious Revolution, 1688–1714* (1969).

Horwitz, H., *Parliament, Policy and Politics in the Reign of William III* (Manchester, 1977).

—— *Revolution Politicks: The Career of Daniel Finch, Second Earl of Nottingham* (1968).

Hosford, D., *Nottingham, Nobles and the North* (Hamden, Connecticut, 1976).

Jones, C. (ed.), *Britain in the First Age of Party, 1680–1750* (1987).

Jones, G. H., *Charles Middleton: The Life and Times of a Restoration Politician* (1967).

Jones, J. R., *Charles II: Royal Politician* (1987).

Jones, J. R., *The First Whigs* (1961).
—— (ed.), *The Restored Monarchy, 1660–1688* (1979).
—— *The Revolution of 1688 in England* (1972).
Kenyon, J. P., *The Nobility in the Revolution of 1688* (Hull, 1963).
—— *Revolution Principles* (Cambridge, 1977).
—— *Robert Spencer, Second Earl of Sunderland* (1958).
—— (ed.), *The Stuart Constitution* (2nd edn.; Cambridge, 1986).
Kishlansky, M., *Parliamentary Selection: Social and Political Choice in Early Modern England* (Cambridge, 1986).
de Krey, G. S., *A Fractured Society: The Politics of London in the First Age of Party, 1688–1715* (Oxford, 1985).
Landau, N., *The Justices of the Peace, 1679–1760* (1984).
Macaulay, T. B., *The History of England from the Accession of James II*, ed. C. H. Firth, (6 vols.; 1914).
Miller, J. (ed.), *The Glorious Revolution* (1983).
—— *James II: A Study in Kingship* (1978).
—— *Popery and Politics in England, 1660–1688* (Cambridge, 1973).
Pinkham, L., *William III and the Respectable Revolution* (Cambridge, Mass., 1954).
Pocock, J. G. A. (ed.), *Three British Revolutions: 1641; 1688; 1776* (1980).
Roberts, C., *Schemes and Undertakings: A Study of English Politics in the Seventeenth Century* (Columbus, Ohio, 1985).
Schwoerer, L. G., *The Declaration of Rights* (1981).
—— *No Standing Armies* (1974).
Trevelyan, G. M., *The English Revolution* (1938).
Turner, F. C. *James II* (1948).
Watts, M., *The Dissenters from the Reformation to the French Revolution* (1978).
Western, J. R., *Monarchy and Revolution: The English State in the 1680s* (1972).

2. *Articles and Essays*

Ashcraft, R., and Goldsmith, M. M., 'Locke, Revolution Principles and the Formation of Whig ideology', *Historical Journal*, 27 (1983), 773–800.
Beddard, R. A. 'The Commission for Ecclesiastical Promotions, 1681–1684: An Instrument of Tory Reaction', *Historical Journal*, 10 (1967), 11–40.
Bennett, G. V. 'Loyalist Oxford and the Revolution', in L. S. Sutherland and L. G. Mitchell (eds.), *The History of the University of Oxford*, v. *The Eighteenth Century* (Oxford, 1986). 9–29.
—— 'The Seven Bishops: A Reconsideration', in D. Baker (ed.),

Religious Motivation (Studies in Church History, 15; (1978), 267–87.

Chandaman, C. D., 'The Financial Settlement in the Parliament of 1685', in H. Hearder and H. R. Loyn (eds.), *British Government and Administration: Essays Presented to S. B. Chrimes* (Cardiff, 1974), 144–54.

Cruickshanks, E., Ferris, J., and Hayton, D., 'The House of Commons Vote on the Transfer of the Crown, 5 February 1689', *Bulletin of the Institute of Historical Research*, 52 (1979), 37–47.

Cruickshanks, E., Hayton, D., and Jones, C., 'Divisions in the House of Lords on the Transfer of the Crown . . .', ibid. 53 (1980), 56–87.

Fletcher, A., 'The Enforcement of the Conventicle Acts, 1664–1679', in W. Sheils (ed.), *Persecution and Toleration* (Studies in Church History, 21; 1984), 235–46.

Frankle, R. J., 'The Formulation of the Declaration of Rights', *Historical Journal*, 17 (1974), 265–79.

Goldie, M., 'The Revolution of 1689 and the Structure of Political Argument', *Bulletin of Research in the Humanities*, 83 (1980), 473–564.

Gwynn, R. D., 'James II in the Light of his Treatment of Huguenot Refugees in England, 1685–6', *English Historical Review*, 92 (1977), 820–33.

Horwitz, H., 'Parliament and the Glorious Revolution', *Bulletin of the Institute of Historical Research*, 47 (1974), 36–52.

—— '1689 (and all that)', *Parliamentary History*, 6 (1987), 23–42.

Jones, C., 'The Protestant Wind of 1688: Myth and Reality', *European Studies Review*, 3 (1973), 201–20.

Jones, G. H., 'The Irish Fright of 1688', *Bulletin of the Institute of Historical Research*, 55 (1982), 148–57.

—— 'The Recall of the British from the Dutch Service', *Historical Journal*, 25 (1982), 423–35.

Jones, J. R., 'A Representative of the Alternative Society of Restoration England?', in R. S. Dunn and M. M. Dunn (eds.), *The World of William Penn*, (Philadelphia, 1986), 55–69.

Kenyon, J. P., 'The Earl of Sunderland and the Revolution of 1688', *Cambridge Historical Journal*, 11 (1953), 272–96.

LeFevre, P., 'Tangier, the Navy and its Connection with the Glorious Revolution of 1688', *Mariner's Mirror* (1987), 187–90.

McInnes, A., 'When was the English Revolution?', *History*, 117 (1982), 377–92.

Miller, J., 'The Crown and the Borough Charters in the Reign of Charles II', *English Historical Review*, 100 (1985), 53–84.

—— 'The Glorious Revolution: "Contract" and "Abdication" Reconsidered', *Historical Journal*, 25 (1982), 541–55.

Miller, J., 'The Potential for "Absolutism" in later Stuart England', *History*, 69 (1984), 187–207.

Murrell, P. E., 'Bury St. Edmunds and the Campaign to Pack Parliament, 1687–8', *Bulletin of the Institute of Historical Research*, 54 (1981), 188–206.

Nenner, H., 'Constitutional Uncertainty and the Declaration of Rights', in B. Malament (ed.), *After the Reformation: Essays in Honour of J. H. Hexter* (1980), 291–308.

Plumb, J. H., 'The Elections to the Convention Parliament of 1689', *Cambridge Historical Journal*, 5 (1937), 235–54.

Schwoerer, L. G., 'The Role of lawyers in the Revolution of 1688–9', in R. Schnur (ed.), *Die Rolle der Juristen bei der Entstehung des Modernen Staates* (Berlin, 1986), 473–98.

—— 'Propaganda in the Revolution of 1688–9', *American Historical Review*, 132 (1977), 843–74.

Slaughter, T. P., '"Abdicate" and "Contract" in the Glorious Revolution', *Historical Journal*, 24 (1981), 323–37.

Speck, W. A., 'The Orangist Conspiracy against James II', ibid. 30 (1987) 453–62.

Styles, J., 'An Eighteenth-century Ruling Class? Interest Groups, Lobbying and Parliament in Eighteenth-century England', unpublished paper (1987).

3. *Unpublished Theses*

Beddard, R. A., 'William Sancroft as Archbishop of Canterbury, 1677–1691', D.Phil. thesis (Oxford, 1965) is missing from the Bodleian Library and was therefore unavailable.

Child, M. S., 'Prelude to Revolution: The Structure of Politics in County Durham, 1678–88', Ph.D. thesis (Maryland, 1972).

Davies, D., 'The Seagoing Personnel of the Navy, 1660–1689', D.Phil. thesis (Oxford, 1986).

Harris, T., 'The Politics of the London Crowd in the Reign of Charles II', Ph.D. thesis (Cambridge, 1985).

Marshall, D. N., 'Protestant Dissent in England in the Reign of James II', Ph.D. thesis (Hull, 1976).

Murrell, P. E., 'Suffolk: The Political Behaviour of the County and its Parliamentary Boroughs from the Exclusion Crisis to the Accession of the House of Hanover', Ph.D. thesis (Newcastle upon Tyne, 1982).

Pickavance, R. G., 'The English Boroughs and the King's Government: A Study of the Tory Reaction, 1681–1685', D.Phil. thesis (Oxford, 1976).

Rosenheim, J. M., 'An Examination of Oligarchy: The Gentry of Restoration Norfolk', Ph.D. thesis (Princeton, 1981).

Simpson, A., 'The Convention Parliament, 1688–1689', D.Phil. thesis (Oxford, 1939).

Sinner, R. J., 'Charles II and Local Government: the Quo Warranto Proceedings, 1681–1685', Ph.D. thesis (Rutgers, 1976).

Spaeth, D. A., 'Parsons and Parishioners: Lay-Clerical Conflict and Popular Piety in Wiltshire Villages, 1660–1740', Ph.D. thesis (Brown University, 1985).

Index

Absolutism 1, 10, 16–17, 21, 57, 125, 139, 153–4, 162, 166, 205, 242–3
Addison, Joseph 195
Agriculture 189–91
Ailesbury, Thomas Bruce, earl of 46, 58, 162, 204, 205, 238–9
d'Albeville, Sir Ignatius White, marquis 71 and n., 84, 86
Aldborough 207–8
America, North 11–13
Ancient Constitution 1, 5, 8
Anne, Princess 138, 229
Argyll, Archibald Campbell, earl of 16, 51
Aristocracy 7, 191–2, 197–8, 249–50
Arlington, Henry Bennet, Lord 36
Army 9–10, 47, 55–7, 82, 145–6, 152–3, 154–6, 219
Arnold, John 97
Arundel, Lord 50, 63
Association 230–2

Barnardiston, Sir Samuel 147
Barrillon, Paul 43–4, 53, 55, 125–7, 137, 174
Bath, John Granville, earl of 85, 86–7, 133, 192, 209, 231
Beaufort, Henry Somerset, duke of 132
Beddard, R. A. 224–5
Bellasis, John, Lord 50, 63, 127
Belloc, Hilaire, 127
Bennett, G. V. 65
Bentinck, Willem 217–18
Bethel, Slingsby 204
Bill of Rights, see Declaration of Rights
Birch, Colonel John 37, 107
Birmingham 203
Bishops 199–200, 221
Bloody Assizes 53–5, 148
Bohun, Edmund 173

Boroughbridge 208, 234
Boscawen, Hugh 97, 103
Bramston, Sir John 59, 61, 63, 135, 194, 231
Brent, Robert 130, 216
Bristol 155, 203
Buckingham 45
Buckingham, George Villiers, duke of 36
Burnet, Gilbert 46, 51, 54, 76, 88, 108, 125, 138, 174, 181, 214, 230, 235–6
Butler, Nicholas 130
Butterfield, Herbert 4

Cambridge 65, 144
Cambridge, Group for the History of Population and Social Structure 189
Capel, Sir Henry 95
Care, Henry 175–6
Carlisle 193
Carlton, Charles 119
Carswell, John 130
Cartwright, Thomas, bishop of Chester 128, 222
Catholicism 10–11, 26, 31–2, 34, 66, 126, 166, 168–9, 233–5, 243
Catholics 170–2, 182
Chandaman, D. C. 47, 158
Charles II 3, 9, 26, 28, 34, 36, 40–1, 125, 167, 179
Cheshire 173
Child, Sir Josiah 204
Childs, John 10, 82
Church of England 28, 29, 43, 49, 50, 72, 73, 214–15
Churchill, John 82, 87, 138, 219, 229
Churchill, Sarah 229
Civil Wars 4, 7, 213
Clarendon, Edward Hyde, first earl of 25, 28, 29, 31, 36

Clarendon, Henry Hyde, second earl
    of 14, 60, 64, 88, 99, 100,
    109–10, 127, 200, 236–7
Clarges, Sir Thomas 60, 95, 103
Clergy 198–9, 221–2
Coke, John 57–8
Coke, Sir Edward 149, 151
College, Stephen 28, 206
Commission for Ecclesiastical Causes
    63–4, 66, 68, 69, 74, 143–4, 151
Commons, House of 6, 48–51,
    56–61, 94–5, 96–9, 140
Comprehension 177–8, 186
Compton, Henry, bishop of London
    61, 63–4, 74, 84, 90, 144, 220,
    226, 229
Conventicle Act, 1670 27, 172–3
Convention, 1689 19, 94–113, 235
Coronation oath 165
Corporation Act of 1661 29, 31, 214
Corporations 39, 160–1

Danby, Thomas Osborne, earl of 32,
    60, 85–6, 93, 99, 102, 108,
    191–2, 193, 220, 226–8, 238–9
Darcy, John 60
Dartmouth, George Legge, earl of 83,
    137, 237
Declaration of Indulgence:
    1662 28, 142
    1672 31, 142
    1687 65, 142, 160, 171, 173, 204
    1688 67–8, 142, 184–5, 221
Declaration of Rights 19, 104, 107–8,
    110–14, 140–53, 162–3, 164,
    236, 245
Delamere, Henry Booth, Lord 100,
    191, 228–9
Derbyshire 92
Devon 225
Devonshire, William Cavendish, earl
    of 191–2, 220, 226, 228–9
Dispensing Power 141, 149–50, 223
Dissent, *see* Nonconformists
Dolben, Gilbert 96–7
Dominion of New England 12–13
Downing, Sir George 157
Dryden, John 26, 33, 204
Dumblain, Peregrine Osborne, Lord
    110
Duncombe, Sir Charles 195

Eachard, John 198–9

Elections:
    1679–81 34–5
    1685 44–6
    1688 campaign 66–7, 88, 93,
        129–36, 146, 153, 218
    1689 92–3
Electoral system 207–9
Exclusion 33–4, 36–7, 42, 45, 50,
    123–4
Exeter 86, 202, 209, 225

Fagel, Gaspar 79, 134, 184, 217
Falkland, Anthony Carey, Lord
    104–6
Faversham 117
Feversham, Louis Duras, earl of
    52–3, 87, 89
Filmer, Robert 18, 139–40, 246
Fleming, Sir Daniel 172, 196
Fox, Charles 60
Frankle, R. J. 19

George, Prince of Denmark 229
Glassey, Lionel 160, 195
Godden versus Hales 62–3, 141, 223
Godolphin, Sidney, Lord 50, 88
Goodricke, Sir Henry 226–7
Gother, John 179–82
Grey, Anchitel 107
Grey, Ford, Lord 52–3

Habeas Corpus Act 2, 125–6
Haffenden, Philip 13
Halifax, George Savile, marquis of 3,
    50, 60, 61, 73, 88, 95, 100, 108,
    109, 126, 157, 173, 176–7, 183,
    209, 218, 220
Hampden, Richard 96, 97
Hanmer, Sir John 228
Harley, Sir Edward 95, 112
Harris, Timothy 210
Hayton, David 14
Henning, B. D. 131
Herbert, Arthur 55, 64 and n., 82–3
Herbert, Sir Edward 55, 141
Heywood, Oliver 40
Hill, Christopher 1 n., 3
Hobbes, Thomas 73
Hopkins, Paul 14–15
Hosford, D. H. 7, 132
Howard, Sir Robert 97
Huguenots 206
Hull 155, 227–8

Immortal Seven 219–20
Innocent XI, Pope 77–8
Ireland 13–14

James II:
    aims of 10, 43–4, 64–6, 125–9,
        136–7
    Catholicism of 31, 78, 127, 178–9,
        243
    character of 71, 118–21, 125
    Charles I and 25–6
    Charles II and 40–1, 162
    Church of England and 42–3,
        67–9, 126–7, 214–17, 223, 237–8
    Dissenters and 173–4, 211–12
    early career of 121–4
    Marxist view of 4, 6
    Monmouth's rebellion and 51–4
    Parliament and 47–9, 56–8, 60,
        66–7, 129–35, 232–3
    Providence and 121, 135–8
    Scotland and 15–17
    Whig view of 1–2
    William of Orange's invasion and
        80–2, 89, 117–19
James Francis Edward, Prince of
    Wales 84, 102, 103
Jeffreys, George, Lord 53–5, 61, 62,
    121
Jenkins, Sir Leoline 37
Jennings, Sir Edmund 60
Johnson, Samuel 148
Jones, J. R. 9, 130–1, 161
Judiciary 156–7
Justices of the Peace 159–60, 193, 215,
    226–7

Kaye, Sir John 216–17
Ken, Thomas, bishop of Bath and
    Wells 200
Kent 194–5
Kenyon, J. P. 7, 19
King, Gregory 189, 195, 199, 201
Kirke, Percy 82, 219
Kishlansky, M. 35

Lake, John, bishop of Chichester 200
Lancashire 193–4, 224
Landau, Norma 194
Leeds 202–3, 234
Leicestershire 199
Lenman, Bruce 16
Licensing Act 207

Lilliburlero 235
Liverpool 203
Locke, John 17, 18, 140, 162, 246–7
London 90, 168–9, 203, 205–6, 250–1
Lords, House of 51, 56, 61–2, 95–6,
    99–102, 108–10, 113, 129, 140
Louis XIV 76–8, 154
Lovelace, John, Lord 192
Lowther, Sir John 48, 51–2, 55, 93
Lumley, Richard, Lord 86, 192, 220,
    226

Macaulay, Thomas Babington 1, 2,
    141, 144, 188, 195, 196, 197, 200,
    201
MacFarlane, Alan 197
Magdalen College 65, 74, 120–1
Manchester 203
Marvell, Andrew 27
Marxist interpretation 3, 4, 6, 8, 242
Mary of Modena 75
Mary, Princess 102, 103, 108, 238
Maynard, Sir John 61, 106–7
Middleton, Charles, earl of 58–60,
    79, 244
Militia 56–7, 146, 193
Miller, John 10, 20, 171
Monmouth, James Scott, duke of 33,
    39, 41, 124
Monmouth's rebellion 7, 51–3, 56,
    74, 145, 210–11, 243
Murrell, Pat 131
Musgrave, Sir Christopher 193
Mutiny Act, 1689 163–4

Nantes, Edict of 174
Navy 82–3, 122–3
Newcastle upon Tyne 92
Nonconformists 28–31, 45, 66, 201,
    204
Norwich 202–3, 209–10
Nottingham 229
Nottingham, Daniel Finch, earl of 60,
    88, 95, 99, 109, 110, 200, 220–1

Oates, Titus 148, 168
Oxford 65, 144, 155, 232

Paget, Lord 90
Papillon, Thomas 204
Parker, David 154
Parker, Samuel, bishop of Oxford 65,
    128, 222

Parliament:
  1679–81 35–8
  1685 46–51, 56–62, 65, 215–16
  1689, *see* Convention
  'Free' 232–3, 244–5
Patrick, Simon 200–1
Pembroke, Thomas Herbert, earl of
  101
Penn, William 174, 183
Pepys, Samuel 30, 115–18
Petre, Edward 68–9, 78
Pilkington, Sir Thomas 147
Pinkham, Lucille 17, 75
Player, Sir Thomas 37
Pontefract 93
Pope, Alexander 195–6
Popish plot 32, 36, 42, 51, 168
Population of England and Wales 189
Powle, Henry 94
Presbyterians 14, 27, 29
Preston, Richard Graham Lord 58–9

Quakers 30, 173–4, 183
Queenborough 132

Religious toleration 167, 175, 221
Reresby, Sir John 37, 40, 43, 47, 53,
  60, 61, 194, 198, 209, 210,
  214–15, 226–7
Restoration 26–9, 213–14
'Revolution' 1 and n., 241–2, 248–51
Rochester, Lawrence Hyde, earl of
  41, 50, 60, 62, 64, 88, 89, 100,
  121, 126–8, 200, 215
Russell, Edward 75, 82, 86, 220
Rye House Plot 39, 147

Sancroft, William, archbishop of
  Canterbury 64, 128, 136, 185,
  200–1, 215, 237–9
Sawyer, Sir Robert 97, 247
Scarborough 156, 227
Schwoerer, Lois 20, 105
Scotland 14–17 and n.
Secretaries of State 158
Sedley, Catherine 62, 119
Seven Bishops 67–8, 142–3, 152, 157,
  199–200, 222–4
Seymour, Sir Edward 48, 94, 230
Shaftesbury, Anthony Ashley
  Cooper, earl of 7, 33, 34, 38
Shakerley, Peter 237
Sharp, John 63, 160

Sheffield 202–3
Shrewsbury, Charles Talbot, earl of
  192, 220
Sidney, Algernon 3, 39
Sidney, Henry 218–20
Skocpol, Theda 241, 250
Slaughter, T. P. 19
Somers, John 111
Sovereignty 140
Sprat, Thomas, bishop of Rochester
  69
Stafford, William Howard, Lord 51
Stillingfleet, Edward 181, 200–1, 221
Street, Baron 141–2
Styles, John 250
Sunderland, Robert Spencer, earl of
  44, 50, 60, 62–4, 66, 68–9, 71–3,
  76, 126–7, 133, 137, 182
Supremacy, Act of, 1559 150–1
Suspending Power 141, 142–3,
  150–1, 223

Tancred, Christopher 227
Temple, Sir Richard 98 and n., 103,
  111
Tenison, Thomas 200–1
Test Act:
  1673 31, 56, 57, 74, 80, 129, 214
  1678 32, 80, 171
Tewkesbury 134
Thomas versus Sorrel 149
Thoresby, Ralph 234
Tillotson, John 200
Toleration Act, 1689 2, 26, 166, 187
Tories 2, 9, 18, 26, 32, 33, 35, 45, 72,
  96–101, 104–5, 107, 214
Treasury 157
Treby, Sir George 88, 107, 112, 236
Trelawny, Charles 219
Trelawny, Sir Jonathan, bishop of
  Bristol 200
Trevelyan, G. M. 1, 2
Trevor, Sir John 59
Triennial Act:
  1664 9, 38, 153
  1694 245–6
Turner, F. C. 119–20
Turner, Francis, bishop of Ely 89, 99,
  200
Twysden, Sir William 60
Tyrconnell, Richard Talbot, earl of
  13–14, 64, 90

Uniformity, Act of, 1662 26, 27, 73

Watts, Michael 201
Webb, Stephen Saunders 12–13
Wells 210–11
Welwood, James 131
Western, J. R. 8, 158
Wharton, Thomas 93, 104, 165 and
   n., 235
Whig interpretation 1–5, 8, 17–18,
   188–9, 242, 247
Whigs 1, 2, 26, 33, 35, 45, 72, 73,

96–8, 101, 104, 107, 210, 214
White, Thomas, bishop of
   Peterborough 200
Whitehaven 203
William of Orange 1, 2, 17, 18, 53,
   74–6, 106, 112, 118, 185–6, 207,
   217, 220, 225–6, 239–40
Williams, Sir William 147

York 39–40, 155–6, 193, 202, 209,
   226–7
Yorkshire 44–5, 85, 93–4, 201, 207–8

OXFORD

MORE OXFORD PAPERBACKS

Details of a selection of other books follow. A complete list of Oxford Paperbacks, including The World's Classics, Twentieth-Century Classics, OPUS, Past Masters, Oxford Authors, Oxford Shakespeare, and Oxford Paperback Reference, is available in the UK from the General Publicity Department, Oxford University Press (JN), Walton Street, Oxford OX2 6DP.

In the USA, complete lists are available from the Paperbacks Marketing Manager, Oxford University Press, 200 Madison Avenue, New York, NY 10016.

Oxford Paperbacks are available from all good bookshops. In case of difficulty, customers in the UK can order direct from Oxford University Press Bookshop, 116 High Street, Oxford, Freepost, OX1 4BR, enclosing full payment. Please add 10 per cent of published price for postage and packing.

REBELLION OR REVOLUTION?

G. E. Aylmer

'This is an ideal book, either to give an initial report of the state of the field, or to sum it all up . . . The conciseness and the accuracy are formidable, and so is the unfailing intellectual fairness.' Conrad Russell in *London Review of Books*

Civil war, regicide, republic, the Cromwellian protectorate, the restoration of the monarchy: some of the most exciting and dramatic events in English history took place between 1640 and 1660. Gerald Aylmer conveys the massive and continuing psychological and emotional impact of those times, and offers an up-to-date analysis of the causes, significance, and consequences of what happened.

The period was dominated by such powerful personalities as Charles I, John Hampden, John Pym, Oliver Cromwell, and John Lilburne; but Dr Alymer also attempts to discover the views of the anonymous mass of the population who lived through the political and religious upheavals of the mid-seventeenth century.

An OPUS book

LOCKE

John Dunn

Although John Locke's *Essay concerning Human Understanding,* in which he set out his theory that men's knowledge reaches them exclusively through their senses, is his best-known and most admired work, it is still curiously misunderstood. By restoring Locke's theory of knowledge to its proper context, John Dunn explains how Locke came to the conclusions he did, and why his views on this fundamental question have so profoundly influenced later generations of philosophers and natural scientists. He also explores Locke's exposition of the liberal values of tolerance and responsible government which was to become the backbone of enlightened European thought in the eighteenth century.

'In eighty lucid and lively pages Dunn has stripped the myths and given us a new key to Locke.' *New Society*

Past Masters

THE ECONOMY OF ENGLAND, 1450–1750

D. C. Coleman

Two centuries ago the Industrial Revolution began transforming the economy of England into the form in which we know it today. But what sort of economy did England have in preceding centuries? Professor Coleman gives us an account of three centuries of English economic life, stretching from the Wars of the Roses almost to the accession of George III. He never allows us to forget that the economic world in which the men and women of the day lived and died was only one aspect of their historical context. And just as he puts the economy of England into its social and political setting, so he also presents it in its changing relationship with the economy of Europe and the wider world. In this last connection the period from 1650 to 1750, rarely treated as a whole, receives particular emphasis as marking the economic divergence of England from the Continent.

'Professor Coleman brings a welcome freshness of learning and originality of style to the subject-matter which makes this work an excellent statement of the more temperate position which lies between 'old' and 'new' economic historians.' Barry Supple, *Times Literary Supplement*

An OPUS book

PHILOSOPHERS AND PAMPHLETEERS

Political Theorists of the Enlightenment

Maurice Cranston

The philosophers of the French Enlightenment wrote for a large public with the aim of promoting political reforms. In this lively and readable book, Maurice Cranston demonstrates the richness and variety of their ideas.

Professor Cranston studies Montesquieu's parliamentarianism and Voltaire's royalism as rival ideologies reflecting competing interests in the *ancien régime*; he analyses Rousseau's debts to the republican experience of the city-state of Geneva, traces the movement from utilitarianism to liberalism in the thought of Diderot and Holbach, and examines Condorcet's endeavour in the first years of the French Revolution to reconcile democracy with the rule of the wise.

CULTURE AND ANARCHY IN IRELAND
1890–1939

F. S. L. Lyons

Winner of the Wolfson Literary Prize for History, 1980, and the Ewart-Biggs Memorial Prize, 1980

'. . . this book is a balanced attempt to come to honest grips . . . with the problem of the Irish body politic and with the seeds of those problems in the more recent past. He has isolated various commonly conflicting, overlapping strands in the Irish mind with a clarity not normally encountered in such discussions, and . . . his presentation will undoubtedly contribute much to our understanding of our own past and of its ramifications into the present.' *Irish Independent*

'Dr. Lyons' discussion of Ulster, with regard to both its internal structures and to its relationship to the rest of the country, shows the same scholarly broadmindedness and the same lucidity of exposition that mark the book as a whole . . . one can hardly read it without feeling its relevance to the present day.' *Irish Press*

THE SIEGE OF DERRY

Patrick Macrory

On 7 December, 1699, the Protestant citizens of Londonderry were anxiously watching from their walls the approach of a regiment of Catholic Soldiers. Rumours were widespread that the soldiers had come to massacre them, yet to deny entry to the King's troops would be high treason.

But who was the rightful King? James II's Lord Deputy ruled in Dublin, but the Protestant cause of William of Orange was gathering support in England. The city fathers were still dithering and the soldiers only sixty yards away, when thirteen apprentice boys siezed the keys of the town and slammed the gates shut. This act of defiance led to the siege of Derry—the siege which Macauley was to call 'the most memorable in the annals of the British Isles'.

'A splendid tale of courage and endurance, with plenty of civilian chutzpah as well as military derring-do . . . A sensible and lucid narrative.' *Observer*

REVOLUTION AND REVOLUTIONARIES

A. J. P. Taylor

Violent political upheavals have occurred as long as there have been political communities. But, in Europe, only since the French Revolution have they sought not merely to change the rulers but to transform the entire social and political system. One of A. J. P. Taylor's themes in this generously illustrated book, is that revolutions and revolutionaries do not always coincide: those who start them often do so unintentionally, while revolutionaries tend to be most active in periods of counter-revolution. He traces the line of development of the revolutionary tradition from 1789 through Chartism, the social and national upheavals of 1848, the 'revolutionaries without a revolution' of the following sixty years—Marx, Engels, Bakunin, and others—to the Bolshevik seizure of power in 1917.

'Based on his 1978 television lectures, a dry, witty, often heterodox glance at some of Europe's political mutterings and upheavals from the French Revolution to Lenin. Amply illustrated.' *Observer*

THE RESTORATION

A Political and Religious History of England and Wales 1658–1667

Ronald Hutton

'Hutton's account of the complicated events leading to the Restoration is the best we have.' John Kenyon in *Observer*

The years 1658–1667 form one of the most vital and eventful periods in English history, witnessing the Plague, the Great Fire of London, the naval wars against the Dutch, and, above all, the transformation of Oliver Cromwell's Commonwealth into the Restoration monarchy of Charles II.

Ronald Hutton has provided the first detailed study of the period, returning to nearly all the extant manuscript sources and reworking every issue afresh. The result is an absorbing and perceptive account of national experience as government policy changed, influenced by the interaction of central concerns, local perspectives, and the various social, political, and religious groups.

ROMAN CATHOLICISM IN ENGLAND

from the Elizabethan Settlement to the Second Vatican
Council

Edward Norman

'a brilliantly objective account . . . he has written about English
Catholicism in a manner for which English Catholics can be
grateful and of which he can be proud'

Lord Longford in *Contemporary Review*

'eruditely benign, fair, well-mannered and handling his theo-
logical, social and political researches with consummate ease.
Few scholars could take us from half-way through the Reformation to 1962 in fewer than 129 pages of text without
unbalancing history, but that is what the author has done.'

Sunday Telegraph

'full of insights . . . a model of clear and concise historical
writing' *Universe*

'a taut and sensitive history' *Church Times*

An OPUS book

THE INDUSTRIAL REVOLUTION
1760–1830

T. S. Ashton

The Industrial Revolution has sometimes been regarded as a
catastrophe which desecrated the English landscape and
brought social oppression and appalling physical hardship to
the workers. In this book, however, it is presented as an important and beneficial mark of progress. In spite of destructive
wars and a rapid growth of population, the material living
standards of most of the British people improved, and the
technical innovations not only brought economic rewards but
also provoked greater intellectual ingenuity. Lucidly argued
and authoritative, this book places the phenomenon of the
Industrial Revolution in a stimulating perspective.

An OPUS book

THE DIARY OF THOMAS TURNER,
1754–1765

David Vaisey

Thomas Turner (1729–93) was a key figure in the village of
East Hoathly, Sussex, where he was shopkeeper, undertaker,
schoolmaster, tax-gatherer, churchwarden, overseer of the
poor, and much besides. In his diary he recorded, in all its
colourful and intimate detail, eleven years of everyday life in
a Georgian village.

'a fascinating depiction of a particular society in eighteenth-
century England' Antonia Fraser, *Standard*

'Turner has a powerful advantage . . . over perhaps any published English diarist—the panoramic view his official position
gave him of his neighbours' social behaviour . . . Turner's diary . . .
becomes (a classic) in the hands of its exemplary editor.'
Marilyn Butler, *London Review of Books*

'David Vaisey's editing . . . is unobtrusive and wellnigh impecc-
able.' J. P. Kenyon, *Listener*

BERKELEY

J. O. Urmson

Unlike Dr Johnson in his famous jibe, J. O. Urmson achieves
an unusually sympathetic assessment of Berkeley's philosophy
by viewing it against a wider intellectual background than is
customary. He sees Berkeley's work as a serious critical analysis
of the scientific thought of Newton and his predecessors, and
of its metaphysical basis; and he gives a clear account of the
relationship between Berkeley's metaphysics and his analysis
of the concepts of science and common sense.

'Professor Urmson's *Berkeley* is welcome, not just because he
makes Berkeley's view that there is no such thing as matter
perfectly intelligible and rather persuasive . . . but because he
devotes some time to explaining the moral and political positions which Berkeley thought materialism threatened.' *Listener*

Past Masters

THE OXFORD HISTORY OF BRITAIN

Edited by Kenneth O. Morgan

The Oxford History of Britain tells the story of Britain and her peoples over two thousand years, from the coming of the Roman legions to the present day.

The dramatic narrative of developments throughout the British Isles is taken up in turn by ten leading historians, who offer the fruits of the best modern scholarship in an authoritative and accessible form. The relationship between the political, economic, social, and cultural transformations in British history is explored revealing a vivid and sometimes surprising picture of a continuous turmoil of change in every period. But there also emerges a pattern of continuity in British cultural and social ideals, and a special awareness of nationality and patriotism which has been such a distinctive feature of British society.

'Without doubt, this will serve as the standard one-volume history of Britain for the rest of the century.' *Sunday Times*

THE OXFORD ILLUSTRATED HISTORY OF THE BRITISH MONARCHY

Edited by Kenneth O. Morgan

'the best buy of the year in historical publishing. It belongs in every school satchel, on every student's desk, in every library's catalogue . . . on everyone's coffee table . . . wherever readers have a real curiosity to discover, in words and pictures, the current stage of historical inquiry in the field of British history, from the Romans to Thatcher.'
Peter Clarke in *History Today*

'Without doubt, this will serve as the standard one volume history of Britain for the rest of the century.' *Sunday Times*